D0215850

OXFORD MONOGRAPHS ON MUSIC

Fortepianos and their Music

Germany, Austria, and England, 1760–1800

KATALIN KOMLÓS

CLARENDON PRESS · OXFORD
1995

Oxford University Press, Walton Street, Oxford OX2 6DP
Oxford New York
Athens Auckland Bangkok Bombay
Calcutta Cape Town Dar es Salaam Delhi
Florence Hong Kong Istanbul Karachi
Kuala Lumpur Madras Madrid Melbourne
Mexico City Nairobi Paris Singapore
Taipei Tokyo Toronto
and associated companies in
Berlin Ibadan

Oxford is a trade mark of Oxford University Press

Published in the United States
by Oxford University Press Inc., New York

British Library Cataloguing in Publication Data
Data available

Library of Congress Cataloging in Publication Data
Komlós, Katalin, 1945–
Fortepianos and their music: Germany, Austria, and England, 1760–1800 / Katalin Komlós.
(Oxford monographs on music)
Includes bibliographical references and index.
1. Piano music—Europe—18th century—History and criticism.
2. Piano—Europe—History—18th century. I. Title. II. Series:
ML720.3.K66 1995 786.2'094'09033—dc20 94-33590
ISBN 0-19-816426-2

1 3 5 7 9 10 8 6 4 2

Typeset by Best-set Typesetter Ltd., Hong Kong
Printed in Great Britain
on acid-free paper by
Biddles Ltd Guildford & King's Lynn

To the Memory of my Parents

Preface

As we rapidly approach the end of the twentieth century, the examination of the music of the past in its own contemporary terms becomes more or less obligatory for any serious musician, whether active on the concert stage, or in the academic world. Wonderful new musical–sociological series offer historical background, expensive editions make more and more music available, and organological research expands our knowledge of the instruments of bygone centuries. And while highly sophisticated disputes and philosophical duels revolve around the correct approach to the music of the past, the scrutiny of the *music* itself often remains undone.

That there is a close relationship between the instrument and the music written for it does not need to be argued here; but further refinement is due in that area. Concerning the pianoforte of the second half of the eighteenth century, the fundamental difference in mechanical design between the German/Viennese and the English instruments has long been recognized, but the effect of that difference on the composition of the music has not been seriously addressed. The subject of this book is the comparative study of the late eighteenth-century European piano repertory, in terms of texture and of specific keyboard writing. An examination of the practical rather than the technological aspects of the instruments themselves, and the manner of playing them, completes the central topic.

The major portion of the volume (The Music) is mainly concerned with the solo piano repertory of the period. This means the omission of the concerto genre, which includes the outstanding series of the Mozart concertos: perhaps the most important group of works in classical keyboard music. The extension of the musical–instrumental discussion beyond the solo literature, however, would have exceeded the reasonable size and framework of this study. As it is, most investigations are carried out within the universal genre of the sonata.

Since the purpose of the book is the overall examination of the reciprocal relationship between the late eighteenth-century pianoforte and its repertory, I have tried to extend my attention to a wide range of pianist-composers, instead of the usual concentration on the work of the great composers. My first consideration was the scrutiny of the various keyboard styles, and if Mozart or Beethoven receives not much more space on these pages than the music of Johann Christian Bach, or Jan Ladislav Dussek, the enormous literature on the former composers surely compensates for these proportions. Joseph Haydn is singled out from the three great Viennese classical masters, for he alone was exposed to the inspirations and possibilities of both types of the eighteenth-century pianoforte.

The content of the following chapters is the result of approximately fifteen years of playing and studying the early piano. The thoughts and observations presented here do not pretend to give a comprehensive account of the subject, but I hope they may draw attention to the interrelationship between instruments, composers, and performers, within the first important period of the history of the pianoforte.

Acknowledgements

My interest in the eighteenth-century fortepiano was awakened by Malcolm Bilson in 1977: his pioneer work and rare artistry has been a source of inspiration ever since. Encouragement and support from Peter Williams gave me the confidence to write this book.

In the course of the work, I received a great deal of help and advice from colleagues and friends. Neal Zaslaw and Peter Williams read the central part (The Music), Howard Ferguson the entire manuscript; I am very grateful for their detailed comments. I owe special thanks to Mary Hunter and James Parakilas, who not only read through my chapters from the beginning, and gave expert guidance in style, but supplied source material that was not available to me in Hungary. Linda Nicholson and Christopher Hogwood let me see and play the instruments of their respective private collections; their kindness is much appreciated. For information regarding instruments, I am indebted to Wolfgang Gamerith (Oberschützen, Austria), John Barnes (Edinburgh), Eszter Gát (Budapest), and Michael Cole (Cheltenham). The fruitful discussions and correspondence with Miklós Spányi alerted me to some specific musical–organological questions, and it has been a relief to be able to count on the prompt linguistic help of Paul Merrick and Pamela Pecko.

For the use of musical and documentary sources I owe thanks to the following libraries: The British Library (London); Bodleian Library (Oxford); Oxford University Music Faculty Library; Rowe Music Library, King's College (Cambridge); Pendlebury Library of Music (Cambridge); Cambridge University Music Faculty Library; Library of the Royal College of Music (London); National Library of Scotland (Edinburgh); Reid Music Library (Edinburgh). The willingness and the help of the librarians of the Liszt Academy of Music, Budapest, has been indispensable for my daily work.

An essential part of my investigations, the examination and the playing of original eighteenth-century pianos, took place in various museums and musical instrument collections. For these opportunities, I am deeply grateful to the following persons and institutions: Dr Peter Germann-Bauer (Museum der Stadt Regensburg); Dr Dieter Krickeberg (Germanisches Nationalmuseum, Nuremberg); Göran Grahn (Stiftelsen Musikkulturens Främjande (Nydahl Collection), Stockholm); Richard and Katrina Burnett (Finchcocks Historical Keyboard Instrument Collection, Goudhurst, Kent); Mr Spiers (The Colt Clavier Collection, Bethersden, Kent); Mimi Waitzman (The Benton Fletcher Collection at Fenton House, Hampstead, London); Elizabeth Wells (Royal College of Music, Museum of Instruments, London); John Raymond (The Russell Collection of Early Keyboard Instruments,

Edinburgh); Dolmetsch Collection of Musical Instruments at Ranger's House, Blackheath, London.

A generous research grant from the British Council (1989) made my extensive work in British libraries and instrument collections possible; a further recent grant enabled me to go for a short working visit to Oxford. I am thankful for both of these opportunities.

András Székely prepared the musical examples with conscience and patience. Bruce Phillips, music books editor at Oxford University Press, has been a kind and encouraging guide from the beginning. I thank him and his colleagues for all their help in the production of this volume.

Budapest,
December 1993 K.K.

Contents

Author's Note

1. Since the names 'fortepiano' and 'pianoforte' were used equally in Europe in the second half of the eighteenth century, with no distinction between them, I also apply them interchangeably; for convenience, I use the short form 'piano' as well. The German nomenclature of keyboard instruments (*Flügel*, *Klavier*, *Hammerflügel*, *Tafelklavier*) will be clarified in context.

2. The numerous citations from contemporary non-English sources are given in bilingual form, unless the original is available in a standard modern edition. All English translations, if not noted otherwise, are my own.

3. The letter-names of the octave-pitches, in relation to the keyboard compass, appear as follows:

$$CC\text{–}C\text{–}c\text{–}c^1\text{–}c^2\text{–}c^3\text{–}c^4$$

(c^1 = Middle C).

Abbreviations

AM	*Acta Musicologica*
CCLN	*The Collected Correspondence and London Notebooks of Joseph Haydn*, ed. H. C. Robbins Landon (London, 1959).
EM	*Early Music*
HSt	*Haydn-Studien*
JAMS	*Journal of the American Musicological Society*
JHW	*Joseph Haydn: Werke*, ed. J. Haydn-Institut, Cologne (1962–).
JM	*Journal of Musicology*
JRMA	*Journal of the Royal Musical Association*
MGG	*Die Musik in Geschichte und Gegenwart*, ed. Friedrich Blume (Kassel, 1949–68)
MJb	*Mozart-Jahrbuch*
ML	*Music and Letters*
MQ	*The Musical Quarterly*
MR	*The Music Review*
NMA	*W. A. Mozart: Neue Ausgabe sämtlicher Werke* (Kassel, 1955–91)
SM	*Studia Musicologica*

Part One
The Instruments

1

Squares and Grands

BARTOLOMEO CRISTOFORI, keeper of instruments at the Medici court in Florence, was a man of inquisitive mind and ingenious technical imagination. He experimented with keyboard mechanisms and produced special types of instruments. The 'gravicembalo col piano e forte' (*c*.1698) was only one of these inventions, but it was the only one that eventually played a decisive role in the history of keyboard instruments.[1]

If we can believe the correspondent of the *Giornale dei letterati d'Italia*, Scipione Maffei, the invention was inspired by the wonderful art of Italian string players of the late seventeenth century. The famous orchestral concerts held at Cardinal Ottoboni's in Rome, the *Accademie Poetico-musicali*, led by Arcangelo Corelli, set a new example in musical performance. Maffei, in his report on Cristofori's new instrument (1711), explains the motivation that prompted the invention as follows:

It is known to everyone who delights in music, that one of the principal means by which the skilful in that art derive the secret of especially delighting those who listen, is the piano and forte in the theme and its response, or in the gradual diminution of tone little by little, and then returning suddenly to the full power of the instrument; which artifice is frequently used and with marvellous effect, in the great concerts of Rome. . . . Now, of this diversity and alteration of tone, in which instruments played with the bow especially excel, the harpsichord is entirely deprived, and it would have been thought a vain endeavour to propose to make it so that it should participate in this power. Nevertheless, so bold an invention has been no less happily conceived than executed in Florence, by Signor Bartolommeo Cristofali [*sic*], of Padua, harpsichord-player, in the service of the most serene Prince of Tuscany.[2]

[1] For the most recent and exhaustive evaluation of Cristofori's achievement, along with a survey of the development of the hammer mechanism, starting from the 15th cent., see Konstantin Restle, *Bartolomeo Cristofori und die Anfänge des Hammerclaviers: Quellen, Dokumente und Instrumente des 15. bis 18. Jahrhunderts* (Munich, 1991). Further important contributions concerning Cristofori's work are Stewart Pollens, 'The Pianos of Bartolomeo Cristofori', *Journal of the American Musical Instrument Society*, 10 (1984), 32–68; and Giuliana Montanari, 'Bartolomeo Cristofori: A List and Historical Survey of his Instruments', *EM* 19 (1991), 383–96.

[2] 'Nuova invenzione d'un gravecembalo col piano, e forte, aggiunte alcune considerazioni sopra gl'instrumenti musicali', *Giornale dei letterati d'Italia*, 5 (Venice, 1711), 144. Quoted in English in Edward Francis Rimbault, *The Pianoforte: Its Origin, Progress and Construction, with Some Account of the Clavichord, Virginal, Spinet, Harpsichord etc.* (London, 1860), 95–7.

The German translation of Maffei's description was published in Mattheson's *Critica musica* (1725),[3] and attracted the attention of the organ maker Gottfried Silbermann of Saxony, who started to experiment with Cristofori's hammer mechanism.[4] Eventually he built similar instruments, during the 1730s. On the strength of the alleged criticism of J. S. Bach, he improved his construction in the 1740s, when King Frederick the Great of Prussia, a musical enthusiast, bought all fifteen fortepianos that Silbermann had built up to that date. J. S. Bach improvised his three-part Ricercar on one of them, on the occasion of his 1747 Potsdam visit; two years later, his approbation prompted him to act as sales agent for Silbermann.[5]

The royal whim of Frederick II explains the fact that his court musicians, J. J. Quantz and C. P. E. Bach, write about the fortepiano as a matter of course in their respective treatises, in the early 1750s.[6] To be sure, square pianos were not uncommon in Germany by then, but the presence of several new Silbermann instruments in the Potsdam palaces evidently gave plenty of opportunity to become acquainted with the novelty. Other musicians were not in such a good position. The eminent Erfurt scholar, Jakob Adlung, reported in 1758 that he had not yet had occasion to see a fortepiano instrument, and asked his more fortunate readers to supply him with information.[7]

Cristofori and Silbermann built *Flügel*-shaped (grand) instruments, with a similar action.[8] Around 1740, however, the small, clavichord-shaped *Tafelklavier* started to appear in Germany. The earliest surviving example, made by Johann Socher in Sonthofen (Bavaria) in 1742, is a pretty instrument of four and a half octaves compass (C–f^3).[9] Since it has a simplified version of Cristofori's action (*Stossmechanik*), it seems to follow Silbermann's construction. The subsequent production of square pianos, however, introduced the Germann *Prellmechanik*, or at least an early version of it. This extremely simple mechanism hardly differs from that of the clavichord, except that little

[3] 'Musicalische Merckwürdigkeiten des Marchese, Scipio Maffei, Beschreibung eines neuerfundenen Claveceins, auf welchem das piano und forte zu haben, nebst einigen Betrachtungen über die Musicalische Instrumente, aus dem Welschen ins Teutsche übersetzet von König', in Johann Mattheson, *Critica musica*, ii (Hamburg, 1725), 335–42.

[4] According to the hypothesis of K. Restle, the 1717–19 Dresden visit of Antonio Lotti might have occasioned an earlier inspiration. Following the invitation of Frederick Augustus II of Saxony, Lotti arrived with some other musicians from Venice (where Maffei's report on Cristofori's invention had been published) to produce operas at the Dresden court: perhaps he brought news about the instrument, or, as Restle speculates, even brought a *cembalo col piano e forte*, to accompany his singers. See Restle, *Bartolomeo Cristofori*, 259.

[5] See Christoph Wolff, 'New Research on Bach's *Musical Offering*', *MQ* 57 (1971), 379–408.

[6] Johann Joachim Quantz, *Versuch einer Anweisung die Flöte traversière zu spielen* (Berlin, 1752); Carl Philipp Emanuel Bach, *Versuch über die wahre Art das Clavier zu spielen* (Berlin, 1753, 1762).

[7] *Anleitung zu der musikalischen Gelahrtheit* (Erfurt, 1758), 563.

[8] Three Cristofori and three Silbermann pianos are extant. The former are housed in New York (Metropolitan Museum of Art), Leipzig, and Rome; the Silbermann instruments are exhibited in Potsdam (Sanssouci Palace; Neues Palais), and in Nuremberg (Germanisches Nationalmuseum).

[9] This instrument is in the collection of the Germanisches Nationalmuseum, Nuremberg.

hammers replace the tangents. The *Tafelklavier* was inexpensive to make, therefore to buy as well, and it required little space. It became a popular domestic instrument. In the first period of fortepiano making, the square type was cultivated in Germany: *Hammerflügel* were rare.[10]

In Germany, where the clavichord was considered the ideal keyboard instrument, professional musical opinion showed a resistance towards the newfangled fortepiano for a long time.[11] The great artist and authority in clavichord playing, C. P. E. Bach—besides some cautious recognition—expressed his reservations in his *Versuch*, and his reputation was so high that his view influenced German musical thinking for decades. As late as 1783, Carl Friedrich Cramer wrote in an indignant manner in his *Magazin der Musik*:

Traurig freylich ists für die Tonkunst, diese Gattung Instrumente unter ganzen Nationen so herrschend zu finden, und selbst in Deutschland, dem wahren Vaterlande der Claviere, besonders den südlichern Provinzen, zwanzig gute Pianofortes, Fortpiens, Clavecin-royals und wie die Hackbrettart weiter heisst, gegen ein einziges erträgliches Clavier anzutreffen.

It is indeed a sad thing for music to find this sort of instrument [fortepiano] so widespread in every country, even in Germany, the real home of the clavichord, and especially in the southern districts, where there are twenty good pianofortes, *Fortpiens*, *Clavecin-royals*, and whatever else this species of *Hackbrett* is called, to a single tolerable clavichord.[12]

Notwithstanding the distribution of instruments, noted by Cramer, D. G. Türk wrote his important *Klavierschule* in 1789 still for the clavichord.

Cristofori's invention seems to have made an impact in the Iberian peninsula. The Portuguese infanta (later the Spanish Queen), Maria Barbara, and her brother, Don Alfonso, both taught by Domenico Scarlatti in Lisbon, must have been interested in the pianoforte. Queen Maria Barbara's inventory of musical instruments (1758) includes five pianofortes of Florence;[13] and Lodovico Giustini, composer of the first music ever written specifically for the pianoforte, dedicated his work to Don Alfonso of Portugal.[14] The famous castrato, Farinelli, who lived at the Spanish court from 1737 to 1759, received a piano from his royal patrons: this favourite instrument of his was made

[10] See John Henry van der Meer, *Germanisches Nationalmuseum Nürnberg: Wegweiser durch die Sammlung historischer Musikinstrumente*, 3rd edn. (Nuremberg, 1982), 46.

[11] See Carl Parrish, 'Criticisms of the Piano when it was New', *MQ* 30 (1944), 428–40; also Katalin Komlós, 'On the New Fortepiano in Contemporary German Musical Writings', *Harpsichord and Fortepiano Magazine*, 4 (1988), 134–9.

[12] *Magazin der Musik*, i (Hamburg, 1783), 1246–7. Quoted and trans. in Parrish, 'Criticisms of the Piano', 436.

[13] See Ralph Kirkpatrick, *Domenico Scarlatti* (Princeton, NJ, 1953), App. iii.

[14] *Sonate Da Cimbalo di piano, e forte detto volgarmente di martelletti | Dedicate A Sua Altezza Reale Il Serenissimo D. Antonio Infante di Portogallo E Composte Da D. Lodovico Giustini di Pistoia | Opera prima | Firenze 1732.*

in 1730 by Ferrini, a Florentine from Cristofori's workshop.[15] According to recent research, pianoforte instruments were built quite early in Iberia. In Spain, instruments with hammer mechanism survive from around the middle of the century;[16] in Portugal, the first piano extant was built by Henrique van Casteel in Lisbon, 1763.[17]

No pianoforte was produced in England before the 1760s,[18] when German *émigré* makers started businesses there. Johannes Zumpe achieved the most brilliant career: he set up his London shop in 1761, and in twenty years' time could boast of the title 'the inventor of the Small Piano-forte and maker to her Majesty and the Royal Family'. Zumpe made square pianos exclusively, using the so-called English single action, and a keyboard compass of GG–f^3. His instruments were extremely popular and widespread; the Queen's Music Master J. C. Bach's preference for them made the modest instruments even more fashionable.[19] Other German makers of square pianos active in England included Johannes Pohlmann (who sent one of his instruments to Gluck in 1772), Frederick Beck, and Christopher Ganer, to name but a few.

Early advertisements appeared from the late 1750s, offering the new instrument. The 15 July 1758 issue of the *Amsterdamse Courant* included a notice from the organ maker Hendrik Blötz, who announced two 'superbe Forte Piano, zijnde Hamerwerk' for sale.[20] A certain Frederic Neubauer advertised 'pianofortes, lyrichords, and claffichords', in addition to harpsichords, in *The Universal Director* (London, 1763).[21] The first recorded concert performance on a 'fortipiano' took place in the same year, in the Viennese Burgtheater.[22]

When in 1761 John Broadwood from Scotland was accepted as an apprentice in the London harpsichord workshop of Burkat Shudi in Great Pulteney Street, nobody could have guessed that a new chapter had begun in the history of the pianoforte. Eight years later, through the marriage of Broadwood and Shudi's daughter, a partnership resulted, and in 1771 John Broadwood became the head of the firm. He began to build square pianofortes in the early 1770s, using the Zumpe-type single action, but a keyboard compass of five full octaves

[15] See documents concerning the activity of Ferrini in Luigi Ferdinando Tagliavini, 'Giovanni Ferrini and his Harpsichord "a penne e a martelletti"', *EM* 19 (1991), 399–408.

[16] See Beryl Kenyon de Pascual, 'Francisco Pérez Mirabel's Harpsichords and the Early Spanish Piano', *EM* 15 (1987), 503–13.

[17] See Stewart Pollens, 'The Early Portuguese Piano', *EM* 13 (1985), 18–27.

[18] The oft-quoted pianoforte by Father Wood (1752), and the instrument bought by the Revd W. Mason in Hamburg (1755), were not of English make. See Stanley Sadie (ed.), *The Piano* (The New Grove Musical Instruments Series; London, 1988), 19.

[19] See the results of the latest research on Zumpe's instruments in Richard Maunder, 'The Earliest English Square Piano?', *Galpin Society Journal*, 42 (1989), 77–84.

[20] See Clemens von Gleich, *Pianofortes uit de Lage Landen* (The Hague, 1980), 9.

[21] Quoted in Sadie (ed.), *The Piano*, 21.

[22] See Eva Badura-Skoda, 'Prolegomena to a History of the Viennese Fortepiano', *Israel Studies in Musicology*, 2 (1980), 78.

(FF–f^3). In the 1780s Zumpe developed the English double action, which then became generally applied in English squares.

After the pioneer work of Gottfried Silbermann, and of his nephew, Johann Heinrich Silbermann of Strasburg, the development of the *Hammerflügel* (grand pianoforte) reached an important stage, on the Continent and in England as well. The outstanding personalities at this period were Johann Andreas Stein in Augsburg and Americus Backers in London.

One of the finest makers in the history of the piano, J. A. Stein started to experiment with the hammer mechanism in the 1750s. Besides home experience, he gained new impulse through a Paris journey in 1758; the trip included a visit to the workshop of Silbermann in Strasburg. Johann Adam Hiller, editor of the *Wöchentliche Nachrichten und Anmerkungen die Musik betreffend*, wrote about the work of Stein in a 1769 issue of his journal:

Ein geschickter Orgel- und Instrumentmacher, der zugleich Organist an der evangelischen Barfüsserkirche zu Augspurg ist, Herr Johann Andreas Stein, hat an der Verbesserung der Mängel, die sich bey dem Pianoforte finden, seit zehn Jahren gearbeitet.

A capable organ and instrument maker, who is also the organist of the Lutheran *Barfüsserkirche* in Augsburg, Herr Johann Andreas Stein, has been working on the improvement of the defects of the pianoforte for ten years.[23]

The major 'defects' of the instrument were the inefficient damping and the lack of proper escapement. Several German makers tried to solve these problems. Concerning the question of damping, we read in Forkel's *Musikalischer Almanach für Deutschland*:

Man hat diesem Uebel [dem Nachklingen] auf mancherley Weise abzuhelfen gesucht; dennoch sind nur wenige Instrumentmacher glücklich darinn gewesen. Die beste Art der Einrichtung, die sich in diesem Falle anwenden lässt, findet man an den Spath und Schmahlschen Instrumenten zu Regenspurg. Hier ist eine Dämpfung über den Saiten angebracht, die mit dem Tasten zugleich steigt oder fällt. So lange der Taste in der Höhe gehalten wird, so lange bleibt auch die Dämpfung von der Saite entfernt. So bald man den Finger vom Tasten nimmt, fällt die Dämpfung auf die Saite zurück.

They [the instrument makers] tried to get rid of this evil [reverberation of sound] in many ways, but so far only a few makers have succeeded. The best solutions are to be found in the instruments of Spath and Schmahl of Regensburg. Here the dampers are on the strings, and they rise or fall together with the keys. As long as the key is depressed, the damper is lifted from the string. As soon as one's finger is removed from the key, the damper falls back on to the string.[24]

Forkel does not mention the name of Stein, yet the perfection of the German action (*Prellmechanik*) with escapement must be attributed to him. W. A.

[23] *Wöchentliche Nachrichten* (Leipzig), 24 July 1769.

[24] *Musikalischer Almanach für Deutschland auf das Jahr 1782* (Leipzig, 1782), 16.

Mozart's oft-quoted letters from Augsburg in 1777 have brought everlasting credit to the great master.[25] A quarter of a century later, the *Musikalisches Lexikon* of Heinrich Christoph Koch could already place Stein's work in a historical perspective:

Nur dem Orgelbauer J. A. Stein zu Augsburg war es vorbehalten, im letzten Viertel des verwichenen Jahrhundertes diesem Instrumente einen Grad der Vollkommenheit zu geben, der wenig mehr zu wünschen übrig lässt.

It was reserved for the Augsburg organ builder J. A. Stein in the last quarter of the last century to achieve a degree of perfection on this instrument [fortepiano] that hardly leaves anything to be desired.[26]

The creator of the first English grand pianoforte, and the inventor of the 'English grand action', Americus Backers, is a somewhat enigmatic figure.[27] Neither the date nor the place of his birth is known. James Shudi Broadwood thought he was Dutch; according to Burney, he was German.[28] All we know for sure is that Backers was active in London from 1763, and died there in 1778. His 1771 announcement regarding the public exhibition of a new model of grand pianoforte suggests that he had been experimenting with the mechanism for some time previously.[29] The notice appeared in the 1 March 1771 issue of *The Public Advertiser*, addressed 'To the PUBLIC':

At the Long Room in the Thatched House, St. James's Street, on Monday, Tuesday, Friday and Saturday Mornings, may be seen and heard a new invented Instrument, of the Size and Shape of a Harpsichord, which answers all the Purposes that have been hitherto wanted in an Instrument of the Harpsichord Kind. It is played on in the same Manner, but differs in all other Respects, as the Tone and Expressions are far superior to any Musical Instrument yet offered for public Inspection. This instrument is made by Americus Backers, of Jermyn-street, St. James's, who calls it an Original Forte Piano; and thereby means that it is no Copy, being entirely his own Invention. There are many Things made under the Denomination of Forte Pianos, but as this is the real one, Mr. Backers takes this Method of informing the Public, that they may form a Judgment how much this is superior to those which have been offered under that Name. A fine Harpsichord Player is engaged to play on it from One 'till Two o'Clock: After which Time it will be left at Liberty for any Lady or Gentleman to make Trial thereof. Admittance 2s. 6d. each.[30]

[25] See, especially, the letter of 17 Oct. 1777, in *The Letters of Mozart and his Family*, ed. and trans. Emily Anderson, 3rd edn. (London, 1985), 327–30.

[26] 'Fortepiano', in *Musikalisches Lexikon* (Frankfurt am Main, 1802), 591–2.

[27] The following paragraphs are based on the excellent recent account of Warwick Henry Cole, 'Americus Backers: Original Piano Forte Maker', *Harpsichord and Fortepiano Magazine*, 4 (1987), 79–85. The article contains important firsthand data, based on new research.

[28] See 'Some Notes Made by J. S. Broadwood, with Observations and Elucidations by Henry Fowler Broadwood' (London, 1862); for the assumption of Burney, see n. 31 below.

[29] According to J. S. Broadwood, his father, John Broadwood, and Robert Stodart assisted Backers in his pioneer work, see 'Some Notes Made by J. S. Broadwood'.

[30] Quoted in Cole, 'Americus Backers', 79.

Fortunately, we can inspect the same type of instrument today in the Russell Collection of Early Keyboard Instruments in Edinburgh, in its original condition. This example, made in the year following the above advertisement, bears the inscription 'Americus Backers No 21 Londoni Fecit 1772'. A fine specimen with a mahogany case and five-octave compass ($FF,GG-f^3$), it exhibits all the important features of the English grand pianoforte for the first time. Not only the action, but the operation of the two front pedals as well (the left for una corda, the right for raising the dampers), served as models for the subsequent types of Stodart, Broadwood, and Kirkman.

Judging from the opinion of Charles Burney, Backers must have had a fine reputation by the early 1770s. In the course of his travels is Germany, Burney wrote in 1772:

I must observe, that the Germans work much better out of their own country, than they do in it, if we may judge by the *harpsichords* of Kirkman and Shudi; the *piano fortes* of Backers; and the *organs* of Snetzler; which far surpass, in goodness, all the keyed instruments that I met with, in my tour through Germany.[31]

Burney recommended Backers's instruments as the best available pianofortes in a letter to Thomas Twining, who asked his advice in the matter.[32]

The first patent for the English grand action was issued by Robert Stodart in 1777 (No. 1172), in a combined grand pianoforte and harpsichord. Broadwood followed with his first patent in 1783 (square piano), after he had remodelled and strengthened the case of the instrument, and placed a second soundboard in the construction. The original description of the patent (*Specification of John Broadwood Pianofortes*, AD 1783, No. 1379) gives exact details of the 'New Constructed Piano Forte, which is far superior to any Instrument of the Kind heretofore Discovered'.[33]

Broadwood built the first grand piano in 1781 or 1782. The production of the grands started as a slow and gradual process.[34] According to the records of Broadwood's manuscript Notebook, only about forty instruments were finished within the first six years. The number of squares by the same date, 1788, was above 900. A new impetus occurred around the turn of the decade: between 1788 and 1792, the factory made nine times as many grands as had been made up to 1788 altogether. In the subsequent years of the 1790s, Broadwood produced an average of 140 grand pianos per annum.

[31] *The Present State of Music in Germany, The Netherlands, and United Provinces* (facs. of the 1775 London edn.; New York, 1969), ii. 147.

[32] Letter of 21 Jan. 1774, quoted in Cole, 'Americus Backers', 83.

[33] Printed by George E. Eyre and William Spottiswoode, London; pub. at the Great Seal Patent Office, 1856.

[34] All data in the following two paragraphs is taken from David Wainwright, *Broadwood by Appointment: A History* (London, 1982), 326–8. Some of the figures concerning the yearly production of Broadwood conflict with those of other sources; see 'Broadwood', in *The New Grove Dictionary of Music and Musicians*, ed. Stanley Sadie (London, 1980), iii. 324; Laurence Libin, 'Keyboard Instruments', *Metropolitan Museum of Art Bulletin*, 47 (1989), 40.

Amazingly high as these figures are, they seem modest when compared to the mass production of Broadwood's square pianos. Within a single year, between 1784 and 1785, more than 200 squares were sold; by the 1790s, this figure increased to an average of 250 per year. Squares were much more saleable than grands, of course, their price being one-third of that of a grand piano. Broadwood had agents throughout the country, and could boast of an international, even transatlantic market.[35] This enormous scale of production, apart from the unlimited demand of music consumers, cannot be separated from the general economic growth of the Industrial Revolution in England.[36]

Piano manufacture proceeded on a more modest scale in other European countries. Sébastien Erard, the most important French maker of the late eighteenth century, produced his first square pianoforte in Paris in 1777; prior to that, most instruments in Paris were English imports, mainly by Zumpe. Pascal Taskin made the first grand pianofortes in France from the late 1770s, then Erard, after a long and fruitful stay in England, built his first grand piano with English action in 1796. Other Paris makers produced pianos in the last quarter of the century, however, as shown in the notices of contemporary journals and almanacs.[37] The *piano-forte organisé*, a combination of the pianoforte and the organ, seems to have been favoured in France at the time.[38]

According to the recent research of John A. Rice, piano manufacture is well documented in the 1780s in Tuscany. Inspired rather by the contemporary English square than by the tradition of the Cristofori school, Tuscan makers built small (presumably square) pianos. The instruments are described in the various issues of the *Gazzetta toscana*, 1784–7.[39] In the Low Countries, as Clemens von Gleich reports, 'Dutch instrument builders have concentrated almost exclusively on the production of square pianos. This type was the most current in living-rooms, certainly up to about 1840.'[40]

In the German-speaking countries, both the vogue and the manufacture of the fortepiano were spreading fast in the direction of Vienna. Perhaps the most significant maker of the *Hammerflügel* after Stein, Anton Walter, established

[35] In 1796, John Jacob Astor bought six square pianos from Broadwood, to be sent to America.

[36] For the economic and sociological background of late 18th-cent. English piano manufacture see Cyril Ehrlich, *The Piano: A History*, 2nd edn. (London, 1990), 16–20.

[37] See the comprehensive account of French piano making and piano music of this period, in Adélaïde de Place, *Le Piano-Forte à Paris entre 1760 et 1822* (Paris, 1986). The book includes an index of all the makers, and a catalogue of all the pianoforte compositions published in Paris between these dates.

[38] On this particular type of instrument, see Peter Williams, 'The Earl of Wemyss' Claviorgan and its Context in Eighteenth-Century England', in Edwin M. Ripin (ed.), *Keyboard Instruments: Studies in Keyboard Organology, 1500–1800* (New York, 1971), 77–87; id., 'Claviorgan', in *The New Grove Dictionary of Musical Instruments*, ed. Stanley Sadie (London, 1984), i. 429–30.

[39] See John A. Rice, 'The Tuscan Piano in the 1780s: Some Builders, Composers and Performers', *EM* 21 (1993), 4–26.

[40] *Pianofortes uit de Lage Landen*, 11.

his workshop there around 1780.[41] As the famous virtuosos of the London Pianoforte School (Dussek, Cramer, Clementi) played their brilliant performances on Broadwood grand pianos, so the greatest musicians of Vienna favoured Walter's concert instruments. W. A. Mozart premièred his mature concertos on his (still extant) Walter fortepiano, and Beethoven used one at least until 1800. Johann Schantz took over the workshop of his brother, Wenzel Schantz, in 1791; Nannette Stein, with her husband Johann Andreas Streicher, opened her Viennese shop in 1794. The *Jahrbuch der Tonkunst von Wien und Prag* (1796) characterized the instruments of these outstanding makers as follows:

Derjenige Künstler, der sich bisher am berühmtesten gemacht hat, und der gleichsam der erste Schöpfer dieses Instruments bei uns ist, ist Hr. Walter, wohnhaft an der Wien, im Fokanetischen Hause, im hintern Hofe. Seine Fortepiano haben einen vollen Glockenton, deutlichen Anspruch, und einen starken vollen Bass. Anfänglich sind die Töne etwas stumpf, wenn man aber eine Zeitlang darauf spielet, wird besonders der Diskant sehr klar. Wird aber sehr viel darauf gespielet, so wird der Ton bald scharf und eisenartig, welches jedoch durch frisches Beledern der Hämmer, wieder zu verbessern ist. . . .

Der zweite berufene Meister ist Herr Schanz [*sic*], wohnhaft an der Wien, oberhalb dem k. Heumagazine, beim Ochsen, hinten im Hofe. . . . Der Ton derselben [seiner Instrumenten] ist nicht so stark, als jener der Walterschen, aber eben so deutlich, und meistens angenehmer, auch sind sie leichter zu traktiren, indem die Tasten nicht so tief fallen, auch nicht so breit sind, wie jene. . . .

Der dritte grosse Meister, oder vielmehr Meisterinn ist Madame Streicherinn, in der rothen Rose auf der Landstrasse. . . . Ihre Instrumente haben nicht die Stärke der Walterschen, aber an Ebenmaass der Töne, Reinheit, Schwebung, Anmuth, und Sanftheit, sind sie unerreichbar. Die Töne sind nicht anstossend, sondern schmelzend, das Traktament erfordert eine leichte Hand, elastischen Fingerdruck und ein fühlbares Herz. . . .

Ueberhaupt aber ist es gewiss, dass wir gleichsam zwei Originalinstrumentenmacher haben, näml. Walter und Streicher, alle Uebrigen ahmen entweder dem Erstern oder dem Andern nach; vornehmlich findet Walter sehr viele Kopisten, weil mancher derselben aus seiner Schule abstammt. . . .

Da wir nun zwei Originalinstrumentenmacher haben, so theilen wir unsere Fortepiano in zween Klassen: die Walterischen und Streicherischen. Eben so haben wir auch bei genauer Aufmerksamkeit zwei Klassen unter unsern grössten Klavierspielern. Eine dieser Klassen liebt einen starken Ohrenschmauss, das ist, ein gewaltiges Geräusche; sie spielt daher sehr reichtönig, ausserordentlich geschwind, studirt die häckeligsten Läufe und die schnellsten Oktavschläge. . . . Den Virtuosen dieser Art empfehlen wir walterisches Fortepiano. Die andere Klasse unserer grossen Klavierspieler sucht Nahrung für die Seele, und liebt nicht nur deutliches, sondern

[41] For a recent account of the types of Walter's fortepianos, complete with pictures and diagrams, see Kurt Wittmayer, 'Der Flügel Mozarts: Versuch einer instrumentenbaugeschichtlichen Einordnung', in Rudolph Angermüller, Dietrich Berke, Ulrike Hofmann, and Wolfgang Rehm (eds.), *MJb 1991: Bericht über den Internationalen Mozart-Kongress 1991* (Kassel, 1992), i. 301–12.

auch sanftes, schmelzendes Spiel. Diese können kein besseres Instrument, als ein Streicherisches, oder sogenanntes Steinisches wählen.

[In Vienna], the artist who has made himself the most famous so far, and who is the first maker of this instrument [fortepiano], is Herr Walter of Vienna, who lives in the Fokanetisch house, in the back courtyard. His fortepianos have a full, bell-like tone, a clear response, and a strong, full bass. The tone is a bit dull at first, but later, after one has played the instrument for a certain time, the treble especially becomes very clear. After too much playing, on the other hand, the tone will be sharp and metallic, which can be remedied through the re-leathering of the hammers. . . .

The second qualified master is Herr Schanz, resident in Vienna, above the imperial hay-store, at the sign of the Ox, at the back of the yard. . . . The tone of his instruments is not as strong as that of Walter's, but it is just as clear, and usually more pleasing; furthermore, the touch is lighter, for the keys do not fall so far, and are not as wide as those [of Walter's]. . . .

The third great *Meister*, or rather *Meisterinn*, is Madame Streicherinn, at the Red Rose in the Landstrasse. . . . Her instruments have not the strength of the Walter type, but the evenness, clarity, lightness, sweetness, and softness of their tone are unmatched. The sound is not jarring, but melting; the touch requires a light hand, flexible fingers, and a sensitive heart. . . .

We can say in summary: we have two original instrument makers, namely Walter and Streicher, and the others imitate the one or the other. Walter especially has many followers, some of whom come from his school. . . .

As we have two original instrument makers, so we divide our fortepianos into two classes: the *Walterisch*, and the *Streicherisch*. By close observation we can also detect two classes of players amongst our best piano players. One of these classes loves a great musical treat, that is, a powerful sound; to that end they play with a rich texture, extremely fast, study the most difficult runs and the fastest octaves. . . . For the virtuosos of this kind we recommend the Walter style of piano. The other class of player seeks nourishment for the soul, and loves playing that is not only clear but also soft and melting. These can choose no better instrument than the Streicher or so-called Stein type.[42]

Besides the legion of instrument makers who made *Tafelklaviere*, a large number of makers built fine *Hammerflügel* in Germany and Austria. This is a major difference from England, where the Broadwood firm fairly monopolized the production of grand pianos for a long time. Within the distinct tone-quality and construction that separate these German/Austrian instruments from their more numerous English counterparts, there is a refreshing variety that one can still enjoy among the surviving original examples. A list of eminent makers, active in the last quarter of the eighteenth century, includes:

[42] Johann Ferdinand von Schönfeld, *Jahrbuch der Tonkunst von Wien und Prag* (Vienna, 1796; facs. repr., ed. Otto Biba, Munich and Salzburg, 1976), 87–91. Trans. partially by Michael Latcham. According to the opinion of Michael Latcham, the presence or absence of the check in the action (Walter versus Stein/Streicher) has an important effect on the 'Walterisch' and 'Streicherisch' styles of playing. See 'The Check in Some Early Pianos and the Development of Piano Technique Around the Turn of the Eighteenth Century', *EM* 21 (1993), 29–42.

Dulcken, Johan Lodewijk (Munich)
Heilman, Matthäus (Mainz)
Könnicke, Johann Jakob (Vienna)
Schantz, Wenzel and Johann (Vienna)
Schiedmayer, Johann David (Erlangen)
Schmahl, Christoph Friedrich (Regensburg)
Schmidt, Johann (Salzburg)
Späth, Franz Jakob (Regensburg)
Stein, Johann Andreas (Augsburg)
Stein, Nannette and Matthäus Andreas (Vienna)
Walter, Anton (Vienna)

Several observations and documents from various sources, partially discussed already in this chapter, support the fact that the common pianoforte instrument of the second half of the eighteenth century was not the grand, but the small square piano. This important detail has not been sufficiently emphasized in the literature. The 'fortepiano' or 'pianoforte' of the time, mentioned and evaluated in various contexts in musical and sociological writings (past and present), suggests the notion of the wing-shaped instrument as a matter of course; whereas the latter was basically the instrument of professionals, made and sold in considerably smaller numbers than the universally used domestic instrument, the square piano.

Carl Philipp Emanuel Bach, one of the most original keyboard artists of the century, owned only a *Tafelklavier* in the last period of his life. The catalogue of his estate includes the following list of instruments:[43]

Ein fünf Octäviger Flügel von Nussbaum Holz schön und stark von Ton.
Ein *Fortepiano* oder *Clavecin Roial* vom alten Friederici, von Eichenholz und schönem Ton.
Ein fünf Octäviges Clavier von Jungcurt, von Eichenholz und schönem Ton.
Ein fünf Octäviges Clavier vom alten Friederici, von Eichenholz, der Deckel von Feuernholz, schön von Ton. An diesem Claviere sind fast alle in Hamburg verfertigte Compositionen componirt worden.
Ein Helfenbeinerner Zinken, der aus einem einzigen Elephanten-Zahn gedrehet ist, und desswegen in eine Kunstkammer aufgenommen zu werden verdient.

Thus C. P. E. Bach, in his late Hamburg years, possessed a harpsichord, a fortepiano, and two clavichords. The second item in the list, 'Ein *Fortepiano* oder *Clavecin Roial*', can not be a *Flügel*-shaped instrument, since Christian Ernst Friederici, the well-known organ maker of Gera, did not build grand pianos. He first specialized in a light upright piano (1740s); from the late 1750s, however, he started to build square pianos (*Fortbiens*) that became very

[43] *Verzeichnis des musikalischen Nachlasses des verstorbenen Capellmeisters Carl Philipp Emanuel Bach* (Hamburg, 1790), 92; facs. edn. with Preface and Annotations, Rachel W. Wade, *The Catalog of Carl Philipp Emanuel Bach's Estate* (New York, 1981).

popular. Bach's instrument was in all likelihood one such small *Tafelklavier*; the term 'clavecin roial' (or 'royal') was reserved for this type of case.[44] Philipp Emanuel was clearly partial to the instruments of Friederici. 'I have a greater preference for the clavichords of Friderici [*sic*] than for those of Fritz and Hass. . . . The *Fortbiens* are very good, and I sell many of those,' he wrote in a 1773 letter to Forkel.[45] The first statement of the letter is supported by the 'fünf Octäviges Clavier' listed in the estate; the second statement proves that Bach acted as sales agent for Friederici. More important is that Philipp Emanuel, who wrote the last five volumes of his late *Kenner & Liebhaber* series 'fürs Fortepiano' (pub. 1780–7), presumably thought in terms of the *Tafelklavier*.

The very first keyboard treatise written exclusively for the piano, J. P. Milchmeyer's *Die wahre Art das Pianoforte zu spielen* (Dresden, 1797), teaches how to play the square piano. The opening paragraph of Chapter 5 reads thus:

Hat man unter Instrumenten verschiedener Art die Wahl, so würde ich anrathen, dass man das kleine viereckige Pianoforte, dem grösern vorziehe. Das grose braucht mehr Platz, vermehrt die Unkosten des Transports auf Reisen, und hat weniger Veränderungen, als die kleinen. . . . Bei den grosen Pianoforte's habe ich auch gefunden, dass die beiden obersten Octaven, verhältnismäsig selten einen schönen, hellen, durchdringenden Ton hatten, die Bässe waren meistens auserordentlich stark, und die obern Töne schmachtend.

If one has the choice of different kinds of instruments, my advice would be to give preference to the small square pianoforte, as opposed to the grand. The latter needs more space, its transport costs more when travelling, and has fewer alterations of colour than the small one. . . . I also find that the two upper octaves of the grand pianofortes comparatively seldom have a beautiful, clear, and penetrating tone; the bass is mostly very strong, and the treble is weak.[46]

Milchmeyer does not name any maker whose instruments he would consider as a model for his tutor, but the detailed description of the four *Veränderungen* ('Pedalen', as Milchmeyer puts it)[47] seems to point in the direction of the instrument maker Johann Gottlob Wagner, active in Dresden, where Milchmeyer's book was published. Wagner's 1774 invention, the square piano named *clavecin royal*, had identical *Veränderungen*: lute,[48] raising the

[44] Concerning its invention by J. G. Wagner see n. 49 below.

[45] 'Die Fridericischen Clavicorde haben bey mir einen grösseren Vorzug vor den Fritzischen und Hassischen. . . . Die Fortbiens sind sehr gut und ich verkaufe Viele davon.' See Carl Hermann Bitter, *Carl Philipp Emanuel und Wilhelm Friedemann Bach und deren Brüder* (Berlin, 1868), i. 336.

[46] Milchmeyer, *Die wahre Art*, 57.

[47] On the various stops of pianoforte instruments, operated by hand, knee, or foot, see the next chapter.

[48] According to Rosamond Harding, the 'Harfen- oder Lederzug', described by Milchmeyer, means 'lute' colour. See *The Piano-Forte: Its History Traced to the Great Exhibition of 1851*, 2nd edn. (Cambridge, 1978), 127.

dampers, una corda, and swell (raising the lid).[49] On the other hand, Milchmeyer's characterization of the ideal pianoforte sound is quite different from the harpsichord-like tone of Wagner's instruments, which have uncovered wooden hammers. The above set of *Veränderungen* seems to have been a standard arrangement on square pianos, in other countries as well. A 1789 instrument by Thomas Haxby of York, housed in the Colt Clavier Collection, and a square of *c.*1810 by the Dutch makers Meincke and Pieter Meyer, in the Haags Gemeentemuseum, have the same four tone-colours, operated by pedals, one of which serves to raise the lid.

As sketched above, the Broadwood firm made only square pianos before the 1780s. But in the official ledgers, even after 1800, 'Piano forte' designated the regular square, and 'Grand Piano forte' as a distinct term was used for the more rare, and more expensive instruments.[50]

While Continental instruments hardly ever found their way to the British Isles, English pianos appeared occasionally in Germany. (In France, importing from England was a regular practice from the beginning.) In the majority of cases, the presence of English instruments was connected with the person of Jan Ladislav Dussek. As early as 1782, Dussek gave a concert in Hamburg on an English fortepiano 'von ganz neuer Erfindung', as the *Staats- und Gelehrte Zeitung des Hamburgischen unpartheyischen Correspondenten* advertised.[51] Between 1800 and 1802 Dussek lived in Hamburg, and, according to his letters, he promoted the sale of the grand pianos of Clementi there. On 16 May 1800 he wrote to Longman, Clementi & Co.:

> I have at last received the Forte Piano in a pretty good state, and having played upon it to Several Amateurs, some of them are very anxious of possesing a Like instrument, therefore I hope it will be no objection with you to pay me the Two above mentioned works [sonatas and concertinos] with Instruments. . . . Be so good therefore, and as soon as you have received my manuscripts, send 2 Grand Forte Pianos.[52]

Another, impatient letter followed on 12 June:

> I beg You would do your possible to send me the Two Grand Instruments immediately, for the Two Gentelmen who I have persuaded to purchaise them after they have heard my Own, are very impatient about it.

[49] For a detailed discussion of Wagner's instrument, see Wolfgang Wenke, 'Das "clavecin roial" des Dresdener Instrumentenmachers Johann Gottlob Wagner von 1774', in Günter Fleischhauer, Walter Siegmund-Schultze, and Eitelfriedrich Thom (eds.), *Studien zur Aufführungspraxis und Interpretation von Musik des 18. Jahrhunderts*, Beilage zum Heft 29: *Zur Entwicklung der Tasteninstrumente in der zweiten Hälfte des 18. Jhs.* (Blankenburg, 1986), 13–15.

[50] For access to the materials of the Broadwood Archive (Ledgers 1–2, and Letter Book 1801–10), housed in the Surrey Record Office of Surrey County Council, I owe thanks to Dr D. B. Robinson, County Archivist.

[51] Issue of 12 July 1782, quoted in Howard Allen Craw, 'A Biography and Thematic Catalogue of the Works of J. L. Dussek (1760–1812)', Ph.D. diss. (Univ. of S. California, 1964), 27–8.

[52] The letters are quoted ibid. 109 and 112–13.

Finally, Dussek could register the successful transaction on 22 August:

I have this Momment [*sic*] received your letter and *connaissement* of the 2 Instruments . . . I assure You that great deal of Business may be done here, as since they have heard me play upon English Forte Pianos, and particularly the one You send [*sic*] Last Winter, they are grown mad for them.

It was presumably on these instruments that Dussek and F. H. Himmel played the latter's two-piano sonata on 25 April of the following year, in the Freemasons' Hall of Hamburg, with great success. The performance, 'upon two beautiful and matched English pianos', as the *Allgemeine Musikalische Zeitung* wrote, 'could only be described as perfect'.[53]

The greatest collector of English pianos in Germany was surely Prince Louis Ferdinand of Prussia. Like his royal uncle, Frederick the Great, who bought over a dozen Silbermann fortepianos earlier, Louis Ferdinand obtained thirteen English instruments, mainly under the influence of Dussek, who entered his service in 1804 in Magdeburg. The prince, by all accounts, was a fine keyboard player and amateur composer; Beethoven, who made his acquaintance in 1796 in Berlin, dedicated his C minor Concerto to him.[54] Louis Ferdinand fell in battle at Saalfeld (1806), aged 34: Dussek wrote his F sharp minor Sonata Op. 61 on the untimely death of his aristocratic patron and friend ('Élégie Harmonique Sur la Mort de Son Altesse Royale, le Prince Louis Ferdinand de Prusse, En forme de Sonate').

Broadwood produced the last recorded harpsichord (No. 1155), a solid, five-octave instrument with Venetian swell shutters, in 1793. (The instrument is part of the Russell Collection of Early Keyboard Instruments in Edinburgh.) The firm, however, continued to sell and tune harpsichords beyond that date. The last entry in the Letter Book concerning a harpsichord is in answer to one Miss Wilkinson, Grove Hillhouse, who wished to sell or exchange her harpsichord; the date is August 1802. The entry reads: 'The Harpsichord we cannot allow anything for as from their almost total disuse they are unsaleable.'[55]

[53] Quoted in Craw, 115.

[54] See the musical biography of Prince Louis Ferdinand in Friedrich Gustav Schilling, *Encyclopädie der gesammten musikalischen Wissenschaften oder Universal-Lexicon der Tonkunst*, iv (Stuttgart, 1837).

[55] Letter Book 1801–10, in the Broadwood Archive (Surrey County Council, Surrey Record Office).

2

Keyboard and Compass

THE mechanical differences between the German/Viennese and the English pianoforte have been described several times in the literature; much less has been said about the keyboard itself. Naturally, the pressing of the key cannot be discussed separately from the structure of the mechanism; still, it is through the keys that the player is in direct contact with the instrument.

The touch of the German/Viennese fortepiano is lighter, and the fall of its key is shallower than on the English instruments. These qualities largely determine the manner of playing on the two types of pianos; ultimately, they have an effect on the composition of the music itself. The Viennese fortepiano requires a light hand, and the quick action produces a graceful swiftness that is essential to the keyboard style of Mozart and his Viennese contemporaries. Milchmeyer, the German champion of the *Tafelklavier*, emphasizes the importance of the above qualities of the keyboard in his 1797 treatise: '[When choosing the proper instrument], one should observe whether the touch is not too hard, or the keys do not fall too far, for both of these hinder rapid playing.'[1]

The more sluggish action of the English pianoforte, with a deeper fall of the key, made the instrument more suitable for heavier and fuller textures.

The dimensions of the keys (length, width, depth of touch) have a certain effect on the position of the hands, and consequently on touch and fingering. The degree of curvature of the fingers, for instance, is determined by the length of the natural keys in front of the sharps. The shorter the key, the more curved the finger must be, in order to keep the old rules of keyboard playing: still hand, and even touch. The width of the naturals affects the stretch of the fingers, and the horizontal orientation of the fingers on the keyboard in general. Agility and dexterity are decisively influenced by the depth of touch ('key-dip'): the shallower the dip, the lighter the passage-work.

As a general rule, the dimensions of the keys are smaller on the German/Viennese fortepianos than on the English ones (see Table 1).[2] The length of the

[1] 'Auch darauf siehet man, ob etwa die Tasten sich zu hart spielen, oder zu tief fallen, weil beides an einem geschwinden Spiele hindert.' *Die wahre Art*, 57.

[2] The instruments in Table 1 are all originals, from the collections of the Germanisches Nationalmuseum (Nuremberg), the Victoria and Albert Museum (London), the Russell Collection of Early Keyboard

TABLE 1. Measurements of Keys on 18th-Century German/Viennese and English Pianos

(All measurements in millimetres)

	Length of natural keys in front of sharps	*Overall length of naturals, front to back*	*Width of naturals*	*Key-dip*
G. Silbermann grand, 1749	34	120	20	4
Zumpe square, 1767	41.5	127	21	7.5
Backers grand, 1772	40.5	125	22	7.5
Steinbrück square, 1782	40	127	22	5
Stein grand, 1788	35	124	19	6
Walter grand, *c*.1790*	41	142	22	5
Broadwood grand, 1787	43	132	23	7.5
Steinway modern grand	50	150	22	11

* The overall length of the naturals varies widely among Walter's instruments. On several others the overall length is only 131 mm.

natural keys in front of the sharps is considerably shorter on the Silbermann and Stein instruments than on any other in the table. The longest keyheads are on the Broadwood pianos: they are almost one-third of an inch longer than those of the Stein type. Broadwood used keys of the exact same dimensions well into the nineteenth century; up to the 1820s, for certain. We find similar measurements on Clementi's pianos.

As far as the depth of touch is concerned, there is a conspicuous difference between the German/Viennese and the English instruments, the latter being characterized by a deeper fall of the keys. Interestingly, the early models (squares and grands, by Zumpe and Backers, respectively), have the exact same key-dip (7.5 mm) as the later standard type of Broadwood.[3] This is a crucial point that affects the physical aspect of playing profoundly. Just how profoundly, a letter of the eminent fortepiano maker, Andreas Streicher of Vienna, might illustrate.

The background to this document is that the Leipzig publishing firm, Breitkopf & Härtel, as an active dealer of Viennese fortepianos, had contacts with Viennese instrument makers. The relationship between Gottfried Härtel

Instruments (Edinburgh), and the Colt Clavier Collection (Bethersden, Kent). For the measurements of the Walter fortepiano, in private possession, I owe thanks to Professor Wolfgang Gamerith in Oberschützen (Austria).

[3] The pianos of Robert Stodart are somewhat different in this respect. The original grand pianoforte in the Dolmetsch Collection of Musical Instruments (with the nameboard 'Robertus Stodart & Co London Fecerunt 1790') has a key-dip of 6 mm.

and Andreas Streicher was a particularly friendly one, and their correspondence illuminates the questions and problems connected with the instrumental ideals of the time. Being familiar with the English type of piano as well, Härtel wrote to Streicher about the demand of Clementi and other partisans of the English instruments for a bigger tone and heavier action in the Viennese models.[4] Streicher answered on 2 January 1805 as follows:

> There is one remark in your letter with which I cannot concur, namely the heavier action and deeper [key] fall of pianos such as Clementi demands. I can assure you from twofold experience that a pianist can become accustomed much sooner to a poor tone, dragging, sticking of the keys, and all kinds of evils than to the heavy action and even less to the deep fall of the keys. This summer I too have manufactured some of such instruments [the action of] which, however, is far from the action demanded by Mr Clementi, and now I have every reason to regret it. To be sure the English pianos gain an advantage over ours if we construct the keyboard according to their way, and this also seems to be Clementi's goal. Only it is also certain that then the fortepiano certainly will not be the universal instrument any longer, whereby at least nine-tenths of the keyboard amateurs will have to give up their playing.[5]

Later, Streicher tried to achieve some compromises on his instruments, without, however, changing their fundamental character.

Longer keys result in smoother playing and fingering;[6] the heavy action and the deep fall of the keys, at the same time, produce a robust and resonant sound. Both of these characterize modern piano playing. The early English grand is much closer to the modern piano than the contemporary Viennese fortepiano is; naturally, this likeness is manifest in the manner of playing as well.

The compass of the keyboard was expanded by exactly two octaves during the eighteenth-century history of the pianoforte. The expansion was a gradual one, of course, the more important intermediate stages of which are summarized in Table 2.

The four-octave range of Cristofori's piano (*C*–*c*³) would be normal for an Italian keyboard of around 1700, or after (sometimes with short octave, *C*/*E*–*e*³).[7] A half-octave extension in the treble is characteristic of German instruments; the *C*–*f*³ compass of the earliest surviving *Tafelklavier* (Socher) is

[4] Dussek's activity, as a sales agent of Clementi's pianos in Hamburg from 1800 on, surely did a great deal for the promotion of the English instruments in Germany. See his letters cited in the previous chapter.

[5] See Wilhelm Lütge, 'Andreas und Nannette Streicher', *Der Bär* (Jahrbuch von Breitkopf & Härtel), 4 (1927), 65–6; quote and trans. taken from William Newman, 'Beethoven's Pianos versus his Piano Ideals', *JAMS* 23 (1970), 498.

[6] The relationship between key-length and playing technique, through the gradual process from short to longer keys, has a long history, of course, starting at least in the 16th cent.

[7] Not all the surviving Cristofori pianos have this compass, however, contrary to the generalizing observation of John Henry van der Meer, *Musikinstrumente* (Munich, 1983), 189. The 1720 instrument, in the possession of The Metropolitan Museum of Art, New York, presently has a *C*–*f*³ compass; but, according to Libin ('Keyboard Instruments', 34), it is the result of a later alteration of the original range of *FF*–*c*³.

TABLE 2. The Gradual Extension of the Compass in the Course of the 18th-Century History of the Piano

Instrument	*Year*	*Compass*
Cristofori grand	1726	C–c^3
J. Socher square	1742	C–f^3
G. Silbermann grand	1746	FF–d^3
J. Zumpe square	1767	GG–f^3
A. Backers grand	1772	FF, GG–f^3
J. A. Stein grand	1784	FF–f^3
Broadwood grand	1787	FF–f^3
Broadwood grand	1790	FF–c^4
Broadwood grand	1794	CC–c^4

typical of clavichords. With the additional half-octave in the bass we reach the five-octave standard of the second half of the eighteenth century. Apart from some English variants (GG–f^3 of the Zumpe square, or the usual omission of *FF#* in the otherwise five-octave keyboard of Backers), the FF–f^3 compass characterized German/Viennese as well as English pianos up to *c.*1790.

One or two additional keys appeared in the treble register of the Viennese fortepiano during the 1790s. Half of the surviving Walter instruments have an FF–g^3 compass;[8] so does a 1796 *Hammerflügel* by J. J. Könnicke (Germanisches Nationalmuseum, Nuremberg). The notable *Pedalhammerflügel* made by Johann Schmidt of Salzburg (*c.*1795, Germanisches Nationalmuseum), and an original Schantz fortepiano of *c.*1795–7,[9] have the similar range of FF–a^3.

Radical extensions were carried out on Broadwood's pianos, mainly as a response to the initiatives of J. L. Dussek. It seems that a half-octave in the treble was added as early as 1790 (FF–c^4); and, by 1794, some Broadwood grands reached the six-octave compass (CC–c^4). John Broadwood's letter of 13 November 1793 to Thomas Bradford confirms the former event:

> We now make most of the Grand Pianofortes in compass to CC in alt. We have made some so for these three years past, the first to please Dussek, which being much liked Cramer Jr had one of us so that now they are become quite common and we have just begun to make some of the small Pianofortes up to that compass.[10]

Broadwood's ambition was to gain the favour of the star pianists of London; the additional half-octave in the bass in 1794 might have been likewise Dussek's idea. In any case, apart from the six-octave instrument Burney commissioned from J. J. Merlin in 1777, specifically for the playing of his

[8] See Wittmayer, 'Der Flügel Mozarts', 307.
[9] In the private collection of Linda Nicholson, London.
[10] Quoted in Wainwright, *Broadwood by Appointment*, 75.

four-hand music, and from such monsters as the peculiar six-manual, six-octave piano of Könnicke ('Piano Forte pour la parfaite Harmonie', 1795), Broadwood produced the only pianofortes with a compass of six octaves before the turn of the century.

The standard compass still remained five octaves, however, and customers had to pay extra for the 'additional keys'. Factory records show that the same type of instrument was available in different price categories, depending on the accessories fitted. Squares were offered 'with additional keys', 'with Pedal', or 'ornamented'; grands only 'with additional keys'. 'A New Grand Piano Forte with additional keys we cannot afford to sell under Fifty Guineas,' wrote John Broadwood to one Miss Patterson of Glasgow, in April 1802. Fashion demanded the wider compass: from 1794 on, the majority of the 'Grand Piano Fortes' sold were those with additional keys.[11]

The modification of sound through various devices had appeared on the earliest pianos, and remained part of the instrument's construction. As a legacy from the older types of keyboard instruments, the organ and the harpsichord, in the first period hand stops operated such mechanisms. The later knee-levers were characteristic of German/Viennese instruments, mainly of the *Hammerflügel*. Pedals, the only devices that have survived till modern times, were applied earlier on English than on Continental pianos, at least on those of the grand type. (Some German squares had pedals quite early, in the 1770s.)[12]

The device that became most important in a historical perspective, the raising of the dampers, was to be found on pianos as early as the first half of the eighteenth century. Presumably, C. P. E. Bach was familiar with the effect through the Silbermann instruments of Frederick the Great, for he wrote in the last chapter of his *Versuch*, Part II ('Von der freyen Fantasie'):

> The best instruments for our purpose [improvisation] are the clavichord and the pianoforte. . . . The undamped register of the pianoforte is the most pleasing and, once the performer learns to observe the necessary precautions in the face of its reverberations, the most delightful for improvisation [*zum Fantasiren*].[13]

According to this information, Philipp Emanuel had practical experience of improvising on the pianoforte during his Berlin years. He must have found the undamped register 'most pleasing' in the broken-chord passages of extemporizations. (Series of arpeggios occur typically in the fantasias of C. P. E. Bach, beginning with his celebrated C minor piece of the *18 Probestücke*.)

[11] The details in this paragraph are taken from the materials of the Broadwood Archive.

[12] For a recent summary of the subject, see Kenneth Mobbs, 'Stops and Other Special Effects on the Early Piano', *EM* 12 (1984), 471–6.

[13] C. P. E. Bach, trans. William J. Mitchell, *Essay on the True Art of Playing Keyboard Instruments* (New York, 1949), 431.

Gottfried Silbermann's grand pianos introduced 'split damping', that is, separate raising mechanisms for the treble and the bass register. This feature, which remained in use in many types of instruments up to the end of the century, may have inspired players to achieve special sound effects, through the 'undamping' of either the higher or the lower range of the keyboard alone. The dampers were raised through hand stops, on Silbermann's grands as well as on various square models of later times, a circumstance which restricts the use of this device. Presumably, players kept the dampers raised for longer passages, since they could only operate the stops during pauses in the music.

The other basic modification of the sound, the one to produce piano colour, was achieved either through the *Verschiebung* (una corda), or the moderator. We find an una corda device on the earliest grand pianos. The lateral shift of the action is operated by two iron levers (placed underneath the keyboard) in Cristofori's instrument, and by a hand stop on G. Silbermann's piano. The eighteenth-century English grand followed the Cristofori model in this respect, too, only here pedals operate the mechanism, from the earliest type of Backers. German/Viennese makers preferred the moderator or celeste stop (a cloth strip between the hammer and the string, to muffle the tone), operated by hand stop or knee-lever. The una corda pedal did not appear on Viennese instruments before the nineteenth century.

It is neither possible nor necessary to give a complete account of all the additional colour variants on the early pianoforte, be it square or grand, German or English; whether operated by hand, knee, or foot. On the earlier types, *cembalo* or lute stops made the instrument sound like a harpsichord or a clavichord. In fact, the fortepiano was still considered a kind of harpsichord, with pedals and stops to achieve dynamic and colouristic variety. Several documents suggest this tendency. J. N. Forkel wrote in the *Musikalischer Almanach für Deutschland*:

So wie man um mehrerer Mannichfaltigkeit des Tons willen, an den Flügeln verschiedene sogenannte Register und Züge erfand, so suchte man aus eben der Ursache auch auf dem Pianoforte dergleichen anzubringen. Man sieht daher jetzt selten ein gutes Piano forte, an dem nicht wenigstens so viele Züge angebracht seyn sollten, dass man durch verschiedene Combinationen derselben 10 bis 12 Veränderungen hervorbringen kann.

As different stops and *Züge* for variety of sound were desired on the harpsichord, the same experiments were made on the pianoforte too. So now one can hardly see a good pianoforte that would not have at least as many stops, that through their different combinations ten or twelve *Veränderungen* could be produced.[14]

Regarding German instruments, the use of several *Veränderungen* was more typical of the *Tafelklavier* than of the *Hammerflügel*. As cited in the first

[14] *Musikalischer Almanach für Deutschland auf das Jahr 1782* (Leipzig, 1782), 16.

chapter, Milchmeyer recommended the purchase of square pianos, for '[the grand piano] has fewer alterations of colour [*Veränderungen*] than the small one'.[15] The more or less standard four *Veränderungen* (see the description of the Wagner-type square piano in the previous chapter) included the swell, that is, the raising of the lid, which helped to increase the volume of the sound through the gradual opening of the lid, or the dust plate (*Staubschutzdeckel*).

The mechanical arrangement and operation of such devices varied among different makers; sometimes even among the instruments of one and the same maker. Johann Gottlob Wagner, for instance, advertised his newly invented 'clavecin roial' in 1775 as an instrument with four pedals ('Vermittelst dieser Pedaltritte . . . werden alle Veränderungen in der grössten Geschwindigkeit, mitten im Spielen bewirket'); surviving Wagner *Hammerklaviere*, however, including the one in the *Bach-Haus* in Eisenach (made 1788), have knee-levers instead of pedals.[16]

Early English squares had hand stops within the case, at the left-hand side of the instrument. Zumpe provided two stops, to raise the bass and treble dampers. Broadwood squares were made without stops or pedals, but, at the customer's wish, could be equipped with any sort of mechanism, at extra charge.[17] Thus in 1796 Mr Bartolozzi ordered 'a pianoforte ornamented without additional keys with 2 pedals to act by the knee, one of them to raise the lid, the other dampers'.[18] The document shows that Broadwood used knee-levers as well as stops and pedals; also, a mechanism to raise the lid.

As a general rule, English grands had two pedals, from the start: one to raise the dampers, the other to achieve an una corda effect. Pedals did not appear on Viennese grand pianos before the nineteenth century.

The fashion for descriptive and programmatic music, mainly for amateurs, prompted instrument makers to install various percussive and other mechanisms in the pianoforte. For the imitation of the orchestral effects of battle music, Turkish music, and the like, pedals to operate drums, triangles, and cymbals were added to the piano. Although patented first in England (Rolfe and Davis, 1797), such noisy accessories became more typical of German and Viennese instruments. Upright pianos of particular shapes (*Giraffenflügel*, *Pyramidenflügel*, *Lyraflügel*), especially, were equipped with an arsenal of sensational effects, including bassoon, janissary music, etc. A number of surviving instruments from the early part of the nineteenth century have as many as six pedals. Highly popular among *Liebhaber*, such gadgets, however, were disapproved of by the more serious musicians of the time.[19]

[15] *Die wahre Art*, 57. [16] See Wenke, 'Das "clavecin roial"', 15.

[17] As mentioned earlier in this chapter, 'Piano forte' and 'Piano forte with Pedal' belong to different price categories in the contemporary Broadwood price-lists. See Broadwood Archive, Letter Book 1801–10.

[18] Quoted in Wainwright, *Broadwood by Appointment*, 326.

[19] See further details in Ch. 9. The most exhaustive treatment of the subject is in Harding, *The Piano-Forte*, 112–50.

3

Aesthetics of Sound

AROUND 1800 Andreas Streicher prepared a booklet which was presented with each of his instruments sold in Vienna. He entitled the brochure *Kurze Bemerkungen über das Spielen, Stimmen und Erhalten der Fortepiano, welche von [Nannette Streicher] [geborne] Stein in Wien verfertiget werden*. The very important chapter 2 'On Tone' (*Vom Tone*) starts as follows:

Es ist sehr schwer, wo nicht unmöglich, den schönsten Instrumentalton zu bestimmen. Jeder Mensch hat sein eigenes, von einem andern mehr oder weniger verschiedenes Gefühl. Diesem müssen wir es zuschreiben, dass einige nur *scharfe*, *schneidende*, *grelle*; andere hingegen *volle*, *runde*, *molligte* Töne lieben.

It is very difficult, if not impossible, to agree upon what constitutes a really beautiful instrumental tone since everyone has a more or less different idea about it. For this reason, some prefer a *sharp*, *cutting*, or *shrill* tone; others, on the contrary, prefer a *full*, *well-rounded* tone.[1]

Certainly no justification is required here for saying that the tone-quality of an instrument is of fundamental importance for any serious player, up to the present day. Contrary to the more or less uniform sound ideal of our uniform modern world, however, the instruments of bygone centuries had much more character and variety of sound.

As the previous chapters have already suggested, the two basic types of early pianos produced sounds utterly different from one another. German/Viennese instruments had a light, clear, ringing tone; English ones a fuller, more resonant tone. Apart from the mechanical differences of the action, the heaviness of the strings, and the size and construction of the hammers, this discrepancy is the result of the differing ideals and execution of the damping. The immediate decay of the sound after releasing the key was a *sine qua non* of the German/Viennese fortepiano, whereas the advocates of the English instruments liked a kind of 'halo' around the sound. Both were for musical reasons. The rhetorical, *sprechend* manner of German keyboard music could only be communicated through perfect articulation; the more 'public' and flamboyant concert style of the London Pianoforte School, on the other hand, sought volume and a legato effect.

[1] *Kurze Bemerkungen* . . . (Vienna, 1801), 12; trans. from Richard Fuller, 'Andreas Streicher's Notes On the Fortepiano, Chapter 2: "On Tone"', *EM* 12 (1984), 463.

How to produce efficient damping was a crucial question for German instrument makers, as shown earlier, through the citation from Forkel's *Musikalischer Almanach*, in Chapter 1. When the young Mozart became acquainted with the instruments of Johann Andreas Stein in Augsburg, his very first statement was this: '[Compared to the claviers of Spath] now I much prefer Stein's, for they damp ever so much better than the Regensburg instruments.'[2] Milchmeyer likewise emphasizes the importance of good damping:

Nun geht man zu den Dämpfern über, und probirt, ob sie alle Noten, vorzüglich auch die untersten Bassnoten, gut dämpfen. . . . Auch muss man beim Dämpfen aller Töne genau Acht geben, ob der Ton kurz aufhöre und nicht einen gewissen unangenehmen Nachhall oder ein Zischen hinter sich lasse.

[When selecting a proper pianoforte,] one turns to the dampers, and tries whether all the notes, including especially the lowest bass notes, are damped well. . . . One also must give close attention whether the tone stops quickly, and does not leave behind a certain unpleasant reverberation, or a buzz.[3]

While German/Viennese pianos were equipped with leather dampers, English pianos had 'feather-duster' dampers that did not quite hinder the after-vibration of the strings. Consequently, complete silences, so essential for the minutely prescribed articulation of the rhetorical style, are practically impossible to achieve on English instruments.

Two authors of the time discussed the tone-quality of the German type of pianoforte in detail: Milchmeyer in Dresden, and Andreas Streicher in Vienna. Interestingly, both compare proper piano tone to that of wind instruments on the one hand, and to the human voice on the other. Milchmeyer writes:

Vor allen Dingen muss der Spieler, der ein Pianoforte untersucht, wohl aufhorchen, ob die Töne hellsingend sind, und der Nachhall von langer Dauer ist, wenn er mit den obersten Tönen einen Accord anschlägt, und hält, denn daraus lässt sich ein Schluss auf die Güte des Resonanzbodens machen, sodann ob diese Töne einer schönen Frauenzimmerstimme gleichen, und ein wenig in den Klerinettenton übergehen. Hierauf spielt man die Töne von oben bis unten einen nach dem andern langsam, und merket genau auf, ob sie etwa verschiedene Eigenschaften haben, ob z.B. einige schreiend, andre zu sammetartig, wieder andre zu hölzern klingen. Im Ganzen müssen alle Töne von einerlei Beschaffenheit seyn.

The player who tests a pianoforte must above all carefully listen whether the tone is clear and singing, and whether the after-ring is of long duration when he strikes a chord with the upper notes, and holds it, for by this one can judge the quality of the soundboard, and whether the tone resembles a beautiful woman's voice, with a shade of clarinet tone. Hereupon one should play the notes one after another, from top to bottom, slowly, and listen carefully as to whether they have diverse qualities, for

[2] Letter of 17 Oct. 1777; see *Letters*, 327. [3] *Die wahre Art*, 57–8.

instance, whether some have shrieking, others a too velvety, still others a too wooden sound. All the notes of the keyboard must have the same quality [of sound].[4]

The precision of the tone-production of wind instruments demonstrates very well the fortepiano ideal of both the player and the maker. A. Streicher writes:

. . . wenn so wohl die . . . Töne des Fortepiano Gefallen erwecken oder rühren sollen; sie sich, so sehr als nur möglich, dem Tone der besten Blasinstrumente nähern müssen. . . . Bey einem Steinischen Fortepiano ist der Ton ganz nach dem angegebenen Ideale gebildet, so wie in seiner Tastatur schon alles vorbereitet ist, was der Spieler zu jeder Gattung des musikalischen Vortrags braucht.

If the tone of the fortepiano is both to move and please the listener, it should, as much as possible, resemble the sound of the best wind instruments. . . . The tone of the Stein fortepiano is modelled completely according to this ideal, so that in its keyboard, everything that the player needs for every type of musical performance is already prepared.[5]

Streicher also mentions the desirable resemblance to the human voice; among wind instruments, his preference is, especially in regard to the treble register, the tone of the flute (*flötenartig*).

Streicher lays great emphasis on the role of light touch, in order to achieve a beautiful tone. 'A "silver tone" . . . very soon . . . becomes an "iron tone" if played too heavily,' he warns.[6] Streicher gives a long, and at times humorous description of proper versus agressive performance on the fortepiano. Strongly against 'overplaying', he offers a penetrating explanation of this evil:

Alle Saiten- und Blasinstrumente liegen, während des Berührung des Spielers, *dem Ohre näher*, als das Clavier. Bey diesem ist der Spieler in keiner so nahen Verbindung mit dem Tone, als die übrigen Instrumentisten, sondern er hat nur die Tastatur, die den Ton hervor bringt, ihn selbst aber nicht gibt, *nahe bey sich*, aber gerade das, was den eigentlichen Ton schafft, den Resonanzboden *entfernt von sich*. . . .

Daher kommt es, dass diejenigen, welche dem Spieler gegen über stehen, alles, auch in einer weiten Entfernung, auf das deutlichste vernehmen, während jener selbst glaubt, sein Instrument gebe *gar keinen Ton*; daher kommt es, dass er in einem grossen Saale noch weniger von sich hört, als in einem Zimmer; weil dort die *entfernten Wände* den Ton nicht so schnell zurück werfen können, als hier die *näheren*. Für den Zuhörer geht aber darum nichts verloren. Der Ton verbreitet seine Schwingungen bis zu ihm hin, und lautet nicht schwächer, wohl aber sanfter und schöner.

During playing, all string and wind instruments are situated *nearer the ear* than is the keyboard. For this reason, the fortepianist has in no way so close a command of his tone as the other instrumentalists. Rather, he has only the keyboard, which produces the tone not in his direction, *near him*, but straight out. The soundboard *carries away from him* the sound that is actually produced. . . .

[4] *Die wahre Art*, 57.

[5] *Kurze Bemerkungen*, 12–13; trans. in Fuller, 'Andreas Streicher's Notes', 463–4.

[6] '. . . ein so genannter *Silberton*, der aber sehr bald, besonders bey starkem Spielen, *Eisenton* wird.' Ibid. 12; trans. 463.

> *This is the reason* that those who are standing opposite the player, even at a distance, can hear everything distinctly, while the player himself thinks his instrument is producing *hardly any tone*; this is also the reason he hears even less of his playing in a large room than in a small one, because *distant walls* cannot reflect the sound as quickly as those which are *nearer*. For the listener, however, nothing is lost. The tone spreads its vibrations to wherever he is and it sounds not weaker, but truly gentler and more beautiful.[7]

English grand pianos had a broader, fuller sound from the start. Quite early, around 1788, John Broadwood introduced a significant change in the design of his instruments: to equalize the scale in string tension and striking point, he divided the bridge. By this, he achieved a more even tone-colour throughout the range. The gain, however, carried a loss as well: the sacrifice of the colouristic variety between the treble and bass registers[8] (a quality that points in the direction of the modern piano ideal).

The correspondence between musical aesthetics and instrumental character is formulated in a somewhat obscure printed source. The document is an informative essay, titled 'Desultory Remarks on the Study and Practice of Music, Addressed to a Young Lady while under the Tuition of an Eminent Master', written by an unknown author in 1790–2, and published in the 1796–7 issues of the *European Magazine* (London). Although not indicated in the title, the author's subject is piano performance. According to the editorial comments of the January 1797 issue, 'the master spoken of in them ['Desultory Remarks'] is the now celebrated Mr Dussek'.

Among the various aspects of performance, the article reflects upon the question of tone:

> To acquire a rich, a full, and mellifluous TONE is the DESIDERATUM beyond all other qualities in a Performer; . . . The mellow, impressive, Organ-like Tone is superior in significance and effect to that quilly and vapid sound produced by the Generality of Piano Forte Players.[9]

This passage tells us a great deal about contemporary English taste in keyboard performance. The very adjectives used (rich, full, mellow) would sound quite incongruous in relation to the German-type instruments; the 'organ-like' tone suggests a literal adherence to the sound ideal of the traditional chamber organ. The disparaging remark about 'quilly and vapid sound' is not likely to refer to the German-type piano, for that was scarce in England, and especially not played 'by the Generality of Piano Forte Players'. Rather, the author stresses the importance of the proper touch, to be learnt by all

[7] Ibid. 24–5; trans. 468–9.

[8] My personal experience reinforces this. The earliest Broadwood grand I have played, an instrument of 1787 in the Colt Clavier Collection, still with undivided bridge, has a more distinctive sound than any of the numerous later pianos I played, with divided bridge.

[9] *European Magazine*, 30 Sept. 1796, 181.

piano players. But the issue is, of course, inseparable from the character of the instrument. For, though inefficient touch brings no good results on any instrument, the desired 'mellifluous' tone is only possible on a fine English grand.

Some decades later, the German pianist-composer, Friedrich Kalkbrenner, characterized English instruments as follows:

> English pianos possess rounder sounds and a somewhat heavier touch [than their German counterparts]: they have caused the professors of that country to adopt a grander style, and the beautiful manner of *singing* which distinguishes them; to succeed in this, the use of the loud pedal is indispensable, in order to conceal the dryness inherent to the pianoforte.[10]

This 'singing' quality is one of the recurring attributes of eighteenth- and early nineteenth-century keyboard playing, connected not only with the pianoforte, but with earlier types of keyboard instruments as well. The changing notion of this ideal seems to reflect the changing aesthetics of 'singing' itself.

When C. P. E. Bach advises keyboard players 'to listen closely to good singers',[11] he presumably refers to the art of natural phrasing. Later, he explains in more detail:

> Lose no opportunity to hear artistic singing. In so doing, the keyboardist will learn to think in terms of song. Indeed, it is a good practice to sing instrumental melodies in order to reach an understanding of their correct performance. This way of learning is of far greater value than the reading of voluminous tomes or listening to learned discourses.[12]

Mid-eighteenth-century musical aesthetics advertised the primacy of vocal music, of course, and the representatives of the Berlin *Kulturkreis* were particular advocates of the idea. When discussing the 'singing' manner of keyboard playing, however, C. P. E. Bach did mean the character of the tone as well—surely clavichord sound, in the first place.

The emulation of singing figures prominently in later sources concerning the sound and the playing of the pianoforte, whether German or English. The two types, however, convey different vocal ideals. 'For the fortepiano player, it is essential to have an instrument, on which he can play without exertion in a light, singing, dexterous, and expressive manner,' wrote Andreas Streicher in Vienna around 1800;[13] Milchmeyer, as quoted earlier in this chapter, also considered *hellsingend* tone to be the prerequisite of a good pianoforte.

[10] Friedrich Kalkbrenner, *Méthode pour apprendre le pianoforte à l'aide de guide-mains*, Op. 108 (Paris, 1830); Eng. trans., anon., *Complete Course of Instructions for the Pianoforte* (London, *c.*1835), 10. Quoted in David Rowland, 'Early pianoforte pedalling: The evidence of the earliest printed markings', *EM* 13 (1985), 10–12.

[11] *Essay*, 39. [12] Ibid. 151–2.

[13] 'So wichtig es für den Fortepiano-Spieler ist, ein Instrument zu haben, auf welchem er ohne Anstrengung *leicht, singend, fertig, mit Ausdruck spielen* . . . lassen kann.' *Kurze Bemerkungen*, 3; my trans.

With the increasing tendency towards legato playing, the question took on a new aspect, one that concerned touch and playing style. And this style was primarily connected with the English piano. In the case of English instruments, 'singing' quality meant the ideal of the uninterrupted vocal line in performance. Clementi confessed that the English grand pianoforte formed his 'cantabile, legato style of playing'.[14] According to contemporary opinion, the champion of cantabile performance was J. L. Dussek. 'His fingers were like a company of ten singers,' wrote Václav Tomášek, a compatriot of Dussek.[15]

English pianos were little known in Vienna. When Beethoven received his grand pianoforte from Thomas Broadwood in 1818, the instrument appeared as a curiosity in the imperial city. In 1823, Ignaz Moscheles decided to give a kind of demonstration concert at the Kärntnerthor Theater, using alternately a Viennese and an English piano. The former was represented by an instrument by Conrad Graf; for the latter, Moscheles borrowed Beethoven's Broadwood. The young pianist described the reaction of the audience as follows:

I tried in my Fantasia to show the values of the broad, full, although somewhat muffled tone of the Broadwood piano; but in vain. My Viennese public remained loyal to their countryman—the clear, ringing tones of the Graf were more pleasing to their ears.[16]

The adjective 'muffled', used by Moscheles for the characterization of the tone of the Broadwood instrument, might lead us to the following aspect of piano sound.

Hummel's oft-quoted comparison regarding the tone character of the German as against the English pianoforte draws attention to an important point, namely the timbre and intensity of the sound of the respective instruments, when set against an orchestra. According to Hummel, the incisive tone of the German/Viennese piano rings more clearly against the orchestral texture than the mellow sound of the English piano. Since concerto performances require sizeable halls, the question also involves acoustical phenomena. To quote Hummel:

[The German piano] has a round fluty tone, which in a large room contrasts well with the accompanying orchestra, and does not impede rapidity of execution by requiring too great an effort. . . .

To the English construction, however, we must not refuse the praises due on the score of its durability and fullness of tone. . . .

In the meantime, I have observed that, powerfully as these instruments sound in a chamber, they change the nature of their tone in spacious localities; and that they

[14] Ludwig Berger, 'Erläuterung eines Mozartschen Urtheils über Muzio Clementi', *Caecilia*, 10 (1829), 238–9; quoted in Leon Plantinga, *Clementi: His Life and Music* (London, 1977), 290–1.

[15] 'Wenzel Johann Tomaschek, geboren zu Skutch am 17. April 1774: Selbstbiographie', *Libussa*, 4 (1845–9), 394; quoted in Craw, 'Biography and Thematic Catalogue', 127.

[16] *Recent Music and Musicians As Described in the Diaries and Correspondence of Ignatz Moscheles*, ed. Charlotte Moscheles, trans. A. D. Coleridge (New York, 1873), 89.

are less distinguishable than ours, when associated with complicated orchestral accompaniments; this, in my opinion, is to be attributed to the thickness and fullness of their tone.[17]

Hummel's observations are justified in the reviews of a concert given by Dussek on an Erard grand (with modified English action) in the Odéon Theatre in Paris, on 22 March 1810. The critic of the *Journal de l'Empire* wrote:

L'art merveilleux de M. Dusseck ne peut empêcher que le piano ne soit un instrument bon pour seconder le travail d'un compositeur; excellent pour accompagner la voix d'un canteur, très convenable dans un salon pour la musique de chambre; mais très déplacé sur un vaste théâtre et dans un grand concert, ou chacun des instrumens qui accompagnent vaut mieux que celui qui est accompagné.

The marvellous art of M. Dusseck could not prevent the piano from being an instrument good to second the work of a composer; excellent to accompany the voice of a singer; very appropriate in a salon for chamber music; but very much out of place in a vast theatre and in a grand concert, where each of the instruments that accompany is better than the one that is accompanied.[18]

It seems that the tone of the Erard grand blended too much with the sound of the orchestra: the solo instrument had insufficient sparkle to be the protagonist of the performance. But the criticism also indicates that as the nineteenth century proceeded, the increasing size of the concert halls, and of the accompanying orchestras, gradually demanded fuller sound from the piano, a sound that the eighteenth-century construction of the instrument, with its wooden frame, could not produce.

[17] *A Complete Theoretical and Practical Course of Instruction on the Art of Playing the Pianoforte* (London, 1828), 64–5.

[18] Issue of 24 Mar. 1810, 3–4; quoted and trans. in Craw, 'Biography and Thematic Catalogue', 179. Reviews of other contemporary concerts point out the same deficiency; see A. de Place, *Le Piano-Forte à Paris*, ch. 6, esp. 156–8.

Part Two
The Music

4

Clavier Instruments and Textures

IN 1772 Dr Burney met the German poet and musician C. F. D. Schubart in Ludwigsburg, and his description of the pleasant day concludes as follows:

> In this manner we kept on a loquacious intercourse the whole day, during which, he not only played a great deal on the Harpsichord, Organ, Piano forte, and Clavichord; but shewed me the theatre, and all the curiosities of Ludwigsburg, as well as wrote down for me, a character of all the musicians of that court and city.[1]

Schubart was actually organist and court harpsichordist at the time; the report shows, nevertheless, that a South German musician had both the ability and the opportunity to play all four kinds of keyboard instruments in the early 1770s; and not at all badly. 'He [Schubart] was the first real great harpsichord player that I had hitherto met with in Germany,' says Burney; he adds later: 'He played on the Clavichord, with great delicacy and expression.'[2]

The different natures of these four instruments need no explanation here. Their coexistence in the eighteenth century makes that era special in the history of keyboard music. For although *Claviermusik* before the end of the century is rarely specified for any one instrument, there are certain harpsichord and clavichord idioms, and later, writing that suggests pianistic thinking. The fact that the examples of this are mostly by composers who specialized in one particular instrument does not diminish their importance.

Some of the earliest examples of the Italian keyboard sonata in *style galant* were composed by the Venetian Domenico Alberti. Alberti's *VIII Sonate per cembalo, Op. 1* (published posthumously by Walsh, London, 1748), is true harpsichord music. The simple charm of this music, which is totally devoid of any articulation or dynamic mark, is in the constant tinkling of the left-hand accompaniment, and in the ornamented line of the melody (see Ex. 1, Sonata No. 2). Such pretty harpsichord writing remained essentially unchanged for the rest of the century in Italy, to be seen in the keyboard works of Galuppi, Rutini, Cimarosa, and others. The country of the birth of the pianoforte was in no hurry to make use of that instrument. During the years 1754–62 the youngest Bach, Johann Christian, fully absorbed this style: his earlier studies with his father and with his brother Carl Philipp Emanuel became virtually untraceable in his keyboard compositions.

[1] Burney, *The Present State of Music*, i. 110. [2] Ibid. 108.

Ex. 1 Alberti, Sonata Op. 1/2, i

In mid-century Vienna the most important and most respected exponent of the harpsichord was Georg Christoph Wagenseil. As *Hofklaviermeister* of the Empress Maria Theresia and her children, Wagenseil remained faithful to his instrument to the end of his life.[3] His divertimenti (actually three-movement sonatas) for solo harpsichord are both structurally and instrumentally more elaborate than similar compositions of his Italian colleagues. The articulation is worked out in careful detail. There are hardly any notes without some sort of mark in the score. Staccato, legato, little slurred figures, and tied notes reflect not only an accurate notation, but a considerably more advanced style as well. The young Joseph Haydn had a perfect model for his early keyboard divertimentos and partitas here. In fact, some of his early sonatas can hardly be distinguished from the short, but nicely proportioned movements of Wagenseil.

Wagenseil applied no dynamic marks in his harpsichord music. This feature is more conspicuous in his ensemble works, where the piano and forte indications of the accompanying instruments do not appear simultaneously in the main keyboard part.[4] However, the notation of the solo works suggests a flexible use of the instrument. It conveys the notion that the harpsichord can sustain tone, and that the player can control the duration and the character of the notes through the attack. The opening of the Menuet in No. 2 of the *VI Divertimenti da cimbalo, Op. 1* (1753), for instance, displays a remarkably rich articulation (see Ex. 2). The varied touch of the single and grouped notes of the right hand, and the increasing number of held notes of the left hand,

[3] See Burney's visit to the aged composer in Vienna, *The Present State of Music*, i. 329–30.

[4] The same dichotomy exists in the accompanied keyboard works of some of Wagenseil's Viennese contemporaries. See e.g. the *Divertimento per il Clavicembalo, Violino and Alto Viola* of Anton Zimmermann; the *Partitta a Clavi Cembalo con due Violini e Basso*, and the *Concertino per il Clavi Cembalo, Flauto traverso, Violino, Violoncello e Basso* of Leopold Hoffmann, in Michelle Fillion (ed.), *Early Viennese Chamber Music with Obbligato Keyboard* (Madison, Wis., 1989), Nos. 6, 7, 8.

Ex. 2 Wagenseil, Divertimento Op. 1/2, ii

produce a delicately shaped phrase, one which contradicts the alleged insensitivity of the harpsichord.

Nothing could look (or sound!) more different from the Op. 1 score of Wagenseil than the *18 Probestücke* of Carl Philipp Emanuel Bach, published in the same year, as part of the famous *Versuch*. Herald of an idiosyncratic artistic world, this archetype of clavichord writing could never be attributed to any other keyboard instrument. (The first two sets of solo sonatas of Philipp Emanuel from the early 1740s are titled 'per cembalo'.[5] However, the frequent use of dynamic marks in them suggests that the composer, in his solo works, had always thought in terms of an instrument capable of dynamic shades.) The *Probestücke* exemplify 'the true art of clavichord playing', and the notation certainly reinforces their didactic mission. The idiomatic writing includes not only indications of *Bebung* and *Tragen der Töne*, but extreme juxtapositions of ***pp*** and ***ff***, and constant change of colour and touch as well. The slow movements especially reflect a nervous foreboding of romantic introspection, manifest in the highly unusual appearance of the scores.

Two excerpts might illustrate the instrumental style. The first, from the Largo maestoso of Sonata IV (a movement that starts and ends in different keys), shows the transition from strict 3/4 metre into the closing free section, *senza misura* (Ex. 3). The articulation of the unaccompanied melodic lines conveys a rhetorical style, and the *Bebung* effect of the long notes heightens the expression. The other example is from the end of the B flat minor slow movement of Sonata V (Ex. 4). Almost absurd dynamic contrasts and elaborate rhythms create a theatrical atmosphere here, not unlike a *recitativo accompagnato* from an operatic scena. (Such late examples as the second movement of Beethoven's Fourth Piano concerto seem to originate in this kind of instrumental 'stage music'.)[6] The natural dynamics of the texture, that is, the alternation of one-part melody and eight-part chords, is amplified by the ***pp–ff*** indications; the final ***ppp*** is the only triple dynamic mark in the *18 Probestücke*.

[5] 'Prussian' sonatas (1742), and 'Württemberg' sonatas (1744).

[6] For an unusual interpretation of this movt. see Owen Jander, 'Beethoven's "Orpheus in Hades": The *Andante con moto* of the Fourth Piano Concerto', *19th-Century Music*, 8 (1984–5), 195–212.

Ex. 3 C. P. E. Bach, H. 73, ii

Ex. 4 C. P. E. Bach, H. 74, ii

Christian Gottlob Neefe in the Preface to his *Zwölf Klavier-Sonaten* (Leipzig, 1773), dedicated to C. P. E. Bach, specified the clavichord as the desired instrument for the performance of his compositions:

Diese Sonaten sind Klaviersonaten: Ich wollte daher, dass sie auch nur auf dem Klaviere gespielt würden; denn die meisten werden auf dem Flügel, oder Pianoforte wenig Wirkung thun, weil keines von beyden des Kantabeln und der verschiedenen Modifikation des Tons so fähig ist, als das Klavier.

These sonatas are *Klavier* [clavichord] sonatas. I mean by that that they are only to be played on the *Klavier*, for most of them will have little effect on the *Flügel* [harpsichord] or *Pianoforte*, since neither of the two is as capable of cantabile and the various modifications of tone as the *Klavier*.[7]

Although generally recommended by contemporary German treatises as the most sensitive keyboard instrument, the clavichord is rarely singled out in this manner, as the exclusive performing medium.

Music designated 'for the pianoforte' on printed title-pages begins to appear in the 1760s, in Paris and London.[8] The first known examples are:

J. G. Eckard, *Six Sonates pour le Clavecin, Op. 1* (Paris, 1763) (fortepiano mentioned in the author's Preface).

J. G. Eckard, *Deux Sonates pour le Clavecin ou le Piano Forte, Op. 2* (Paris, 1764).

J. C. Bach, *Six Sonatas for the Piano Forte or Harpsichord, Op. 5* (London: Welcker, 1766).

J. Burton, *Ten Sonatas for the Harpsichord, Organ, or Piano Forte* (London: Welcker, 1766).

Johann Gottfried Eckard, born in Augsburg, was closely connected with J. A. Stein, who took him to Paris in 1758. Through Stein, Eckard knew and understood the early pianoforte well, and he evidently became an exponent of the instrument in Paris. In the Preface to his Op. 1 set he explains:

J'ai tâché de rendre cet ouvrage d'une utilité commune au Clavecin, au Clavichorde, et au Forté et Piano. C'est par cette raison que je me suis cru obligé de marquer aussi souvent les doux, et les forts, ce que eut été inutile si je n'avais eu que le Clavecin en vue.

I have tried to make this work suitable for the harpsichord, the clavichord, and the fortepiano. It is for this reason that I have felt obliged to indicate the soft and the loud

[7] See the facsimile of the Preface in the modern edn. of the sonatas, ed. Walter Thoene, *Denkmäler Rheinischer Musik*, 10–11 (Düsseldorf, 1961, 1964). The Eng. trans. is in William Newman, *The Sonata in the Classic Era* (Chapel Hill, NC, 1963), 378.

[8] The first known music written and published explicitly for the pianoforte, a set of twelve sonatas composed by L. Giustini (1732), was mentioned in Ch. 1. See the description of the sonatas in Rosamond Harding, 'The Earliest Pianoforte Music', *ML* 13 (1932), 194–9.

Ex. 5 (*a*) Eckard, Sonata Op. 1/2, ii

(*b*) Eckard, Sonata Op. 1/4

(*c*) Eckard, Sonata Op. 1/2, iii

so frequently, which would have been pointless if I had had only the harpsichord in mind.[9]

Eckard's eight sonatas reflect a remarkable pianistic thinking. His array of dynamic and articulation marks is surprisingly wide, and their use, in general, is justified musically. Besides the indications ***p***, ***f***, ***pp***, ***ff***, we find in Op. 1 *cresc*, ***m:f:***, ***m:p:***, *legato e piano*; and in Op. 2 *rinf.*, ***fp***, *dolce*, *m. voce*, *tenute*. Dynamic differentiation can accompany harmonic events (dissonance → resolution, see Ex. 5*a*; interrupted cadences, see Ex. 5*b*), or contrast effects produced by opposite kinds of attack (see the juxtaposition of the staccato unison and the legato chromatic passages in Op. 1 No. 2, 3rd movt., Ex. 5*c*).

Pianism, however, is not merely a matter of dynamic signs. More important from the point of view of idiomatic instrumental writing are those passages

[9] Printed in J. G. Eckard, *Œuvres Complètes*, ed. Eduard Reeser (Amsterdam, 1956), p. iii.

where the texture and general character call for pianoforte sounds. In slow movements, for instance, the continuous triplet-figure accompaniment requires a blend that is quite alien to the nature of the harpsichord (see Ex. 6*a*). In some passages the articulation reflects pianistic inspiration. The short excerpt from the Andante movement of Op. 2 No. 2 might serve as an example: the variety of attack, the use of *rinf.* and *portato*, and the detailed articulation of the melody speak for themselves (see Ex. 6*b*).

Ex. 6 (*a*) Eckard, Sonata Op. 1/1, ii

(*b*) Eckard, Sonata Op. 2/2, i

Some of the movement titles also deserve attention: Cantabile; Amoroso (both in Op. 1 No. 1); Affettuoso (Op. 1 No. 3). Such terms are familiar from the German *Empfindsamkeit*, and refer to a sensitive approach.

The most puzzling question about Eckard's sonatas, however, concerns compass. The Sonata Op. 1 No. 2 has the uncommon range of *FF*–g^3. A compass that extends five octaves was very rare before the end of the century.[10] The fact that notes *FF* and g^3 occur in the same sonata (2nd movt., bar 26; 3rd movt., bar 25) excludes the possibility of using different five-octave instruments (*FF*–f^3 and *GG*–g^3) for different pieces. Since the first three sonatas of Op. 1 were probably composed in Augsburg,[11] the 'Forté et piano' mentioned by Eckard must have been Stein's instrument. However, no Stein fortepiano known to us has a greater range than *FF*–f^3, nor do French harpsichords or early piano types anywhere in Europe. The riddle, like many other organological questions, remains to be solved by future research.

[10] K. 485 of Domenico Scarlatti uses the same range, *FF*–g^3.

[11] See Eduard Reeser, 'J. G. Eckard', in *MGG*, iii. 1089.

Leopold Mozart and his two children became acquainted with the newly published sonatas of Eckard in Paris. 'Schobert, Eckardt [*sic*], Le Grand and Hochbrucker have all brought us their engraved sonatas and presented them to my children,' wrote the father to Frau Hagenauer on 1 February 1764.[12] In the same letter we read: 'My little girl plays the most difficult works which we have of Schobert and Eckardt and others, Eckardt's being the most difficult, with incredible precision.' Leopold's description of the Eckard sonatas is quite correct: some of their movements are downright difficult to play. Wolfgang Mozart chose the A major Andante, a one-movement piece (Op. 1 No. 4), for the middle movement of his concerto arrangement K. 40, composed in Salzburg, July 1767. The outer movements of the work are based on pieces by Honauer (Op. 2 No. 1) and C. P. E. Bach ('La Boehmer', H. 81), respectively.

Another German by birth, Johann Christian Bach, became a London celebrity, after an eight-year sojourn in Italy, where instrumental music came second to vocal music, especially opera. As the composer told Dr Burney, in Italy 'his chief study was the composition of vocal Music, . . . [and] during many years he made little use of a harpsichord or piano forte but to compose for or accompany a voice'.[13] In England, on the other hand, there was a strong demand for keyboard music and *Hausmusik* of all sorts, so Christian Bach soon found himself in the position of a keyboard expert. Since the period in question, the 1760s, coincided with the quick spread of the Zumpe type of square piano in England, he became an important exponent of that instrument. Until recently it was thought that J. C. Bach gave the first solo concert on (presumably a Zumpe) pianoforte in London, on 2 June 1768, in the Thatched House Tavern on St James's Street. Richard Maunder, however, challenged this notion with a freshly discovered document, according to which James Hook, organist of Vauxhall Gardens, played a 'Concerto on the Forte Piano' two months earlier, on 7 April 1768, 'at Mr Hickford's Great Room in Brewer-street'.[14] On Bach's early London career we read in Burney:

When he arrived in England, his style of playing was so much admired, that he recovered many of the losses his hand had sustained by disuse, and by being constantly cramped and crippled with a pen; but he never was able to reinstate it with force and readiness sufficient for great difficulties; and in general his compositions for the piano forte are such as ladies can execute with little trouble; and the

[12] Concerning Eckard, 'the engraved sonatas' must have been Op. 1, for Op. 2 was not yet available at this time. See *Letters*, 37.

[13] Burney, *A General History of Music from the Earliest Ages to the Present Period*, ed. Frank Mercer (London and New York, 1935), ii. 866.

[14] See Richard Maunder, 'J. C. Bach and the Early Piano in London', *JRMA* 116 (1991), 201–10. Since the playing of a concerto on a small square piano is unlikely, Maunder suggests that Hook might have used a Backers grand for his performance.

allegros rather resemble bravura songs, than instrumental pieces for the display of great execution.[15]

In J. C. Bach's first set for solo 'Piano Forte or Harpsichord', the Six Sonatas, Op. 5, we can clearly discern two different types of keyboard writing. Sonatas Nos. 1–4 are composed in a modern, *galant* manner, apparently with the new pianoforte in mind. The last two sonatas, on the other hand, display distinctive harpsichord idioms, and baroque features as well. The cyclic structure of the C minor sonata (No. 6) has little to do with the *style galant*: a praeludium-like Grave introduces a three-part fugue, then a Gavotte rounds off the composition. (All three movements are in C minor.) Sonata No. 5 in E major conforms more to the character of the three-movement classical sonata, but the instrumental writing unambiguously evokes the harpsichord. The stormy passages of the 'orchestral' first movement, and particularly those of the brilliant finale, would sound very tame indeed on a small *Tafelklavier* (see Ex. 7). The total lack of articulation and dynamic marks in the last two sonatas of the set shows great contrast with the first four. This suggests that in the choice of instrument the music itself is a much better guide than the alleged 'intention' of the composer; or conversely, that intention is often apparent in the score, and needs no special comment or explanation.

Ex. 7 J. C. Bach, Sonata Op. 5/5, iii

Sonatas Nos. 2–4 sound so much like Mozart that their very beginnings seem to anticipate the main theme of not one, but several Mozart pieces. It is no coincidence that the younger composer chose these three sonatas for his concerto arrangements of 1772 (K. 107).

Perhaps the most important achievement of these sonatas is the well-balanced interaction between instrumental idiom and the moulding of the form. From the potentials of the pianoforte Bach evolves a language that is perfectly suited for the realization of his sonata-form ideal. Some characteristics of this model are highlighted by Bach's use of the instrument: the typical dynamic contrast within a main theme; the more important contrast in character between first and second theme; the finely articulated texture. The softer attack and sensitivity of the pianoforte inspired Bach's lyrical second themes (for instance, in the D major Sonata, see Ex. 8*a*), or the elegantly

[15] *General History*, ii. 866.

Ex. 8 (*a*) J. C. Bach, Sonata Op. 5/2, i

(*b*) J. C. Bach, Sonata Op. 5/4, ii

elaborate refrain of the Rondeaux movement of the E flat Sonata (Ex. 8*b*). The use of dynamic indications, in general, is less detailed than in Eckard. Bach takes advantage of the sustaining power of the low register: the long-held bass octaves that accompany the arpeggio-figuration of the right hand in the development of sonata No. 4 suggest the effect of raised dampers as well (see Ex. 9).

Ex. 9 J. C. Bach, Sonata Op. 5/4, i

The pianistic quality of J. C. Bach's Op. 5 becomes clearer when compared to another Op. 5, the *Six Sonates Pour le Clavecin avec l'accompagnement d'un Violon ou Flute Traversière et d'un Vcelle*, by C. F. Abel, published in London in 1764. Abel, also of German origin, and J. C. Bach's business partner, was a gambist rather than a keyboard player, and had little interest in the different possibilities of new keyboard instruments. His accompanied sonatas, seemingly close in style to Bach's Op. 5, are typical examples of rococo harpsichord music: there are no dynamic or articulation marks, and the easy flow of triplets never goes beyond the level of mere prettiness.

The English organist and harpsichordist John Burton had his own ideas about keyboard writing in the mid-1760s, different from those of his Continental or London *émigré* contemporaries. Of course English keyboard music, strongly dominated by Scarlatti and Handel on the one hand, and by a preference for the organ on the other, had different roots and traditions altogether. 'Handel's harpsichord lessons and organ concertos, and the two first books of Scarlatti's lessons, were all the good Music for keyed-instruments at that time in the nation,' wrote Charles Burney about the English musical scene of the 1740s.[16] Perhaps it is not wrong to suggest that in eighteenth-century English keyboard music the organ played a role similar to that of the clavichord in Continental practice; or, at any rate, it came next to the harpsichord in secular music as well, as the clavichord did elsewhere. The evidence is in the style of some of the music, and in the titles of collections published in England. For instance, the *VIII Sonatas or Lessons for the Harpsichord* of Thomas Arne (London: Walsh, 1756) contain a fugue, and movements that approach the style of the voluntary. Significantly, some harpsichord concertos of Continental composers, like those of Wagenseil and C. P. E. Bach, were designated 'for the organ or harpsichord' in English collections.[17]

Thus the title of the printed collection composed by John Burton (*Ten Sonatas for the Harpsichord, Organ or Piano-forte*) should not be surprising.[18] Dr Burney introduces the composer as follows:

> The late Mr. BURTON, the scholar of Keeble, was an enthusiast in his art; but having in his youth exercised his hand more than his head, he was not a deep or correct contrapuntist. He had, however, in his pieces and manner of playing them a style of his own, to which, from his having been one of the first harpsichord players in our country who attempted expression and light and shade, he excited an interest and attention, which would now perhaps be much more difficult to obtain.[19]

The sonatas show a strange mixture of styles, textures, and movement types. Burton frequently writes thick textures; and although that sort of writing was not uncommon in harpsichord literature, some of his passages suggest that full sonority represented a quality associated with the pianoforte for English composers from the start (see Ex. 10). Sonata No. 1, and its harpsichord version in

[16] *General History*, ii. 1008.

[17] From the two sets of C. P. E. Bach's *Concertos for the Harpsichord, or Organ* . . . (London: Walsh, *c*.1753; Longman, Lukey and Co., *c*.1760) only one opus, H. 444, bears the option of two solo instruments in the original sources. The two sets of Wagenseil (*Six concertos for the harpsichord or organ with accompaniments for two violins and a bass*, Walsh, *c*.1765; *Six concertos for the organ or harpsichord with instrumental parts*, Welcker, *c*.1765) also include compositions originally intended for harpsichord only. See E. Eugene Helm, *Thematic Catalogue of the Works of Carl Philipp Emanuel Bach* (New Haven, Conn., and London, 1989); Helga Scholz-Michelitsch, *Das Orchester- und Kammermusikwerk von G. C. Wagenseil: Thematischer Katalog* (Vienna, 1972).

[18] Another triple designation on a title-page, *Duetto für 2 Claviere, 2 Flügel order 2 Fortepiano*, composed by the German J. G. Müthel (Riga, 1771), naturally names the clavichord as the third—or rather, first—instrument.

[19] *General History*, ii. 1018.

Ex. 10 Burton, Sonata No. 5, i

another collection of Burton, provide a good example. Lesson II ('The Chace') in the *Three Favourite Lessons for the Harpsichord* is a simpler variant of this D major sonata. The difference between the two compositions lies exclusively in the texture. A comparison of bars 9–12 and 41–4 proves that the 'Organ or Piano-forte' designation of the sonatas means something quite concrete here (see Ex. 11*a* and *b*). The dynamic marks in the first sonata excerpt reinforce the natural difference of volume between five-part and two-part textures. (The number of parallel octaves, particularly in bars 43–4, justifies Burney's remark about Burton's lack of proper proficiency in counterpoint.)

Nevertheless, it seems that these sonatas are essentially conceived for the harpsichord. There is very little articulation in the score, and most of the dynamic indications are either meaningless from the point of view of the musical structure and expression, or related to textural considerations, as in Ex. 11. The ***f***, ***p***, ***ff***, ***pp***, crescendo, diminuendo signs, often marked separately for the two hands, are placed rather haphazardly. A tiny example, chosen at random from the Minuetto of Sonata No. 2, illustrates this (Ex. 12). Also, the keyboard range of the sonatas corresponds to that of the English harpsichord

Ex. 11 (*a*) Burton, Sonata No. 1, i
Id., Lesson II, 'The Chace'

(*b*) Burton, Sonata No. 1, i
Id., Lesson II, 'The Chace'

Ex. 12 Burton, Sonata No. 2, ii

of the time: *FF*–f^3, with no *FF#*. The absence of the key *FF#* is apparent in bar 42 of Sonata No. 1 (cited in Ex. 11*b*), where the descending progression of the bass octaves is broken by an upward skip at the end. The note *FF*, on the other hand, occurs in Sonata No. 10, so the *GG*–f^3 range of the Zumpe square piano, practically the only possible pianoforte instrument in our case, could not accommodate the entire set. (The contemporary chamber organ could not accommodate it, either.)

The mention of three different keyboard instruments on a title-page was not unique to Burton's sonatas. John Garth published several sets of accompanied sonatas and also '6 Voluntarys' with similar designation. The first of these, *Six Sonatas for the Harpsichord, Piano Forte, and Organ; with accomp. for 2 Violins, and a Vcello*, Op. 2 (London: Welcker, *c.*1768), written in a much lighter vein than Burton's set, attests to the possibility that in England, the *galant* style could be performed on the organ.

According to certain sources, the first keyboard sonatas of Muzio Clementi also date from the late 1760s. His Op. 1 and Op. 2 (both titled *Six Sonatas for the Harpsichord or Piano Forte*), published in 1771 and 1779 respectively, were

p. 45-47

in fact composed much earlier.[20] Ironically, Op. 2 became famous as the first great example of pianistic writing, yet the sonatas must have been written for, and were certainly played by Clementi on, the harpsichord: his numerous London concert performances, prior to the start of his long Continental tour in 1780, were exclusively on the harpsichord.[21] Clementi was a virtuoso who, in his youth, gained his facility through industrious practicing of baroque keyboard music, and he remained a celebrated performer of Domenico Scarlatti. The breakneck third and octave passages of his music probably owe more to the style of Scarlatti than to the inspiration of the new pianoforte. As late as 1780, his London concert appearances announce 'Lesson for the Harpsichord', or 'a sonata for the harpsichord'.[22] Grand pianos were still scarce at the time in England, and Clementi obviously considered a robust harpsichord a much more brilliant instrument than a modest square piano.

An important source about London musical life in the late eighteenth century, *Recollections of R. J. S. Stevens*, contains remarkable evidence concerning Clementi's choice of instrument. According to the accounts of Stevens, in the second half of the 1770s, the keyboard instrument used at most places of public music-making in London was the pianoforte.[23] Yet, when reporting on the 1777 concerts at the Anacreontic Society, Stevens states: 'At this Concert, I have frequently heard Clementi, and Dance, on the Harpsichord: and Schroeter, on the Piano Forte.'[24] Such differentiation is rare in contemporary documents, therefore the more valuable.

The keyboard idiom of Clementi's Op. 1 shows the influence of Scarlatti (see Ex. 13). In Op. 2, of which only three sonatas are unaccompanied, a bold, new keyboard idiom is initiated. Although we may not be certain that this 'difficult' virtuosic style implies a new instrument, Clementi's later contemporaries were clear on this point. The *Quarterly Musical Magazine and Review* wrote in 1820: 'This admirable work [Op. 2] is the basis on which the whole fabric of modern sonatas for the pianoforte has been erected.'[25] The Zurich publisher H. G. Nägeli opened his representative series of new pianoforte music in 1803 with Clementi's set. (The fact that Op. 2 was later printed in several revised versions, one 'with considerable improvements',[26] does not

[20] Some autograph fragments of Op. 1 date from 1768, and, according to the 1820 volume of the *Quarterly Musical Magazine and Review*, Op. 2 was completed by 1770. See Alan Tyson, *Thematic Catalogue of the Works of Muzio Clementi* (Tutzing, 1967), 13.

[21] See Plantinga, *Clementi*, 35–6, 39. The subject is treated in Katalin Komlós, 'Mozart and Clementi: A Piano Competition and its Interpretation', *Historical Performance*, 2 (1989), 3–9.

[22] Plantinga, *Clementi*, 39.

[23] 'Mr. Sabattier was the Manager of this department, and generally stood behind the Person who was at the Piano Forte,' wrote Stevens about the 1777 events in the Anacreontic Society, where evening entertainments regularly included concerts of instrumental music. An entry of 1779, about the glee club called Friendly Harmonists, which met in Anderton's Coffee House, reads: 'Theodore Aylward . . . used to preside at the Piano Forte.' See *Recollections of R. J. S. Stevens: An Organist in Georgian London*, ed. Mark Argent (London, 1992), 25, 32.

[24] Ibid. 27. [25] Quoted in Tyson, *Thematic Catalogue*, 14. [26] Ibid. 37.

Ex. 13 Clementi, Sonata Op. 1/2, ii

Ex. 14 Clementi, Sonata Op. 2/4, i

alter the novelty of the original conception.) Nobody wrote passages like bars 29–30 of the first movement of the A major sonata before Clementi (Ex. 14), and the second episode of the Rondo in the same sonata outstrips the more famous 'octave lesson', Op. 2 No. 2.

But what do other aspects of the notation tell us? Articulation and dynamic marks are sparse in Opp. 1 and 2: nuances of performance, at least at this early stage, seem not have concerned Clementi.[27] Then, early 'pianistic' writing may have more to do with sensitivity and elaboration of detail than with forceful texture and sonority? As far as the compass of Opp. 1–2 is concerned, Clementi's use of the note *FF#* (in, for instance, the first movement of Op. 2 No. 2) suggests a non-typical English instrument, for that key was missing on most contemporary harpsichords as well as on the first English grand piano of Americus Backers. Apart from some Shudi and Broadwood harpsichords of a wider keyboard compass (*CC*–f^3), full chromatic range from *FF* was not customary on English instruments before the 1780s.

The *galant* pianoforte style initiated by J. C. Bach in England was followed and continued by Johann Samuel Schroeter in the 1770s. Another London

[27] See Mozart's comments and other contemporary opinions on Clementi's playing in Komlós, 'Mozart and Clementi'.

musician of German origin, Schroeter was born in 1752, the same year as Clementi, but his musical background was entirely different. Raised in Leipzig, he studied with J. A. Hiller, and then in the course of a family concert tour appeared in a Bach–Abel concert in London on 2 May 1772. Subsequently he remained in England, professionally supported by the generous Christian Bach, whose position as the Queen's music master he gained after Bach's untimely death.

The light, rococo manner of Schroeter's keyboard music, like that of J. C. Bach, appealed to the young Mozart. The opening theme of one of the Op. 2 accompanied sonatas ('pour le clavecin ou le piano forte', published *c.*1773 in Amsterdam) sums up this style very well (see Ex. 15). The fastidious Mozart considered Schroeter's Op. 3 concertos (*Six Concertos for the Harpsichord or Piano Forte*, London, *c.*1774) 'very fine',[28] and he wrote cadenzas for three of them. On his advice, the concertos found their way into the Salzburg house, where, in December 1778, Nannerl Mozart instructed the castrato (and obviously competent keyboardist) Francesco Ceccarelli on the playing of the first concerto.[29]

Ex. 15 Schroeter, Sonata Op. 2/2, i

Schroeter's first set of sonatas published in London (*Six Sonatas for the Piano-Forte or Harpsichord, with an Accompanyment for a German Flute or Violin*, Op. 4, Napier, *c.*1775), dedicated to a 'Miss Scott', is pleasant and easy chamber music for the amateur. It shows some influence of the current English keyboard idiom; for example, long passages in parallel thirds, such as the rondo theme of the second movement of Sonata No. 4 (Ex. 16), are rare in the

Ex. 16 Schroeter, Sonata Op. 4/4, ii

[28] See letter from Paris, 3 July 1778, *Letters*, 559.

[29] See Leopold Mozart's letter from Salzburg, 10 Dec. 1778, *Letters*, 639.

music of Continental composers. With a modest number of dynamic and articulation marks, this music is eminently suited for (and probably inspired by) the early square piano.

By 1777 Charles Burney found that when two persons were playing keyboard music for four hands, 'particular attention' must be made 'to that clair–obscure which is produced by different degrees of *Piano* and *Forte*'.[30] The important Preface to his *Four Sonatas or Duets For 2 Performers on one Piano Forte or Harpsichord* (London, 1777) explains:

> With respect to the *Pianos* and *Fortes*, each Performer should try to discover when he has the *Principal Melody* given to him, or when he is only to *accompany* that Melody; in order, either to make it more conspicuous, or merely to enrich its harmony. . . . It is hoped, . . . that something analogous to *Perspective*, *Transparency*, and *Contrast* in painting, will be generally adopted in music, and be thought of nearly as much importance, and make as great a progress among its students, as they have lately done in the other art.[31]

This kind of fine shading of loud and soft is only possible on the pianoforte, of course, so Burney must have written his sonatas for that instrument. The score suggests the same: the detailed articulation marks (for instance, the distinction between staccato dots and wedges), the various dynamic instructions (*Mez.For.*, *Rinf.*, *Cres*, *Dim.*), and the *perdendosi* endings of several movements clearly suggest this intention.

A great deal has been written about the early keyboard style of Haydn and Mozart. Here we face two entirely different cases. Haydn, unlike Mozart, was not a keyboard player *par excellence*, and if his splendid pre-1780 sonatas tell us little about his inclination toward any particular type of instrument, there are several reasons for that. His opportunities and experiences regarding keyboard instruments were rather limited in Eszterháza, and we know next to nothing about those instruments. Because of the lack of personal documents or communications (Haydn did not write masses of letters, as Mozart did), we cannot know whether Haydn was alert to the distinct character of the different keyboard instruments before the 1780s. For the players' sake, his practical mind would probably not have wished to make such differentiations anyway. Thus, the greater part of his sonata output, with its dazzling variety of form, musical character, and compositional craftsmanship, was *Claviermusik* of the highest order for any available instrument.[32]

[30] Burney, Preface to his *Four Sonatas or Duets For 2 Performers on one Piano Forte or Harpsichord* (London, 1777).

[31] Ibid.

[32] Of the abundant literature on Haydn's keyboard styles and instruments see, among others, László Somfai, *Joseph Haydn zongoraszonátái* (Budapest, 1979); A. Peter Brown, *Joseph Haydn's Keyboard Music: Sources and Style* (Bloomington, Ind., 1986); Horst Walter, 'Haydns Klaviere', *HSt* 2 (1969–70), 256–88;

In the long series of Haydn's sonatas the development of style brings forth a gradual refinement in notation, and sometimes it is difficult to tell whether this is a *practical* reflection of instrumental thinking, or a more *idealized* elaboration of detail. At any rate, the aspiration for a more precise expression leads to the need for a corresponding medium, and Haydn is certainly on the way to exploring the potential of the fortepiano during the late 1770s. His first set published by the Viennese Artaria in 1780, *Sei Sonate Per il Clavicembalo, o Forte Piano*, Op. 30 (Hob. XVI:35–9, 20), seems to live up to the editorial title. For lack of autographs (save for the fragment of the C minor sonata, 1771) the dates of composition are uncertain, but it is likely that just before sending the scores to be printed Haydn supplied performance indications for the sonatas. The number of dynamic marks, compared to his earlier practice, is surprisingly high: besides ***f*** and ***p*** we find *cresc*, ***ff***, ***pp***, ***fz***. The sound and texture of some of the slow movements requires indeed the sensitivity of the fortepiano. A lovely section of the Adagio of Hob. XVI:39 (bars 12–15), for instance, with its long-delayed resolutions, held bass notes, and *tenuto* descant line, loses much of its fine expressiveness—or needs entirely different means to achieve expressiveness—when played on the harpsichord (see Ex. 17).

Ex. 17 Haydn, Hob. XVI:39, ii

The most expressive of the six sonatas, however, is the justly famous C minor work. The first movement, one of Haydn's deeply personal essays for the keyboard, shows a maximum effort to give meticulous instructions about

'Keyboard Sonatas', Workshop 2, in J. P. Larsen, H. Serwer, and J. Webster (eds.), *Haydn Studies: Proceedings of the International Haydn Conference, Washington D. C. 1975* (New York, 1981), 213–21. For a recent opinion, see Howard Pollack, 'Some Thoughts on the "Clavier" in Haydn's Solo *Claviersonaten*', *JM* 9 (1991), 74–91.

performance. Every single bar is full of detailed information: the eloquence of the music is hardly in the notes themselves, but rather in the variety of touch, articulation, and dynamic shades. Since Haydn always composed at the clavichord (as he himself admitted), he must have conceived the beautiful main theme at that most sensitive of instruments. But when he finished the score for publication, apparently ten years later, his pen probably tried to depict the 'transparency and contrast' possible on the instrument that amplified the virtues of the clavichord.

Mozart was the first great fortepiano composer and performer in the history of music. His flair for this instrument was so strong that from early in the 1770s the fortepiano became his exclusive medium for keyboard composition. The documents regarding his attachment to the instrument are too numerous to cite here.[33]

His earliest solo sonatas from the mid-1770s reflect Mozart's cosmopolitan knowledge of current European styles. In the somewhat affected 'sigh motif' and the continuous triplet accompaniment of the Andante of the first Sonata (K. 279, see Ex. 18) we can recognize Eckard (for instance, Op. 1 No. 1, see Ex. 6*a*) as well as J. C. Bach (Op. 5 No. 5); the Andante amoroso character of K. 281 is also familiar from the rococo keyboard music of the *Vorklassik*. The Presto 3/8 finale (K. 280, 283) is a distinct type in the early Italian sonatas of the *galant* style. (See examples in Alberti's *VIII Sonatas*, Nos. 2 and 8, among others.)

Ex. 18 Mozart, K. 279, ii

Mozart played his first six sonatas repeatedly in Munich, Augsburg, and Mannheim, during the autumn of 1777. 'The last one in D [K. 284] sounds exquisite on Stein's pianoforte,' he wrote on 17 October 1777 from Augsburg.[34] *Galanterie*, as Mozart called refined and articulate performance,

[33] For a survey of various documents and their interpretation, see Eva and Paul Badura-Skoda, *Interpreting Mozart on the Keyboard*, trans. Leo Black (London, 1962); Katalin Komlós, ' "Ich praeludirte und spielte Variazionen": Mozart the Fortepianist', in R. Larry Todd and Peter Williams (eds.), *Perspectives on Mozart Performance* (Cambridge, 1991), 27–54.

[34] *Letters*, 328–9.

indeed plays an important part in the unusual Rondeau en Polonaise middle movement of this sonata. Dynamic differentiation even becomes an element of variation in the *veränderten Reprisen* of the refrain, as Ex. 19 shows.

Ex. 19 Mozart, K. 284, ii

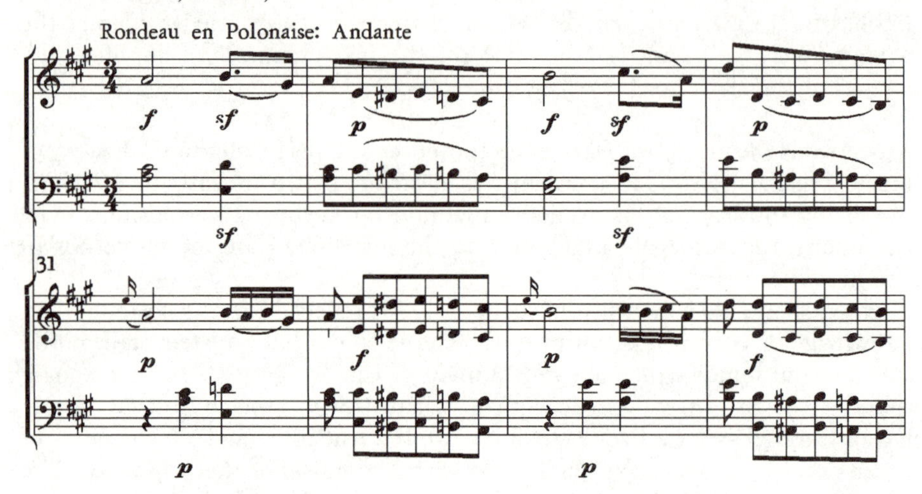

Mozart's acquaintance with the excellent fortepianos of J. A. Stein in October 1777 has been emphasized as a turning-point in his instrumental thinking; yet the glorious 'Jeunehomme' Concerto K. 271, written almost a year earlier, already gives plenty of evidence of the mature pianism of the young composer. The Augsburg sojourn, and the intensive work on Stein's instruments, nevertheless made further impressions on Mozart's keyboard idiom. The immediate result was K. 309, written for Rosa Cannabich during the first Mannheim days. Mozart gave piano lessons to Mlle Cannabich, and his letters of November 1777 report progress in the learning of the sonata. 'The Andante will give us most trouble, for it is full of expression and must be played accurately and with the exact shades of forte and piano, precisely as they are marked,' he explained on 13 November.[35] According to Mozart, the Andante is the portrait of Rosa Cannabich: it truly is a porcelain miniature, painted with infinite care and fine detail.

The 'development' of Mozart's fortepiano language needs no further analysis here. The compositional mastery, the profound expression, and the instrumental virtuosity of the Paris compositions of 1778 (the A minor sonata, and the two great variation sets K. 354 and 264) are far beyond the stage of novelty and experiment.

[35] *Letters*, 374.

5

Vienna and London, 1780–1800[1]

THE last two decades of the eighteenth century brought the first golden age of the pianoforte. The instruments reached an advanced technical level, and the keyboard music of the mature classical style responded to the new possibilities. The grand pianoforte (or *Hammerflügel* in Austria and Germany) became a solo concert instrument, as no earlier keyboard instrument had been. Its first great players were its first great composers as well: Mozart, Clementi, Beethoven, Dussek.

In Vienna Anton Walter built the most robust concert instruments of the early 1780s. Mozart and Beethoven both owned and played Walter pianos, the latter at least until the turn of the century. In England the single action of the earlier square pianos gave way to the English double action in the 1780s. Broadwood squares were made and sold in increasing quantity, and then from about the mid-1780s the Broadwood grand became the most respected instrument of professionals.

The invention and development of musical instruments usually goes hand in hand with musical demands: there exists a reciprocal relationship between the two. The finely articulated language of classical Viennese keyboard music found its medium in the perfectly damped, light sound of the 'Viennese' fortepiano. The quick touch of the German action is ideal for passage-work, and shows up the basically linear structure of the music clearly and transparently. Since the high and low registers have distinct colours, the sound spectrum is delightfully varied. On Walter's instruments the bass register is quite powerful. Due to the sharp, percussive attack, sforzatos and other accents (so important in Beethoven's music) give a sudden, biting effect.

Contemporary English pianos have a fuller and thicker tone, which sounds fine in heavy chords, but is less suited for pearly runs and nuances. The somewhat imperfect damping allows more resonance, but the considerable *Nachklang* makes rhetorical pauses and short notes (for instance, resolutions of appoggiaturas) less effective. The new late eighteenth-century style of piano playing and piano writing strove for homogeneous texture, full sound, legato style, and powerful virtuosity: the very qualities offered by the grand pianos of Broadwood, Stodart, Clementi, and others.[2]

[1] The keyboard music of Joseph Haydn is not discussed in this chapter, since, due to its special status, it is granted a separate chapter to itself.

[2] See the expert discussion of the characteristics of the two types of instruments, and the comprehensive

The musical vogue of Paris and London was quite different from that of Vienna. Although the greatest music of the time was written in Vienna, the imperial city seemed a bit provincial next to the cosmopolitan grandeur of the other capitals. Public concerts were still scarce in Vienna: music was generously patronized by the nobility, so it mainly reflected a private, aristocratic taste. The long tradition of public concerts in Paris and London, on the other hand, gradually established a more popular style that was at once intelligible and effect-oriented. Piano music was no exception.

To demonstrate the two different styles, let us cite the main themes of two sonata movements, written about the same time. One is the beginning of Mozart's K. 570 (Ex. 20), the other is the second movement of the G minor Sonata of J. L. Dussek, Op. 10 No. 2 (Ex. 21). Both works were published as accompanied sonatas as well, with *ad libitum* violin accompaniment. The most obvious difference between the two themes concerns texture. On a trivial level, texture means the number of parts and the relationship between them. The Mozart theme has a lean, fragile texture, whereas the Dussek one is heavy and robust, written mostly in six parts. Articulation, the syntax of musical language, plays an important role in the Mozart melody; it hardly matters among the big chords and octave passages of the Dussek theme. The latter speaks clearly to a large audience, while the former is intimate and personal.

Ex. 20 Mozart, K. 570, i

Ex. 21 Dussek, Sonata Op. 10/2, ii

description of late 18th-cent. piano music, in Malcolm Bilson, 'Keyboards', in Howard Mayer Brown and Stanley Sadie (eds.), *Performance Practice: Music after 1600* (London, 1989), 223–38.

The two composers were from widely different musical backgrounds and had different temperaments, and their ambitions were fulfilled in different ways. Both pursued careers as fortepiano performers, but Mozart, after his spectacular Viennese successes, was buried in his compositional work, and had neither time nor opportunity to organize concert tours for himself. His untimely death then cut short any further ambitions. Dussek, a Bohemian by birth, set out to conquer the audiences of the biggest concert-halls of Europe: he was one of the first international stars of the instrument in the modern sense. His inclinations coincided with the resources of the powerful English pianos. The instrument inspired his imagination, and in return he initiated improvements and innovations on the instruments of John Broadwood.

Perhaps the most famous virtuoso of the time, the Italian-born Muzio Clementi, gained his technique and musical knowledge from baroque keyboard music, played on the harpsichord. He grew up in England during the 1760s and early 1770s on the works of Scarlatti, Handel, Johann Sebastian and Carl Philipp Emanuel Bach, and Paradisi. This circumstance naturally influenced Clementi's compositional style. As we saw in the previous chapter, Clementi's pre-1780 solo performances in London were exclusively on the harpsichord. Apparently he continued to play the harpsichord as well, for in May 1781, during his one-year Paris sojourn, Broadwood shipped him a harpsichord and a square piano.[3] Clementi then spent some time in Strasburg and Munich and arrived in Vienna in December 1781.

The fortepiano competition between Mozart and Clementi on Christmas Eve 1781, in the presence of the Emperor Joseph II and the Grand Duke and Grand Duchess of Russia, became an important source of information about the artistic personalities of the two musicians.[4] On this occasion Clementi played his Sonata in B flat major Op. 24 No. 2, and his Toccata in B flat major, Op. 11. The sonata, in technical respects, is quite a modest piece, compared to the hair-raising difficulties of his earlier Op. 2. The Toccata, however, displays the famous chains of thirds, the hallmark of Clementi's keyboard style. Mozart's condemnation of Clementi's playing ('simply a *mechanicus*')[5] originated from this encounter. We shall discuss the mutual evaluation of the two artists in detail in the last chapter.

Clementi composed no less than a dozen sonatas in Vienna (Opp. 7–10, three pieces in each set). The influence of Viennese musical taste is obvious in them, but it does not overpower Clementi's instrumental originality. The report in Cramer's *Magazin der Musik*, emphasizing Clementi's indebtedness to the 'German' school, may be biased, but is not unfounded.[6] Echoes of

[3] See Wainwright, *Broadwood by Appointment*, 58.
[4] See Komlós, 'Mozart and Clementi'. [5] Letter of 12 Jan. 1782, *Letters*, 792.
[6] Quoted in Leon Plantinga, 'Clementi, Virtuosity, and the "German Manner"', *JAMS* 25 (1972), 329.

Haydn, Koželuch, and Mozart are equally discernible in the sonatas. The opening movement of Op. 7 No. 3 in G minor is a clear reflection of Haydn's C minor sonata, just published by Artaria. The short slow movement of the other G minor sonata, Op. 8 No. 1, also recalls the rhythmic structure and the careful articulation (bar 15) of several Haydn Andante movements. The integration of the motivic/polyphonic work into sonata style points to Leopold Koželuch, the only serious contrapuntalist among Vienna's *Kleinmeister* of the time. Although the angularity of Clementi's normal style is quite different from Mozart's characteristic fluidity, the easy flow of the Allegro con spirito of Op. 10 No. 1 suggests a Mozartian influence.

The truly individual features of these early sonatas are the presence of baroque elements and the prominent role of keyboard virtuosity. Double counterpoint, the simultaneous juxtaposition of two motives, is not at all infrequent. The Presto 3/8 finale of Op. 8 No. 1 applies the compositional procedure of the baroque gigue: the head motif of the first half opens the second half of the movement in inverted form, transposed from the treble register into the bass (Ex. 22). The main theme of another Presto 3/8 finale, Op. 13 No. 6, sounds in canon between the two hands (Ex. 23).

Ex. 22 Clementi, Sonata Op. 8/1, iii

Ex. 23 Clementi, Sonata Op. 13/6, iii

At this stage, technical difficulty and virtuosity were not linked with any particular keyboard instrument in Clementi's works. Born from the brilliancy of a Scarlatti-like harpsichord idiom (see previous chapter), rapid passages of thirds, octaves, and sixths remained second nature to Clementi, whether played on the harpsichord or on the fortepiano, Viennese or other. Besides these, wide stretches of ninth chords and intervals, double trills, and innumerable fermata signs (opportunities for improvised cadenzas)[7] require high technical proficiency from the performer of Opp. 7–10. Even the tempo indications (several Presto and Prestissimo movements) suggest virtuosity. Mozart ridiculed that, too. But even if Clementi played his Prestissimo alla breve pieces Allegro 4/4, as Mozart claims, the achievement is admirable.[8]

Other reports, however, sound quite different. According to a Berne piano maker Clementi 'played like a man with three hands'.[9] The same year, 1784, a correspondent of Cramer's *Magazin der Musik* wrote from Berne:

> When you see his fast passages in octaves for one hand, you can believe they are not easy to play; but he always does far more even than is written—octave trills, no less—and every note sounds clearly distinct from the others.[10]

Like the reference to Clementi's improvised cadenzas,[11] this description shows that Clementi was partial to virtuosic embellishments ('he always does far more even than is written'). In the light of this, it is worth mentioning a curious performance instruction in the Sonata in B flat, Op. 12 No. 1. Towards the end of the exposition of the opening Presto movement (and at the corresponding place in the recapitulation), preceding the final cadential double trill, we find a long held bass octave and a I^6_4 chord, which bears the inscription *senza ornamenti* (see Ex. 24). The obvious deduction must be that normally a cadenza would be played here. The I^6_4 chord is traditionally the signal for a cadenza, though the fermata that customarily marks off such a chord is lacking here. Clementi clearly wanted a strange, frozen effect here, so he verbalized his intention.[12]

Clementi's keyboard works from the 1790s reflect the influence of the English pianos. The most serious sets (Op. 25, 1790; Op. 33, for Therese

Ex. 24 Clementi, Sonata Op. 12/1, i

[7] According to the Clementi student Ludwig Berger, Clementi chose to play the Op. 24/2 Sonata at the competition with Mozart, because its several fermatas offered good opportunities for improvised cadenzas. See Berger, 'Erläuterung eines Mozartschen Urtheils'.

[8] Letter of 7 June 1783, *Letters*, 850.

[9] Quoted in Plantinga, *Clementi*, 72.

[10] Ibid.

[11] See n. 7 above.

[12] The written-out cadenzas of two C major opening movts. (Op. 25/1 and Op. 33/3) give an idea of Clementi's extempore embellishments. The former is rather an *Eingang*, leading to the recapitulation; the latter is part of a highly virtuosic sonata, originally composed as a keyboard concerto.

Jansen, 1794; Op. 37, 1798) continue the technically difficult style of the earlier sonatas, but show some particular features as well. The extension of the five-octave keyboard range (Op. 33 No. 1), the occasional marking of the pedal (Op. 37 No. 3), and the instruction *Legato assai* (Op. 33 No. 2) signify the inspirational presence of the grand pianoforte.

As 'principal composer and performer' at the Hanover Square Grand Professional Concerts, Clementi performed regularly with great success. His last documented solo piano concert, according to Plantinga, took place in May 1790.[13] However, the oboist and composer W. T. Parke mentions further performances in his contemporary memoirs. Of a 7 February 1791 Hanover Square concert he writes: 'Clementi, in a sonata on the piano-forte, astonished the audience by his execution.'[14] Even five years later we read: 'Clementi . . . performed a sonata with his accustomed brilliancy of execution.'[15] But Clementi's public appearances became sporadic, and he dedicated himself to teaching. His professional-level students included Therese Jansen, Benoît August Bertini, Johann Baptist Cramer, John Field, and others.

Unlike Mozart, Haydn and Beethoven had high regard for Clementi. (The reaction of the three composers towards C. P. E. Bach was similarly divided: the music of the 'Hamburg' Bach remained alien to Mozart, even if his response was not violent as in the case of Clementi.) When Artaria published Clementi's Op. 7 and Op. 9 and sent copies to Haydn, Haydn answered graciously in June 1783:

> Many thanks for the pianoforte Sonatas by Clementi, they are very beautiful; if the author is in Vienna, please present my compliments to him when opportunity offers.[16]

Beethoven had most of Clementi's piano works in his library, and he asked Czerny to use Clementi's *Introduction to the Art of Playing on the Piano Forte* to teach his nephew Karl.

Mozart liked music that was warm, elegant, and beautiful. He knew and was able to use practically all styles, but light, singing Italianate music attracted him most. He praised composers of this manner (Schroeter, J. C. Bach, Schuster), even if they were not his greatest contemporaries. It is doubtful whether he would have admired the young Beethoven, had he lived into the 1790s.

The singing melodies and the tinkling accompaniment of Italian rococo keyboard music remained an essential element of mature Viennese classical fortepiano writing, the one we usually identify with Mozart. The fundamental texture of this repertory consists of stereotyped accompaniment figures (Alberti, *Trommel*, murky), melodies of periodic structure, and swift, glittery

[13] Plantinga, *Clementi*, 117.

[14] William Thomas Parke, *Musical Memoirs* (London, 1830), 142.

[15] Ibid. 215–16.

[16] *CCLN* 42. We do not know whether Haydn received Clementi's Op. 7 or Op. 9, or both.

passage-work of running scales. All this is wholly idiomatic, comfortable for the hands, and suitable for a new manner of playing brought about by the emancipation of the thumb. The fortepiano helped to realize the articulation, and to illuminate the details with the distinction of light and shade. There were composers who offered only that; there were some with higher aspirations regarding counterpoint, compositional dexterity, and expression; and there was Mozart, the consummation of classical art.

The well-known label of the eighteenth century, *Kenner und Liebhaber*, plays no less a role in Mozart's keyboard œuvre than in that of his colleagues. Mozart was a teacher of the fortepiano, and he composed the majority of his sonatas (accompanied and unaccompanied) and other fortepiano pieces for his students. Wonderful as they are, they are not too demanding technically. Mozart's instrumental style is quite different when he writes for himself.[17] The great concertos, some of the variation sets, and a few other compositions show Mozart's exceptional pianistic gift.

Although *Geschmack und Empfindung* were all-important for Mozart in performance questions, he was not at all averse to virtuosity. He knew exactly the requirements of the stage, and his improvisations, judging from his large-scale variations, must have been phenomenal. To play the B flat Concerto K. 450, or the almost through-composed last variation set K. 613, is a major task for any pianist today. No wonder they are rarely performed; I have never heard the latter piece on the concert stage.

When Mozart absorbed and integrated the high polyphonic art of Handel and J. S. Bach into his style, his music became more complex than any other composer's of the time. (His early contrapuntal studies with Martini gave him only the fundamentals of learned composition.) The texture of the Rondo in A minor is at once condensed and fragile, charged with deep emotion: to play it on a worthy level takes the highest musical and instrumental sensitivity.

The only other composer-pianist of the Vienna of Mozart's time who even approached a Mozartian synthesis was the Bohemian Leopold Koželuch. A fashionable teacher, Koželuch was actually considered the first fortepianist of the imperial city. The *Jahrbuch der Tonkunst von Wien und Prag* (1796) gives a long account of his importance in the promotion of the new instrument:

Ihm verdankt das Fortepiano sein Aufkommen. Das Monothonische und die Verwirrung des Flügels, passte nicht zu der Klarheit, zu der Delikatesse, und zu dem Schatten und Licht, welches er in der Musik verlangte; er nahm also keinen Scholaren an, der sich nicht auch zu einem Fortepiano verstehen wollte, und es scheint, dass er in der Reformazion des Geschmacks bey der Klaviermusik keinen geringen Antheil hat.

The vogue of the fortepiano is due to him [Koželuch]. The monotony and the muddled sound of the harpsichord could not accommodate the clarity, the delicacy, the

[17] The issue is discussed in detail in Komlós, '"Ich praeludirte und spielte Variazionen"'.

light and shade he demanded in music; he therefore did not accept students who failed to show sympathy for the fortepiano as well, and it seems that he has no small share in the reformation of taste in keyboard music.[18]

The solo sonatas and keyboard trios of Koželuch (he wrote the greatest number of trios in the Classical period) show thematic invention, sense of form, and an ability to organize the musical material through the use of counterpoint. His keyboard idiom lies naturally for the hands; the passage-work is brilliant but not vapid (see Ex. 25, excerpt from the Sonata Op. 35 No. 1, published in 1791). The best works of Koželuch should be in the classical piano repertory today.

Ex. 25 Koželuch, Sonata Op. 35/1, i

The Viennese/German piano style was not unknown in England, thanks to the Continental *émigré* musicians who lived there. During the 1780s Johann Samuel Schroeter represented the pleasing, *galant* manner that was a heritage of J. C. Bach. Some of the English composers cultivated that style, too. Schroeter (and later Clementi) taught the young Cramer, whose musical ideal was and remained Mozart. 'His [Cramer's] interpretation of Mozart, and his own Mozart-like compositions, are like breathings "from the sweet south"', observed Ignaz Moscheles in a poetical mood.[19]

Originality is inexplicable. The immense originality of the young Beethoven cannot be explained either by his Bonn musical background, or by his early Viennese impressions. The teaching of Neefe, the acquaintance with Bach's *Wohltemperiertes Klavier*, the contrapuntal studies with Haydn and Albrechtsberger certainly do not explain the earthquake of the finale of the Trio in C minor, Op. 1, or the fantastic romanticism of the middle section of the Adagio of Op. 2 No. 3. In fact, it is quite astonishing that we classify

[18] *Jahrbuch der Tonkunst* (1796), 34–5. [19] *Recent Music and Musicians*, 34.

Beethoven as the 'fellow-composer' of Haydn and Mozart, within the same style.

By a Mozartian standard, Beethoven's piano playing must have been rough and rhapsodic. (Fashions change quickly: Beethoven, supposedly, had made uncomplimentary remarks about Mozart's playing.)[20] The Bohemian composer Václav Tomášek, who heard all the famous pianists from Mozart to the 1840s, considered Beethoven the greatest.[21] As well as creating a sensation in Viennese salons in the early 1790s, Beethoven did a concert tour of Prague, Dresden, and Berlin in 1796, in the company of Prince Lichnowsky; later in the year he appeared in Pressburg. He extemporized, and played his first two concertos repeatedly.

From the very beginning of his Viennese career, Beethoven stretched the limits of the fortepiano.[22] Disregard of the capabilities of the instrument is a crucial feature of Beethoven's artistic approach which is not evident when the music is played on a modern piano. Op. 27 certainly does not outstrip the resources of a Steinway or a Yamaha concert grand, and thus an essential aspect of the music is lost.[23] In Beethoven's case, the use of an eighteenth-century fortepiano (or replica) may be even more relevant than in Haydn's or Mozart's.

The heavy texture, and the sheer force of Beethoven's early piano writing require all the power of the fortepiano. The delicate touch prescribed by contemporary manuals could not accommodate the repeated blows of thick, fortissimo chords, or the running fire of broken octaves, to be played in unison with the two hands. Not less relevant is the fortepiano sound of some special, lyrical Beethoven movements. I know no precedent in the history of keyboard music for the character of the opening movement of the *Sonata quasi una fantasia* in C sharp minor, or of the finales of Op. 13 and Op. 31 No. 2.[24] On the appropriate instrument these beautiful movements assume a dream-like

[20] What the widely quoted criticism, preserved in Czerny's recollections, was actually based on, is hard to detect. (Beethoven told Czerny that he had heard Mozart perform 'several times', and found his fortepiano playing 'choppy'.) Beethoven could only have heard Mozart play during his unfortunately short, two-week visit to Vienna in Apr. 1787: as far as we know, however, Mozart had not played in public in the course of those months. Beethoven *might* have taken a few lessons from Mozart (a pure hypothesis); but again, he told F. Ries that Mozart had never played 'for him'. See Czerny's account quoted in George Barth, *The Pianist as Orator: Beethoven and the Transformation of Keyboard Style* (Ithaca, NY, and London, 1992), 43.

[21] 'W. J. Tomaschek, . . . Selbstbiographie', 391.

[22] Beethoven used an Anton Walter instrument until about the turn of the century. The compass of his keyboard works exceeds the five octaves *FF–f*³ only after Op. 31.

[23] I owe this observation to the performances and comments of Malcolm Bilson.

[24] The lovely rondo theme of the *Pathétique* finale is much rather the herald of a new era than the famous Grave introduction of the first movt. Slow introductions of the French overture type, with dotted rhythms, occur frequently in the sonatas of Koželuch and Dussek. The integration of the introduction into the sonata-form structure is not without precedent either. In Clementi's G minor Sonata Op. 34/2 (1795), the Lento e sostenuto introduction reappears in the course of the movt. These examples differ from those opening movts. of Koželuch where the slow introduction returns at the end of the movt. (e.g. P. XII:13, 17). The latter seem to recall the pattern of the French overture.

quality, and their 'romanticism' (for lack of a better word) gives a curiously anachronistic effect.

Certain new types of textures and instrumental techniques in Beethoven's early piano music seem to be derived from the London Pianoforte School, although the connection is not yet clear, in spite of some serious efforts on the subject.[25] To take one example: the stormy Prestissimo finale of Beethoven's F minor Sonata Op. 2, the strongest movement of the composition, represents a type that can be found both before and after Beethoven's Op. 2. The Prestissimo finale of Clementi's Sonata in E flat (Op. 9 No. 3, pub. Vienna, 1783) seems to initiate this turbulent motion of continuous, rushing triplets, a kind of belated *Sturm und Drang* in pianoforte music. We meet the same genre in early nineteenth-century Vienna, for instance in the works of *Jan Voříšek*. The fine Fantaisie Op. 12 of the Bohemian-born composer (the succession of a long, romantic introduction, and a tightly knit sonata-form movement) already looks forward to the sweeping, brilliant finales of Mendelssohn (see Ex. 26*a*, *b*, *c*).

The outrageous difficulty of Beethoven's piano music shocked the Viennese devotees of the instrument. With the appearance of Opp. 1 and 2, the sonata (solo or chamber) ceased to be the genre of *Hausmusik*. If the dedicatee of Op. 7, the Countess Barbara von Keglevich, could play that sonata, she was a fabulous player indeed. But Beethoven, clever enough in business matters, did

Ex. 26 (*a*) Clementi, Sonata Op. 9/3, iii

(*b*) Beethoven, Sonata Op. 2/1, iv

[25] See Alexander Ringer, 'Beethoven and the London Pianoforte School', *MQ* 56 (1970), 742–58.

(*c*) Voříšek, Fantaisie Op. 12

compose some music for *Liebhaber* too. Between 1795 and 1800 he published no less than nine sets of variations, written on popular tunes of the day. The more or less conventional writing of the variations includes some remarkable examples of Beethovenian textures; more important are, however, the long codas of WoO 68, 71–3, and 75. Their rambling, improvisatory character and wide tonal scope surely reflect the manner of the extempore playing of the young Beethoven.

Beethoven was barely 9 years old when Jan Ladislav Dussek started on his long European concert tour, as one of the first travelling virtuosos of the pianoforte. After visiting Hamburg, St Petersburg, and various parts of Germany, he settled down in Paris in 1786. His playing set the French capital on fire, and he became a personal favourite of Queen Marie Antoinette. After the outbreak of the revolution he fled to England, and for the last decade of the century he remained there as a celebrated star of London's vigorous concert life.

Pianism is the essential feature of Dussek's compositions. Like most representatives of the London Pianoforte School, he wrote almost exclusively for his instrument, and this fact determines the music in a positive as well as in a negative way. The modern, highly developed pianoforte writing becomes nearly an end in itself, often at the expense of the structure or the more serious content. Unlike their Viennese contemporaries (and not only the greatest!), Dussek and his London colleagues wrote few string quartets: they spent no time on the fine elaboration of motivic work, on the balance of sound and form. They wrote very little vocal or orchestral music and therefore did not face the manifold challenges of compositional work.

The keyboard language of Dussek looks and sounds as if the composer was not even a contemporary of Mozart or Pleyel. There is virtually no trace of the predominantly linear thinking of Viennese or German keyboard writing here; but the music is also distinct from Clementi's austere, often contrapuntal style. The typical texture of a Dussek sonata is thick and difficult to play from a technical point of view, and the performance indications tend to go to extremes. Movement titles are usually long (Andantino ma moderato e con espressione, Op. 39 No. 1), and dynamic signs are exaggerated: the contrast of *fff* and ***ppp*** occurs repeatedly. All this aims at maximum stage effect—quite successfully, according to reports of Dussek's concert performances.

The earliest sonatas, published in Paris, show the influence of Clementi in the lavish use of parallel thirds, octaves, double trills, and the like. In the London years these firework-effects gave way to a fuller and more cantabile style. Dussek was perhaps more inspired by the rich sound of the fully developed Broadwood grand than any other composer. Two short sonata excerpts might illustrate this almost orchestral texture. One is from the Op. 35 set, dedicated to Clementi (pub. 1797), the other is from the *Grande Sonate* Op. 43, dedicated to Mrs Bartolozzi née Therese Jansen (pub. 1800) (Exx. 27 and 28).

Ex. 27 Dussek, Sonata Op. 35/1, i

Ex. 28 Dussek, Sonata Op. 43, i

Whether to attract more attention, or out of real musical concern, Dussek induced John Broadwood to extend the standard five-octave compass of his instruments, first to five and a half, then to six octaves. (See details and documentation in Chapter 2.) It seems that the novelty interested him while it was fresh. The Sonata in B flat major, Op. 24 (Longman, 1793) constantly uses the uppermost range of the keyboard up to c^4, and the title announces the fact: 'A Sonata for the Grand and Small Piano Forte with additional keys'. The next two sets for solo piano (Opp. 35 and 39, 1797 and 1799, three sonatas in each set), however, never go beyond f^3 in their range. The works of *c.*1795 bear the common designation 'with or without additional keys'; no doubt because of publishers' considerations, too. Dussek's first three concertos, for instance, are practically printed in two versions, the *ossia* sections being marked as follows: 'Those lines with the small notes are for the common Piano Fortes, without the extra keys.'

Some clever composers immediately seized the opportunity to write 'special' pieces for the newly extended keyboard. Needless to say, the use of the uppermost half-octave was not a musical necessity, but a pure striving for sensation in these compositions. Antonio Gallassi published the following set in the early 1790s:

Three Sonatas | Composed expressly for those | Grand Piano Fortes | which extend to double C in Alt | with an accompanyment for a | Violin | ad Libitum | By Antonio Gallassi | Op. 7 | London | Printed for William Forster N. 348 Strand

In all three sonatas the general range of the music is so ludicrously high that it sounds more like a musical clock (Ex. 29).

Ex. 29 Gallassi, Sonata Op. 7/2, ii

Nevertheless, a wider keyboard increased the flamboyance of the 'grand style', and Dussek's own performances certainly did not lack flamboyance. In the memoirs of Mrs Charlotte Papendieck we read of a 1793 London concert of Dussek:

A pianoforte of Broadwood's was then brought in with as much ease as a chair, and immediately after Dussek followed, . . . Dussek, now seated, tried his instrument in prelude, which caused a second burst of applause. . . . He then . . . spread a silk handkerchief over his knees, rubbed his hands in his coat pockets, which were filled with bran, and then began his concerto.[26]

This picture of a virtuoso is close to the nineteenth-century image of the instrumental hero, embodied mainly by Franz Liszt. The public's reaction also sounds like that of star-worshippers of a later age. 'The public broke out into one general "Ah" after the first few bars of the solo,' remembered V. Tomášek after a concert by Dussek in Prague.[27] Dussek was also the first pianist who turned the instrument sideways on the stage, because he wanted to show his handsome profile to the audience.[28]

This romantic stage-attitude coincides with the music itself. All evaluations of Dussek's keyboard works recognize that they anticipate the style of romantic composers, notably Schubert, Rossini, Bellini, Mendelssohn, Weber,

[26] Charlotte Papendieck, *Court and Private Life in the Time of Queen Charlotte* (London, 1837), ii. 184–5.

[27] 'W. J. Tomaschek, . . . Selbstbiographie', 393–4.

[28] Ibid. 394.

Schumann, and Chopin. There are resemblances in melody, texture, rhythmic contour, and harmonic usage as well, as the little Schumann 'citation' of Op. 39 No. 1 shows (Ex. 30). We can detect *opera buffa* elements in Dussek's sonatas, just as we can in Viennese classical instrumental music, only here they seem to come from Rossini instead of Piccinni or Paisiello (see Ex. 31). The composer whom we recall most often in the lyrical themes and *Walzer* melodies of Dussek, however, is Schubert. There is no rational explanation for these prophecies, unless we believe that on the threshold of new styles elements of the new language appear ahead of their time, in a premature form.[29]

Ex. 30 Dussek, Sonata Op. 39/1, ii

Ex. 31 Dussek, Sonata Op. 9/3, ii

Romanticism prevails in Dussek's harmonic/tonal language too. His quick, clever modulations to remote keys (see Ex. 32) bring unexpected colour, and often stress the new area with a change of key signature. Although distant key relations are not rare in late Haydn, or Beethoven (both within and between movements), it is their application in the large-scale tonal plan of the form that relates Dussek's procedures to those of the first-generation romantic composers. A typical sonata-form strategy of Schubert, for instance, the tripartite

[29] For a survey of Dussek's sonata output, see Orin Grossman, 'The Piano Sonatas of Jan Ladislav Dussek (1760–1812)', Ph.D. diss. (Yale Univ., 1975).

Ex. 32 Dussek, Sonata Op. 35/1, i

ABA tonal structure of the second group, with a chromatically third-related key in the middle, occurs in several opening movements of Dussek.[30] (See the flat mediant within the dominant area in Op. 24 and Op. 35 No. 3, or the flat submediant in Op. 35 No. 1.) Unfortunately, the rambling sequence of musical events sometimes lacks coherence in Dussek's forms: this, however, is a danger that threatened greater composers than Dussek. With sharp critical sense, Louis Spohr pointed out another weakness of Dussek's compositional practice: the characterlessness of some of his main themes. Spohr heard Dussek play at a musical dinner in Hamburg in May 1802, and he put down his uncomplimentary impressions:

> In conclusion, Herr Dussek played a new quintett he had composed in Hamburgh, which was praised to the skies. However, it did not entirely please me; for, despite the numerous modulations, it became tedious towards the end, and the worst was, that it had neither form nor rhythm, and the end could quite as well have been made the beginning as not.[31]

Notwithstanding deficiencies of various sorts, a composer should always be judged by his best works. Regarding Dussek's output up to the turn of the century, the great work to judge by should certainly be his Sonata in E flat major, Op. 44, 'The Farewell' (pub. Longman, 1800): 'A New Grand Sonata' in four movements, complete with slow introduction, dedicated to Clementi. The 'Les Adieux' title of the French edition (Sieber) is identical with that of Beethoven's only programme sonata, Op. 81*a*, also in E flat, composed some ten years later. The parallel is enigmatic again: there is no evidence of Beethoven's possible knowledge of Dussek's Op. 44. Whereas the programmatic subject of Beethoven's sonata is well known, we can only conjecture about that of Dussek's work. The composer left England in 1799 for good: the grand work, dedicated to his distinguished colleague, must have been his farewell to the country of his great successes.

Dussek's 'The Farewell' has everything that a large-scale sonata of this kind should have: masterful form and character, a classical balance in the cyclic

[30] The question is treated in detail in James Webster, 'Schubert's Sonata Form and Brahms's First Maturity', *19th-Century Music*, 2 (1978–9), 18–35; 3 (1979–80), 52–71.

[31] Louis Spohr, *Autobiography* (London, 1878), 17–18.

TABLE 3. J. L. Dussek, Sonata in E flat major, Op. 44, 'The Farewell': Cyclic Structure

i		*ii*	*iii*			*iv*
Intr. Grave	All° moderato	Molto adagio e sostenuto	Tempo di Minuetto	Trio	Tempo di M.	Rondo
E flat minor	E flat major	B major	G sharp minor	A flat major	G sharp minor	E flat major

structure, brilliant instrumental writing, and deeply felt emotional content. The opening movement proves that Dussek is capable of organizing musical material in a concentrated fashion, without loosing the fire and spontaneity of invention. The slow movement is perhaps the most profound Dussek ever wrote: its richness and complexity of harmony, rhythm, and expression are not often reached by Beethoven himself. Dussek, who devalues the meaning of the word 'espressivo' by using it all too frequently in other compositions, achieves a most moving effect here: the written instructions (*dolcissimo*, *delicatamente*, *piangendo*, *calando*) arise from the essence of the music. The tonal plan of the cycle is remarkable (see Table 3), but we find unusual key-relations within the single movements, too. The E flat–E connection of the opening movement (the development section starts in E major, with appropriate key signature), and the B–B flat relation of the slow movement (B flat minor in the development again) are especially noteworthy.[32] It is a great pity that Dussek's 'Farewell' sonata, like Clementi's masterpiece, the programme sonata 'Didone abbandonata' Op. 50 No. 3 (1821), is missing from the rather conventional piano repertory of today.

Dussek's style influenced the music of the next generation of London pianoforte composers. John Field and George Frederic Pinto, although lesser personalities than Dussek, both learned a great deal from the bold romanticism of the older composer. Dussek himself continued his way towards a more definitely romantic style and expression: his last big sonata in F minor (Op. 77, 'L'Invocation') clearly belongs to the artistic realm of the nineteenth century.

[32] In these romantic harmonic surroundings, the V of VI fermata chord that immediately precedes the recapitulation in the first movement sounds curiously anachronistic. This distinctly baroque feature occurs frequently in Haydn and Clementi too.

6

Joseph Haydn

As Kapellmeister to Prince Esterházy, Joseph Haydn presumably played violin in the princely *Hof- und Cammermusique* band;[1] the various obligations included in his job, however, entailed plenty of keyboard activity as well. He always composed at the clavichord,[2] and produced keyboard music throughout his career, from his earliest years. The documents concerning his instruments prior to the late 1780s, nevertheless, are scarce. It is the more surprising that from that time on he responded so eloquently to the potentials of the fortepianos at hand, Viennese and English.

In fact, it is surprising that Haydn's intimate companion, the highly musical Viennese *Clavier*-enthusiast Marianne von Genzinger, still possessed only a harpsichord in 1790.[3] Capable of transcribing a symphony movement to keyboard to the complete satisfaction of the composer,[4] her skills were surely above those of the general *Liebhaber* of the day, and she could also have well afforded a new instrument. The familiar story of the Sonata Hob. XVI:49 written for her, and its fortepianistic conception stressed so emphatically by Haydn, remains the most important source about the inspiration of an instrument for Haydn.[5]

Haydn's partiality for the light touch and sound of the fortepianos of the Viennese Wenzel Schantz is first expressed in a letter of October 1788.[6] Less than two years later he confessed to Frau von Genzinger: 'I know I ought to have composed this Sonata [Hob. XVI:49] in accordance with the capabilities of your *Clavier*, but I found this impossible because I was no longer accustomed to it.'[7] His words communicate the composer's desire for fine and detailed expression, a desire partly inspired by, and certainly in reciprocal relationship with, the qualities of the instrument:

It's only a pity that Your Grace doesn't own a Schantz fortepiano, on which everything is better expressed.

[1] See Sonja Gerlach, 'Haydns Orchestermusiker von 1761 bis 1774', *HSt* 4 (1976–80), 35–48. The question is treated recently in James Webster, 'On the Absence of Keyboard Continuo in Haydn's Symphonies', *EM* 18 (1990), 599–608.

[2] See Georg August Griesinger, *Biographische Notizen über Joseph Haydn* (Leipzig, 1810), 114.

[3] Haydn's letter, referring to her instrument, first names *Flügl*, then later, in the next sentence, *Clavier*. Although the latter could mean clavichord too, the former excludes that interpretation. See *Joseph Haydn: Gesammelte Briefe und Aufzeichnungen*, ed. Dénes Bartha (Kassel, 1965), 242.

[4] See Haydn's letter of 14 June 1789, *Briefe*, 208.

[5] See Haydn's letters of summer 1790, *Briefe*, 240–5.

[6] To Artaria, *Briefe*, 195.

[7] Letter of 27 June 1790, *CCLN* 106.

I know Herr von Nikl's fortepiano: it's excellent, but too heavy for Your Grace's hand, and one can't play everything on it with the necessary delicacy [*mit gehöriger Delicatesse spiellen*]. Therefore I should like Your Grace to try one made by Herr Schanz [*sic*], his fortepianos are particularly light in touch and the mechanism very agreeable [*haben eine ganz besondere leichtigkeit, und ein angenehmes Tractament*]. A good fortepiano is absolutely necessary for Your Grace, and my Sonata will gain double its effect by it.[8]

The last statement repeats the sentence of a previous letter ('Your Grace could then produce twice the effect').[9]

One need not think, of course, that Haydn was not exposed to the fortepiano before 1788, but the notation of his keyboard works of the late 1780s (especially those of the solo sonatas) undeniably shows a great difference from earlier works. If the Adagio e cantabile of Hob. XVI:49 is a portrait of Marianne von Genzinger, it is also one of the fine Schantz fortepiano. The opening movement of the Sonata in C major, Hob. XVI:48, however, initiates this new language perhaps even more tellingly.[10] The performance instructions regarding expression cover the widest possible range, including the smallest nuances. Immediately the first ten bars require dynamic shades from *f* to ***pp***, crescendo and diminuendo, and at least four kinds of touch or articulation. Tempo rubato is achieved through careful rhythmic notation, containing sextuplet and nonuplets. Here, Haydn leaves little room for the imagination of the performer.

From the 1780s on, the centre of Haydn's keyboard composition was shifted from the genre of the solo sonata to that of the accompanied sonata (that is, keyboard trio). In the pre-London period, there is a marked difference between the instrumental styles of the two genres. Haydn's personal keyboard idiom, characterized by non-conventional left-hand material, a texture conceived mostly in consistent parts (also *notated* in that manner), and by concentration on detail, was reserved for the solo works. In the trios, Haydn's keyboard writing assumed greater expansiveness, and a more leisurely pace. The passage-work became extensive, and approached the conventional contemporary Viennese idiom.[11]

Haydn's most brilliant solo piece from this time, the Fantasia in C (Hob. XVII:4), uses the resources of the Viennese fortepiano to the fullest. Originally called 'Capriccio' by Haydn, it is not as easy to play as Haydn claimed ('nicht gar zu schwer').[12] A *tour de force* in compositional invention and instrumental virtuosity, the fantasia displays special effects that arise directly from the nature of the instrument. The famous fermata, preceding the surprising semi-

[8] Letters of 27 June and 4 July 1790, *CCLN* 106–7. [9] Letter of 20 June 1790, *CCLN* 105.

[10] The so-called 'Bossler' sonatas (Hob. XVI:40–2), composed some years earlier, show a sensitive instrumental approach, but on a less advanced level.

[11] For details, see Katalin Komlós, 'Haydn's Keyboard Trios Hob. XV:5–17: Interaction between Texture and Form', *SM* 28 (1986), 351–400, esp. 353–4.

[12] Letter to Artaria, 29 Mar. 1789, *Briefe*, 202.

tone shift (emphasized by the sudden piano dynamics), bears the inscription 'tenuto intanto, finché non si sente più il suono' (bars 192 and 302). It means a long pause: the longer the delay, the more effective is the unexpected continuation.[13] Haydn's idea cannot be reproduced on the modern piano, of course, with its different response. Another instrumental device enhances the marvellously prepared climax at the end of the piece: the octave glissandos of the right hand, thrice repeated, top the sparkling virtuosity of the texture. Again, the effect is unattainable on a modern instrument.

One of the miracles of the history of music is how the aged Haydn, who had never hitherto moved out of a small geographical area in his life, accommodated himself and his art to the cosmopolitan life and musical demands of England. He accomplished this in no time, without speaking the language, and without compromising in any way his artistic standards or integrity.

Haydn's first London sojourn (1791–2) coincided with an unusual confluence of eminent pianist-composers in that city. In fact, those years of the last two decades of the century could boast more distinguished guests (including Haydn himself) than any other time in that period (see Fig. 1). Besides the permanent residents—the Italian Clementi, the Bohemian Dussek, the German Cramer, and the Alsatian Hüllmandel—the young Johann Nepomuk Hummel spent three years, and the widely travelled Adalbert Gyrowetz four years in London; Haydn's rival Ignaz Pleyel visited in the first half of 1792.

Conscientiously, Haydn drew up lists of the names of well-known London musicians for himself. 'Composers in London' and 'Pianists in London' are of special interest to us (see Table 4). The lists are included in the First London Notebook (1791–2),[14] among several professional and everyday observations of the composer.

Haydn's first London lodging was in the house of the violinist and impresario J. P. Salomon, in Great Pulteney Street, opposite the large pianoforte shop of John Broadwood. For composition, he had a private room in the Broadwood house: thus he had an immediate opportunity to get acquainted with the best and newest English pianos. During Haydn's first summer in England, Dussek himself lent him his own Broadwood grand while he went for a concert tour in Scotland.

Interestingly Haydn, so alert to all novelties and various experiences in London, made no written comments about the pianofortes there. His only observation seems to be an open letter in the *Morning Herald* (27 April 1792), addressed to Charles Clagget, the owner of an obscure little musical museum:

[13] The opinion of Franz Eibner and Gerschon Jarecki, according to which the instruction 'is not to be taken literally', for the fermata 'even on a 1784 "Hammerflügel" . . . would last 15 seconds', lacks foundation. (See *Wiener Urtext Edition* (Vienna, 1975), Critical Notes, p. xxiv.) Haydn, so fond of jokes and extremities, might very well have aimed at a suspension of 15 seconds.

[14] See *CCLN* 262–5.

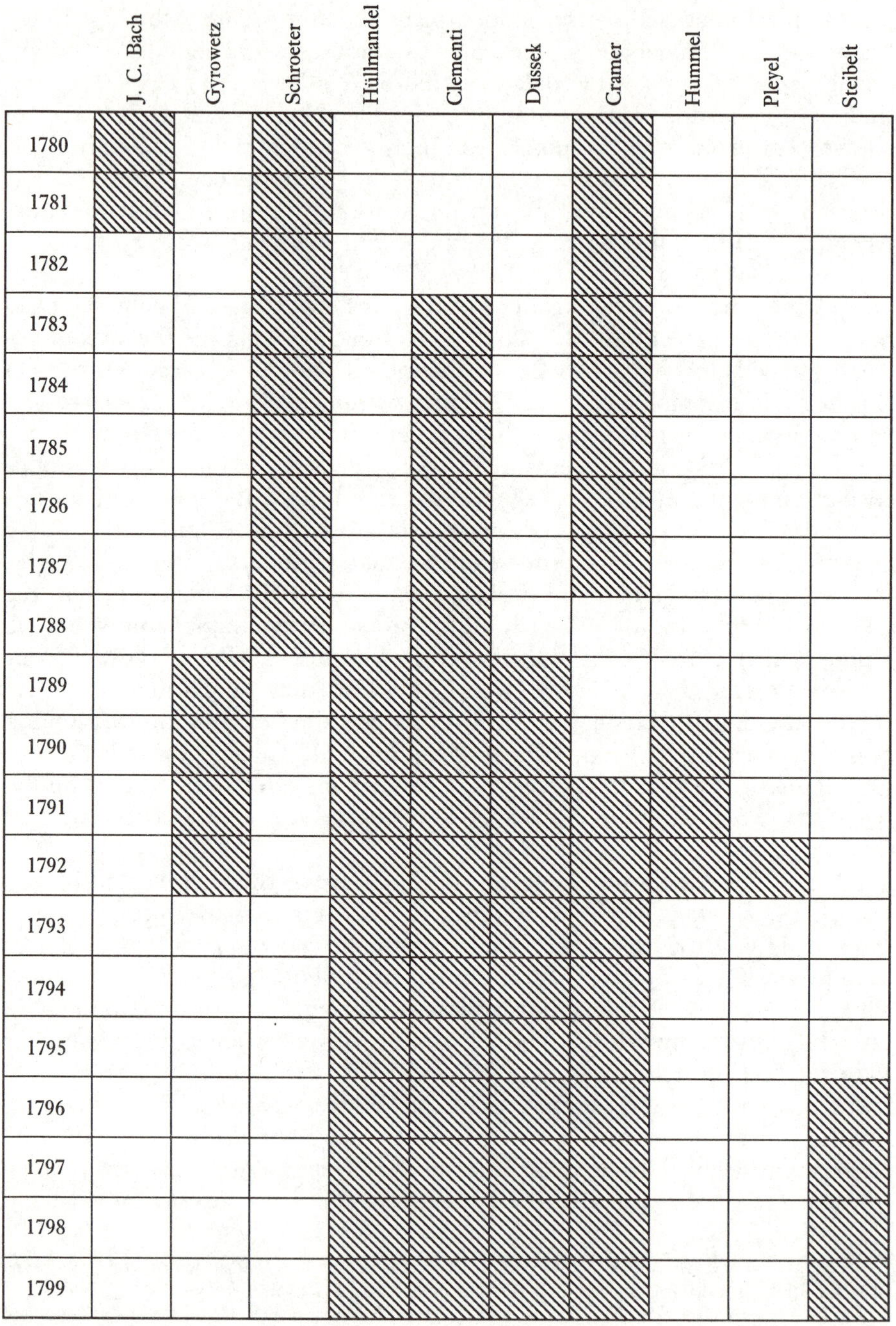

	J. C. Bach	Gyrowetz	Schroeter	Hüllmandel	Clementi	Dussek	Cramer	Hummel	Pleyel	Steibelt
1780										
1781										
1782										
1783										
1784										
1785										
1786										
1787										
1788										
1789										
1790										
1791										
1792										
1793										
1794										
1795										
1796										
1797										
1798										
1799										

FIG. 1. Pianist-Composers Active in London, 1780–1799

TABLE 4. From the First London Notebook of Haydn, 1791–2

Composers in London	*Pianists in London*
Baumgarten	Clementi
Clementi	Dussek
Dussek	Gyrowetz
Gyrowetz	Diettenhofer
Corri	Burney
Burney	Miss Burney
Hüllmandel	Hüllmandel
Graff	Graeff, also flautist
Diettenhofer	Miss Barthélemon
Stephen Storace	J. B. Cramer
Samuel Arnold	Therese Jansen
Barthélemon	J. N. Hummel from Vienna
William Shield	Lenz, still very young
Thomas Carter	
J. B. Cramer	
Francesco Tomich	
Frike	
Callcott	
Latrobe dedicated his piano Sonatas to me	
Mazzinghi	

Sir! I called at your house, during your absence, and examined your improvements on the Pianoforte, and Harpsichords, and I found you had made them perfect instruments.[15]

However, Haydn heard the most famous players (Clementi, Dussek, Cramer) on the stage repeatedly, and the impression must have been profound. His London keyboard style speaks more persuasively than words about the stimulation of the instruments and their virtuosos.

During the first London visit Haydn produced no keyboard music. In addition to his heavy professional and social obligations, adjustment to a foreign environment surely consumed a lot of his energies. The second stay (1794–5), however, brought a rich harvest in various genres: three solo sonatas, fourteen accompanied sonatas (trios), and more than a dozen English songs.

In general, this repertory shows an amazingly renewed style, adapted to different instruments, different players, and different listeners. Consideration

[15] See *CCLN* 135.

for the demands of music consumers—be they *Kenner* or *Liebhaber*—had always been characteristic of Haydn's artistic attitude; now the English audience was the target of this consideration. On receiving the score of Symphony No. 91 from Marianne von Genzinger in Vienna, Haydn wrote to her from London:

> Six days before I had in fact received it [Symphony No. 91] through Herr von Keess from Brussels, but the score was much more useful, for I have to change many things for the English public.[16]

Haydn obviously studied the musical taste of his new surroundings; as his unparalleled success proves, he understood it too.

The most conspicuous sign of the influence of the English pianos on Haydn's keyboard style is the frequent use of repeated thick chords, and a fuller texture in general, in contrast to his former, leaner writing. Passages in thirds and octaves, characteristic of the London idiom, are also more numerous during this period. Some movements or pieces (for instance, the robust accompaniment of the 'Sailor's Song') assume this manner unambiguously; but more interesting are those cases where the finely articulated Viennese language and the massive English style appear together. The B flat slow movement of the Trio in D minor (Hob. XV:23), for instance, with its elaborately worked out *veränderte Reprise*, is very close (even in key!) to the intimate Adagio e cantabile of the 'Genzinger' sonata Hob. XVI:49.[17] The sudden forzando sound of the eight-part chords in the former movement, however, would be inconceivable in the earlier sonata (see Ex. 33).[18]

Ex. 33 Hob. XV:23, ii

Hob. XV:27, the first trio of a set dedicated to Therese Jansen, is probably Haydn's most difficult composition for the keyboard. Its C major brilliance is not mere glitter: it is truly demanding to play. The three movements (the

[16] Letter of 2 Mar. 1792, *CCLN* 131.

[17] The connection of certain keys with certain movt. types or musical characters is not uncommon in Haydn. E minor, for example, seems to be such a key. The linear counterpoint of the Allegretto of Hob. XVI:31 is evoked some twenty years later in the extraordinary, passacaglia-like middle movt. of Hob. XV:28; both represent the *minore* in an E major cycle. The tonal scheme E–Em–E is condensed in a single middle movt. in Hob. XV:14 and Hob. XVI:52. (An extremely remote key in both cases.) Here, the *minore* is cast in a fantastic, improvisatory mood: in a sort of gypsy cimbalom-style in the trio, and reminiscent of the rhapsodic manner of C. P. E. Bach in the sonata.

[18] In the trio excerpts only the keyboard part is reproduced here.

lovely Andante included) abound in third and octave passages, and every bar brings new technical challenges. Unusual sounds are explored in Hob. XV:28: the pizzicato effect of the main theme is a real instrumental *trouvaille* of Haydn, and the full, almost organ-like texture of the A flat version of the same theme in the development is a marvellous tribute to English piano sound.

The sustained tone of the English instruments must have inspired some of the cantabile slow movements of the trios, of which the Andantino et innocentemente of Hob. XV:29 is the loveliest. None the less, cantabile did not necessarily mean a singing legato for Haydn. The middle movements of Hob. XV:23 and 26 bear the inscription 'cantabile', yet both themes are shaped in an articulated, quite unvocal manner. For Haydn, the latter also seemed suitable for string sound, for he arranged it for orchestra, as the second movement of Symphony No. 102.[19]

On the English grand piano, the use of the full range of the keyboard produces a rich, resonant sound. Haydn, who never indulged much in the luscious sonority of keyboard instruments, was evidently inspired by this effect. (A notable exception among his pre-London compositions is the B flat minor middle section of the Adagio e cantabile of Hob. XVI:49. The wonderful sound is achieved here through the crossing of the hands; precisely the device that the dedicatee of the sonata found too hard to play, and requested Haydn to alter for her.)[20] The mellow, romantic tone of some of the London slow movements is quite a new colour in Haydn's palette. As far as the beauty of the general sound is concerned, it is probably the G major middle movement of Hob. XV:22 (originally conceived as a solo piece) that carries off the palm. Two excerpts might illustrate the colouristic variety and the harmonious richness of the texture (Ex. 34*a* and *b*).

Ex. 34 Hob. XV:22, ii

(*a*)

[19] The order of composition (*Klaviertrio* → symphony movt.) is convincingly argued in the Preface to *JHW* XVII/3, ed. Irmgard Becker-Glauch.

[20] See letter of 11 July 1790, *Briefe*, 245. Crossing of the hands, common as it was in classical keyboard music, might have presented difficulties for less dexterous players. Two similar examples from Haydn and Mozart show consideration towards this fact: in both cases the original conception, in which one hand had to reach too far over the other, was changed for a less strenuous solution in the first printed edn. See Haydn, Hob. XV:22/ii, bars 18–19, authorized copy versus 1st edn.; Mozart, K. 457/iii, bars 92–9 and 291–308, autograph versus 1st edn.

(*b*)

The three London solo sonatas are individual masterpieces, with few common characteristics as far as the keyboard writing is concerned. Hob. XVI:52 is a remarkable amalgamation of Viennese and English pianoforte writing. Although cited most often as the crowning example of Haydn's London style, the syntax of the opening movement, the high rhetoric of the Adagio, and the *Contratanz* of the finale speak the personal language of an Austrian composer just as eloquently. The distinguishing quality of the sonata is the joint presence of the two kinds of instrumental idiom, which becomes the very source of the textural variety of the music.

The first four bars immediately expose this doubleness: the heavy chords of the main theme are followed by the carefully articulated figures of the counterstatement. In the latter (bars 3–4), the rests are as important as the notes, so only the quick damping and the light tone of a Viennese-type fortepiano can do real justice to the subtlety of the music. Various other passages of the movement display this contrasting instrumental writing.

The main theme is certainly Haydn's most robust construction for a keyboard instrument. The first chord, by itself, would not be uncommon: several accompanied sonatas of the pre-London period start with a big, broken chord. It is usually an eight-part chord, with arpeggio in the right hand; the identical openings of Hob. XV:14 and 17 include acciaccatura, too (see Ex. 35*a–d*). These chords give impetus to the start of a multi-movement composition. The instrumental effect is harpsichord-like, especially when spiced with acciaccatura. In Hob. XVI:52, on the other hand, the entire theme is built of seven-part chords, and the dotted rhythms enhance the majestic character. In contrast to the earlier examples, Haydn prescribes arpeggio for the left hand in

Ex. 35 (*a*) Hob. XV:11, i

(*b*) Hob. XV:12, i

(*c*) Hob. XV:14, i

(*d*) Hob. XV:17, i

the first chord. It seems a minor detail, and no notation can convey the precise manner of the rolling of a chord anyway; at the same time, Haydn's instruction probably reflects a definite intention.

'Sonata composta per la celebre Signora Terese de Janson', reads Haydn's inscription on the autograph of Hob. XVI:52. On the title-page of the first edition of the Sonata in C major (Hob. XVI:50) the following appears: 'Composed expressly for and Dedicated to Mrs Bartolozzi'. Therese Jansen, later Mrs Gaetano Bartolozzi, must have been a first-rate player. She inspired wonderful and highly demanding compositions from Clementi, Dussek, and Haydn. Hob. XVI:50, with its brilliant opening movement, delicately shaped Adagio,[21] and strikingly Beethovenian finale, deliberately aims to show off some English pianistic features, if not in texture, then in compass and in special pedal effects. As is well known, this is the only keyboard composition

[21] The earlier version of the slow movt. pub. 1794 by Artaria as an independent Adagio, is almost completely devoid of the careful articulation and dynamic marks of the final form.

laydn that exceeds the customary five-octave range: the notes g^3 and a^3 are ·d repeatedly in the third movement.

The two passages marked 'open Pedal' in the opening movement have occasioned much dispute in Haydn literature. Yet, viewed in contemporary context, the term could only indicate raised dampers. Its meaning is made quite clear in piano tutors as well as in actual scores, although these sources are somewhat later than Haydn's sonata. J. B. Cramer states in 1812:

> The open Pedal is chiefly used in slow Movements, when the same harmony is to be prolonged.
> N.B. When a change takes place in the Harmony, the Pedal must be dropt.[22]

According to this explanation, 'open Pedal' indicates the prolongation of the sound, achieved through the raising of the dampers. Naturally, this effect is normally used for the duration of one harmony. (See, for instance, the 'open Pedal' mark at the beginning of the thirty-one-bar *écossaise* theme of Clementi's Op. 37 No. 3, 3rd movt., all above a tonic pedal.)

However, as often happens, practice goes beyond what theory prescribes. Occasionally, 'open Pedal' is used through different harmonies, as a special effect. There is a remarkable section in the finale of Clementi's Op. 40 No. 1, to be played with raised dampers,[23] that can be considered a parallel to Haydn's insert in the recapitulation of the first movement of Hob. XVI:50. Both passages proceed in syncopation, in the treble register, with ***pp*** dynamics, as an aural mirage in the main body of the music (see Ex. 36*a* and *b*). These excerpts

Ex. 36 (*a*) Hob. XVI:50, i

(*b*) Clementi, Sonata Op. 40/1, iv

[22] *Instructions for the Piano Forte* (London, 1812), 43.

[23] In the 1st edn. (Clementi, Banger, Hyde, Collard and Davis, 1802), the sonata is introduced with the following note: 'Ped: is for pressing down the Open Pedal, and * for letting it go again.'

demonstrate that in the early period of pianoforte music the use of the undamped register did not serve the same purpose as it did later, for instance in Chopin: it was a device for special colour.[24]

Haydn moved furthest from Viennese Classicism in the D major Andante of Hob. XVI:51. The looseness of the sonata-form structure and the absence of the double bar after the exposition are uncharacteristic of Haydn's opening movements. Much of the material sounds more like Schubert than Haydn. Sweet melodies follow one another, often proceeding in octaves and thirds, with rocking triplet accompaniment. The style unmistakably recalls the soft lyricism of Dussek; the appearance of a cantabile theme after the opening thought, as a kind of 'second main theme', explicitly resembles Dussek's procedures.

If Haydn paid tribute to the younger composer in Hob. XVI:51, Dussek did the same in his Op. 16, dedicated to Haydn. (The three sonatas, with the accompaniment of 'violon non obligé', were originally published by Sieber in Paris, 1791; Longman & Broderip printed them a year later.) The Larghetto quasi Andante second movement of the Sonata No. 1 functions as an 'hommage à Haydn'. Cast in a ternary form with the middle section in the *minore* (a favourite design of Haydn), the movement betrays an intimate knowledge of Haydn's style. The theme duplicates the main theme of Hob. XVI:26 (see Ex. 37*a* and *b*); more importantly, Dussek successfully simulates Haydn's compositional manner, so different from his own flamboyant pianism.

Ex. 37 (*a*) Hob. XVI:26, i

(*b*) Dussek, Sonata Op. 16/1, ii

The two composers share a number of features, related to the usage of key and harmony. For instance, the change of key signature within a movement,

[24] The famous recitativos in Beethoven's Op. 31 No. 2 are closely related to the cited examples by Clementi and Haydn.

used as a signal of modulation to a distant key, occurs often in the works of both men. Haydn applied it in Hob. XV:14, before the London years; then, in the trios of the 1790s, it became an integral part of his tonal schemes. It is likely that the two musicians influenced each other in this respect, as well as in the tendency of touching the subdominant minor before the close of a movement. The latter gives a romantic colour to numerous endings in Haydn's London sonatas, solo and accompanied.

Some of the most novel textures of Haydn's London pianoforte writing can be found in the English songs and canzonettas of 1794–5. Many of these should be called 'piece for the pianoforte, with the accompaniment of the voice', for the primacy of the instrumental part is indisputable. The songs of the second set (*Six Original Canzonettas*, ii), especially, start with long and substantial piano introductions. The extraordinary Shakespeare setting, 'She never told her love', is actually a pianoforte soliloquy, with words interpolated. When the voice enters in bar 15, almost half-way through the song, it is given two closing phrases, to round off the first formal section; all that follows in the vocal part is some recitative-like material, above the musical action of the instrumental part. The low range and sombre colour of the postlude seem to anticipate the Schubert song 'Nacht und Träume', both in texture and in *Affekt* (see Ex. 38*a* and *b*).

Ex. 38 (*a*) 'She never told her love', Hob. XXVI*a*:34

(*b*) Schubert, 'Nacht und Träume'

Premature romanticism, represented chiefly by Dussek, appears in the later canzonettas. For instance, homogeneous triplet accompaniment, encountered already in Hob. XVI:51, takes over 'Content' (Hob. XXVI*a*:36) completely.

This texture, coupled with romantically coloured harmonies at the end of the song, evokes the nineteenth century (see Ex. 39). The Rossini–Bellini premonitions of Dussek find their counterpart in the introduction to 'O Tuneful Voice', Hob. XXVI*a*:42. The opening triplets could easily preface a cavatina by Bellini or Donizetti; the way the accompaniment lies under the hand also deviates from earlier Haydn. The ninth stretch of the first chord (bar 2), and the middle position of the melody, to be played with the thumb of the right hand (bars 5–8), foreshadow post-classical piano technique (see Ex. 40).

Haydn's English songs were very popular in their time. The composer himself performed them several times in private circles. The most prominent occasion of these was the soirée of the Duke of York in March 1795, where Haydn, 'by the desire of the Queen, sat down to the piano-forte, and, surrounded by Her Majesty and her royal and accomplished daughters, sang, and

Ex. 39 'Content', Hob. XXVI*a*:36

Ex. 40 'O Tuneful Voice', Hob. XXVI*a*:42

accompanied himself admirably in several of his *canzonets*'.[25] One of the publishers of Haydn's settings of Scottish songs, George Thomson in Edinburgh, found the accompaniment of 'The Mermaid's Song' ideal for the kind of drawing-room music that was favoured by amateurs. He wrote to Haydn in December 1803:

> Allow me to mention, that if you find any of the [Scottish] Airs fit for an accompt similar to that in your lst Canzonet in C, published by Corri and Dussek ['The Mermaid's Song'], I am particularly fond of that kind of easy motion in accompt.[26]

'The Mermaid's Song' achieved tremendous popularity in America: it was published in Philadelphia between 1797 and 1799, and six further editions followed in 1808.[27]

A number of London composers honoured Haydn through the dedication of their pianoforte music to him. The sets known to us are as follows:

C. I. Latrobe, *Three Sonatas for the Pianoforte Composed and Dedicated by Permission to Mr. Haydn, Op. 3* (Bland, 1791?).

[25] Parke, *Musical Memoirs*, 198. [26] *CCLN* 223.
[27] See Irving Lowens, 'Haydn in America', in Jens Peter Larsen, Howard Serwer, and James Webster (eds.), *Haydn Studies* (New York, 1981), 37.

J. L. Dussek, *Trois Sonates pour le Piano Forte ou le Clavecin, avec Accompagnement d'un Violon non obligé | Dediées à Joseph Haydn, par J. L. Dussek, Op. 16* (Longman & Broderip, 1792; 1st edn., Paris: Sieber, 1791).

F. Tomich, *Three Sonatas for the Pianoforte, with accompanyments for a Violin and Violoncello, dedicated to Joseph Haydn, by Francisco Tomich* (Longman & Broderip, 1792?).

J. B. Cramer, *Three Sonatas for the Piano Forte, Composed and dedicated to Joseph Haydn by J. B. Cramer, Op. 22* (Clementi, Banger, Hyde, Collard & Davis, 1800–1?; 1st edn., Vienna: Artaria, 1799?).

J. N. Hummel, *Sonate pour le Pianoforte composée et dediée à Monsieur Joseph Haydn Docteur en Musique, . . . par Jean Nep. Hummel de Vienne, Op. 13* (A Vienne au Bureau d'Arts et d'Industrie, 1805).

The last item, Hummel's first published piano sonata, appeared a year after Hummel became appointed *Concertmeister* to Prince Nikolaus II Esterházy in Eisenstadt. His relationship with Haydn, however, started in England. The young Hummel played Haydn's Trio in A flat major in a London concert in 1792; the event is described on the title-page of the 1792 Longman & Broderip edition of Hob. XV:14:

A Favorite Sonata for the Piano Forte or Harpsichord with Accompaniments for a Violin and Violoncello as performed by Master Hummell at Mr. Salomon's Concert Hanover Square, Composed by Dr. Haydn, Op. 68.

When Haydn returned from England to Vienna in 1795, he brought back a Longman & Broderip grand piano. According to Griesinger, he still sat down to it in his late years to improvise [*zu phantasieren*],[28] but eventually a clavichord or small *Tafelklavier* ('ein ganz leicht zu behandelndes Klavier') had to replace his fortepiano instruments, for the latter proved to be too strenuous for his nerves.[29]

In the first years of the new century, publishers still demanded new keyboard music from Haydn. 'I shall never be unthankful, but I regret that at present I am not capable of serving you with new pianoforte Sonatas,' he wrote to G. C. Härtel in Leipzig, July 1800.[30] Ten months later, he seemed to be more generous to Hyde and Clementi in London ('For my part, I shall endeavour to serve you with 3 good pianoforte Sonatas by the end of the Summer');[31] whether he really meant this ambitious project, or simply did not want to appear ungracious, is hard to tell. At any rate, his answer to George Thomson in Edinburgh, who evidently asked for marketable music for amateurs, was straightforward enough. The aged composer wrote in October 1801: 'I am not capable of composing the *Sonatine* for pianoforte and harp, for I am now too weak to do so.'[32]

[28] Griesinger, *Biographische Notizen*, 87. [29] Ibid. 76.
[30] *CCLN* 170. [31] Ibid. 179. [32] Ibid. 192.

7

Sonatas: Accompanied and Unaccompanied

'THE keyboard sonata is set for the keyboard either alone or with another instrument such as the violin or flute,' stated F. W. Marpurg, German theorist and composer, in 1762.[1] This definition clearly reflects the interchangeability of the solo and accompanied keyboard sonata in the second half of the eighteenth century.

The original idea of adding a melody instrument to the keyboard arises from the very nature of early keyboard instruments, mainly that of the harpsichord. As early as 1750, the French *clavecin* composer Simon Simon explained in the 'Avertissement' of his *Pièces de clavecin dans tous les genres avec et sans accompagnement, Op. 1* why he offered the choice of a violin accompaniment to some of his suites:

J'ai cru devoir en composer quelques unes [Suites] avec accompagnement de violon. Elles en seront plus intéressantes, parce que la Mélodie, qui perd les graces de sa rondeur dans les sons désunis du clavecin, sera soutenue par les sons filés et harmonieux du violon.

I thought necessary to compose some [suites] with the accompaniment of the violin. They will be more interesting for this, for the melody, that looses its round gracefulness through the disconnected sound of the harpsichord, will be sustained by the continuous and harmonious sound of the violin.[2]

Ten years later Charles Avison, student of Geminiani, voiced similar thoughts in the 'Advertisement' of his Op. 7:

The accompanying Violins which are intended to enforce the Expression of the Harpsichord, should also be kept *always* subservient to it; for thus an Effect results from the whole, as from the Sound of one improved, or, if I may call it, multiplied Instrument.[3]

Since the tonal decay of the early fortepiano is almost as quick as that of the harpsichord, this *musical* desire for a more melodious, sustained sound applies equally to that instrument.

The other motivation for the addition of an accompanying instrument was clearly *social.* Music as a cultivated amusement was an occasion for pleasant

[1] *Clavierstücke mit einem practischen Unterricht*, i (Berlin, 1762), 6.

[2] Quoted in Eduard Reeser, *De klaviersonate mit vioolbegeleiding in het Parijsche musiekleven ten tijde van Mozart* (Rotterdam, 1939), 62.

[3] *Six sonatas for the harpsichord, with accompanyments for 2 violins, and a violoncello* (London, 1760).

pastime: playing alone was not nearly as much fun as making music together. Ladies usually played the keyboard instrument, and gentlemen contributed the additional part; contemporary iconography gives plenty of evidence for this. To quote Avison again:

This kind of Music is not, indeed, calculated so much for public Entertainment, as for private Amusement. It is rather like a Conversation among Friends, when the Few are of one Mind and Propose their mutual Sentiments, only to give Variety, and enliven their select Company.[4]

As we approach the end of the century, the general dilution of quality that accompanied the enormous increase of the repertory appears in the written comments as well. Accompanied keyboard music, of course, was the exclusive field of the amateur; its advantages were rather trivially explained by J. P. Milchmeyer in 1797:

Was Sonaten mit einer Begleitungsstimme betrift, so gewähren sie den Vortheil, dass man sich einigemal nach den Solos erholen kann, auch wird hier, wo die Aufmerksamkeit der Zuhörer unter zwei Personen getheilt ist, ein kleiner Fehler nicht so leicht bemerkt, als in Stücken ohne Begleitung.

As for sonatas with an accompanying part, they have the advantage that now and then, after the solos, one can relax; also, since the attention of the listener is divided between two persons, a slight mistake is not as noticeable as it is in pieces without accompaniment.[5]

The notion of the *ad libitum* accompaniment originated in the French *clavecin* music of *c.*1730–60. The optional status of the violin part ('si l'on veut') in some of the works of Mondonville, Guillemain, D'Herbain, and others, is described in an 'Avertissement' again, this time in the Op. 13 set of Louis-Gabriel Guillemain:

On pourra si l'on veut executer ces Sonates avec ou sans accompagnement, elles ne perdront rien de leur chant, puisqu'il est tout entier dans la partie du clavecin, ce qui sera plus commode pour les personnes qui n'auront pas toûjours un Violon prest, lorsqu'elles voudront jouer quelques unes de ces pieces.

One can perform these sonatas with or without accompaniment: they will lose none of their melody, for all that is in the harpsichord part; thus it will be convenient for those who do not have a violin always at hand, when they want to play some of these pieces.[6]

The real vogue of accompanied keyboard music, however, arrived with the first generation of fortepiano/harpsichord players and composers that lived in Paris in the 1760s and 1770s, represented by the Silesian Johann Schobert, and the Alsatians Leontzi Honauer and Johann Friedrich Edelmann. In England,

[4] Ibid. [5] *Die wahre Art*, 69.

[6] *Pièces de clavecin en sonates avec accompagnement du violon* (Paris, 1745); quoted in Reeser, *De klaviersonate*, 58.

Felice de Giardini and Charles Avison were the first composers of the new type of chamber music.[7]

The always practical Leopold Mozart knew very well with what kind of compositions his wunderkind should make his début in the international music market.[8] Wolfgang's Opp. 1 and 2 (K. 6–9) were engraved in Paris in 1764, with the title *Sonates pour le clavecin qui peuvent se jouer avec l'accompagnement de violon*. His Op. 3 (K. 10–15) was printed in London the following year with the same title, but the option of 'violon ou flaute traversière', and the *ad libitum* violoncello part made this set even more fashionable. (It is very likely that the violin parts were written by Leopold himself.) Apart from another occasional set composed in The Hague (K. 26–31, 1766), Mozart never wrote accompanied keyboard music with optional accompanying parts again. In his mature duos, trios, quartets, and quintet, the role of the non-keyboard instrument[s] is far from being *ad libitum*, or indeed, subservient in any respect.

Scholars have emphasized that the tempting notion of a 'historical progress' from the early keyboard sonata with *ad libitum* accompaniment to the equal partnership of the keyboard and the violin in Mozart and Beethoven is false.[9] As far as the balance of the instruments is concerned, the two kinds of writing existed in parallel up to the end of the century, if not beyond. Nevertheless, demarcation lines may be drawn in terms of both geographical area and the targeted clientele. The situation in France and England was quite different from that in Austria and Germany, both musically and in terms of the market-place.

France and England

In the cosmopolitan climate of Paris and London in the last quarter of the century, music increasingly became a mass product. The composition, the publication, and the playing of the music were strongly affected by the vast number of amateurs, who consumed enormous quantities of music. For private music-making accompanied keyboard sonatas were the favourite. The

[7] Beside the fundamentally important work of Reeser (n. 2 above), see a detailed discussion of the subject in William Newman, 'Concerning the Accompanied Clavier Sonata', *MQ* 33 (1947), 327–49; Ronald Kidd, 'The Emergence of Chamber Music with Obbligato Keyboard in England', *AM* 44 (1972), 122–44; David Fuller, 'Accompanied Keyboard Music', *MQ* 60 (1974), 222–45. A recent account, with the results of partially new research, is Miklós Dolinszky, 'A műfaj problémája a 18. század közepének billentyűs kamarazenéjében', diss. (Budapest, 1992); id., 'Transition from Solo to Ensemble Genres in Chamber Music with Obbligato Keyboard in the Middle of the Eighteenth Century', *Hungarian Music Quarterly*, 3 (1990), 2–11.

[8] Peter Rummenhöller describes the musical centres of 18th-cent. Europe following the route of the tours of Leopold Mozart and his children during the 1760s and 1770s. See *Die musikalische Vorklassik: Kulturhistorische und musikgeschichtliche Grundrisse zur Musik im 18. Jahrhundert zwischen Barock und Klassik* (Kassel, 1983), ch. 2.

[9] See Kidd, 'The Emergence of Chamber Music', 144; Fuller, 'Accompanied Keyboard Music', 230.

majority of the freshly printed sonatas were supplied with violin accompaniment; it hardly made a difference whether the violin part was called 'ad libitum' or 'obbligato'. Generally speaking, the accompanying part contained little independent material and sometimes none at all. As amateur music, accompanied sonatas were usually shorter, easier, and slighter than the solo sonatas.

The travelling virtuoso J. L. Dussek published almost exclusively accompanied sonatas in the 1780s. His Op. 3 (Berlin and Amsterdam: Hummel, *c.*1786), a set of six short two-movement compositions, bears the title *Sonates faciles*; the pieces in fact qualify as sonatinas, with rondo or variation second movements. Op. 2 (Paris: Author, 1787), with 'violon and basse ad lib.', is a similar set, titled *Sonates non difficiles*. Dussek continued to write moderately easy accompanied sonatas during his London period. In total, he composed exactly three times as many accompanied sonatas as solo keyboard works. Even the sample pieces of his pianoforte treatise are 'Six progressive Sonatinas with Violin accompaniments ad Libitum', borrowed from Ignaz Pleyel.[10]

The main difference in keyboard texture and in general keyboard style between the accompanied and the solo sonata lies in technical difficulty and complexity. In this respect, Muzio Clementi made the most striking differentiation. His accompanied sonatas (either in duo or trio setting) are so embarrassingly unpretentious that it is hard to believe they were written by the composer of some of the most ambitious pianoforte literature of the time. The works are modest in size, and simple in their formal procedures; some binary middle movements, for instance, are a mere 8 + 8 or 8 + 12 bars long.[11]

As far as the cyclic structure of the sonatas is concerned, two- and three-movement pieces are found equally among accompanied and solo sonatas. Two-movement structure, characteristic of the Paris and London repertory, seems to be no more common in accompanied than in solo sets. (In the output of Dussek, for instance, exactly 50 per cent of the accompanied and solo sonatas, respectively, are written in two movements.) On the other hand, the four-movement model of the new 'grand sonata' is reserved for solo compositions. Dussek's magnificent 'The Farewell' (Op. 44), or 'L'Invocation' (Op. 77); Clementi's Op. 40 No. 1, or the famous *scena tragica*, 'Didone abbandonata' (Op. 50 No. 3) would be inconceivable within the realm of the accompanied sonata. The slow introduction, the solemn prelude to a cycle, is also a characteristic of the solo works; it occurs only rarely in accompanied sonatas.

A common feature of the accompanied sonatas is the incorporation of popular songs or operatic tunes in one or more movements. Again, the intent

[10] *Dussek's Instructions on the Art of Playing the Piano Forte or Harpsichord* (London and Edinburgh, 1796).

[11] See Op. 21/2 and Op. 22/2.

TABLE 5. Arrangements of Popular Tunes or Airs in the Accompanied Sonatas of Dussek

Movement type	*Title of tune or air*	*Work [C. = Craw]*	
Middle (slow) movement	'God Save the King'	Op. 12/2 =	C. 65
	'Auld Robin Gray'	Op. 31/3	C. 134
	'Whither my love'		C. 141
	'When to Nina hapless maid', from Dalayrac, *Nina*		C. 142
	'Hope told a flattering tale' ['Nel cor più non mi sento'], from Paisiello, *La molinara*		C. 143
	'Ombra adorata aspetta', from Crescentini, *Romeo et Juliette*	Op. ph.	C. 260
Final (third) movement	Air Russe [Wranitzky?]	Op. 14/1	C. 71
	'The Fife Hunt'	Op. 25/1	C. 126
	'Rule, Britannia'	Op. 25/3	C. 128
	'I thought our quarells ended'		C. 141
	'Lewie Gordon'		C. 142
	'Ma barque légère', from Grétry, *La Rosière de Salency*	Op. ph.	C. 260

is to attract the amateur clientele. Among Dussek's sonatas, only one solo composition includes a borrowed song,[12] whereas the accompanied sonatas use 'favourite airs' quite frequently. The arrangements, mostly in rondo or variation form, occur in middle or final movements (see Table 5). Besides actual quotations, certain finales are cast in national character, like the 'Rondo Cozaque' (Op. 8 No. 1), or the 'Rondo alla Polacca' (Op. 4 No. 2). The commercially minded Ignaz Pleyel surely knew very well which tunes were most popular in contemporary England; his three accompanied sonatas published by Birchall in 1796 (B. 462–4) include no less than five 'favorite Airs', all of them used by Dussek as well.

Clementi was less inclined to compose sonatas on popular melodies, though two of his finales (Op. 12 No. 1 and Op. 24 No. 1) are variations on the French tunes 'Je suis Lindor', and 'Lison dormait', respectively. (Incidentally, both sonatas are solo works.) Mozart's brilliant variations written on the same themes during his 1778 Paris sojourn are well known. The difference is, however, that Mozart, like other Viennese composers, would not consider such show-pieces as parts of sonata cycles. Beethoven's keyboard variations on 'God Save the King', 'Rule, Britannia', or on Paisiello's 'Nel cor più non mi

[12] Op. 31/2 = C. 133, 3rd movt., Pastorale on the Scotch reel 'Cauld be the Rebels cast Oppressors Base and Bloody'.

sento' (very popular in England and France as well) are also independent compositions.

The commercial success of keyboard sonatas with added violin accompaniment induced Clementi to republish his early Op. 2 sonatas, fifteen years after the first print. The famous 'octave lesson', No. 2, appeared as Op. 30 at Dale in 1794, with the following title:

Clementi's Grand Sonata, for the Piano-Forte or Harpsichord, With New Accompaniments, An additional Movement, and·Alterations, as Now Performed and Revised by the Author

Op. 2 No. 4, also originally a solo composition, received a flute accompaniment and was published as Op. 31 in the same year by Dale, with a similar title.

In Paris, the vogue of the accompanied sonata continued to the end of the century. During the 1790s, Daniel Gottlieb Steibelt and Louis Adam were the chief exponents of the genre. Steibelt composed about 180 accompanied sonatas, but he published dozens of his works in solo and accompanied versions as well. The first seven *opera* of the Alsatian Adam contained accompanied sets. He, too, like Clementi, added accompaniment to solo keyboard compositions. The title-page of his 'Grande Sonate pour le fortepiano', Op. 12 (Paris: Frey, *c.*1800) bears the inscription: 'At the request of a large number of amateurs, the author has just added to this sonata an accompaniment for violin and bass that may be used *ad libitum*.'[13]

Austria and Germany

The musical and social hierarchy of the accompanied sonata is admirably described in the famous advertisement of the *Wiener Zeitung*, 1789: 'Wanted by nobleman a servant who plays the violin well and is able to accompany difficult piano sonatas.'[14] It proves that this hierarchy was not at all uncommon in Viennese society, although the musical tradition here and in Germany was quite distinct from that of the Western centres of Europe.

During the last two decades of the eighteenth century the Viennese firm Artaria published around 200 solo keyboard sonatas, around 100 duo-sonatas for violin and keyboard, and about 160 keyboard trios. In the majority of the duos and trios in this repertory, however, the non-keyboard instruments are much more important than typical *ad libitum* parts. Italian style influenced musical taste in Vienna, and the prominence of the violin as melody instrument was very much part of that tradition. In duo sonatas, the singing string sound of Sammartini, Boccherini, or J. C. Bach attracted Viennese ears more than the elaborate manner of Schobert or Hüllmandel.

[13] Quoted in Newman, 'Concerning the Accompanied Clavier Sonata', 342.

[14] Quoted in Karl Geiringer, *Haydn: A Creative Life in Music* (New York, 1946), 38.

W. A. Mozart was by no means the only composer in Vienna whose keyboard and violin sonatas offered equal participation for the two instruments.[15] Yet, the critic of Cramer's *Magazin der Musik* regarded the Mozartian duo-sonata as a new conception in chamber music. (The review concerns the Op. 2 set (= K. 376, 296, 377–380), published by Artaria, 1781.)

Diese Sonaten sind die einzigen in ihrer Art. Reich an neuen Gedanken und Spuren des grossen musicalischen Genies des Verfassers. Sehr brillant, und dem Instrumente angemessen. Dabey ist das Accompagnement der Violine mit der Clavierpartie so künstlich verbunden, dass beide Instrumente in beständiger Aufmerksamkeit unterhalten werden; so dass diese Sonaten einen eben so fertigen Violin- als Clavier-Spieler erfordern.

These sonatas are the only ones of this kind. Rich in new ideas and in evidences of the great musical genius of their author. Very brilliant and suited to the instrument. At the same time the accompaniment of the violin is so artfully combined with the clavier part that both instruments are kept constantly on the alert; so that these sonatas require just as skillful a player on the violin as on the clavier.[16]

Besides other duo-sonatas, contemporary Viennese publications included 'concertante' duos for keyboard and violin, in which the two instruments literally competed in instrumental display (*6 Duetti Concertantes* by F. A. Hoffmeister, 1786–7; *6 Duos Concertantes* by Franz Grill, 1788–9).[17]

The most characteristic and important genre of late eighteenth-century Viennese chamber music with keyboard was the keyboard trio. Its standard designation was still 'Sonata for Harpsichord or Fortepiano, with the accompaniment of Violin and Violoncello', that is, an essentially keyboard genre, with added string parts. (Mozart was an exception: all six of his mature works in this genre appeared as 'Trios' in their first Viennese editions.)

As far as texture and instrumental hierarchy are concerned, the typical Viennese trio has a keyboard part of primary importance, a violin part which shares a fair amount of thematic/melodic material, and a cello part that either doubles the keyboard bass or plays an independent line.[18] The opening movements are often close to the contemporary keyboard concerto in texture: the glittery virtuosity of the keyboard writing of Hoffmeister, Kož eluch, or Pleyel, complete with a cadential trill before the close of the exposition, is particularly comparable to the concerto. Slow movements, on the other hand, are usually

[15] His first inspiration originated in the *6 Divertimenti da camera* by Joseph Schuster (*c.*1777), a German composer who spent several years in Italy. See Mozart's letter to his father from Munich, 6 Oct. 1777, *Letters*, 300.

[16] *Magazin der Musik*, i (Hamburg, 1783), 485. Eng. trans. in Alfred Einstein, *Mozart: His Character, His Work* (New York, 1945), 256.

[17] Hoffmeister applied this instrumental writing to trios as well; see his *6 Trios Concertantes* for keyboard, flute, and violoncello, 1786–7.

[18] See details in Katalin Komlós, 'The Viennese Keyboard Trio in the 1780s: Studies in Texture and Instrumentation', 2 vols., Ph.D. diss. (Cornell Univ., 1986); id., 'The Function of the Cello in the Pre-Beethovenian Keyboard Trio', *Studies in Music*, 24 (1990), 27–46.

Romance, Larghetto, or Cantabile movements for violin solo—a curious exchange of roles in the 'accompanied sonata'.

However, other kinds of instrumentation existed, too. In the trios of Johann Baptist Vanhal, for instance, the role of the violin is at least equal to that of the keyboard. The reviewer of his Op. 29 trios (pub. Artaria, 1782) commented on this: 'There is much fire and good melody in these sonatas as well as in all the works of the composer. The violin is not idle in its accompaniment.'[19] Vanhal's opening movements start with an extensive, violin-dominated first group, then the main theme is restated on keyboard solo, again somewhat in concerto fashion. Vanhal even applies the old compositional technique of thorough-bass. In the opening section of the Trio Op. 29 No. 2 the limitation of the keyboard part to figured-bass accompaniment for twenty-nine bars emphasizes the *tutti* (concerto ritornello-like) character of the music.

When in 1788 Haydn offered Artaria the choice of three new string quartets or three new keyboard trios, he chose the trios.[20] Artaria had in fact requested accompanied sonatas much earlier, in July 1782, but Haydn declined: 'As to the pianoforte Sonatas [*Clavier Sonaten*] with violin [that is, trios], you will have to be patient for a long time.'[21] For Haydn, the composition of trios clearly meant keyboard writing in the first place. This is reflected in the layout of his autographs: the complete keyboard part is on top, followed by two separate systems underneath for the violin and the cello parts respectively (see Ex. 41). This arrangement suggests that Haydn worked out the keyboard part first, then added the string parts below.

Ex. 41 Score arrangement of the autographs of Haydn's keyboard trios

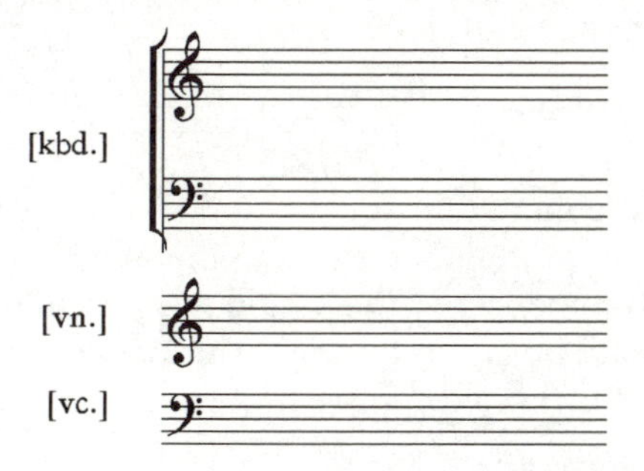

The middle movement of Hob. XV:22 goes beyond that. This beautiful Adagio survived in a solo keyboard version, in the hand of Haydn's copyist Johann Elssler, signed (that is, authenticated) by the composer.[22] The manu-

[19] 'Auch in diesen Sonaten, herrscht so wie in allen Werken des Verfassers, viel Feuer und guter Gesang. Die Violin ist beym Accompagnement nicht müssig.' *Magazin der Musik*, i (Hamburg, 1783), 927.

[20] Letters of 10 and 17 Aug. 1788, *CCLN* 77–8. [21] Ibid. 37–8.

[22] National Széchényi Library, Budapest, Ms. mus. I. 151.

script, written on English paper (Elssler accompanied Haydn on his second London journey), is identical with the keyboard part of the printed trio version, save for an additional bar before the recapitulation, and for the absence of the dynamic marks that appear in the trio.[23] Whether Haydn originally intended the piece as a solo movement, or knew that additional parts would follow, is impossible to tell. At any rate, the final result is definitely an 'accompanied' keyboard essay, where the string instruments bring only colour and background to the eloquence of the pianoforte.

Interestingly, the autographs of Mozart's keyboard trios show different score arrangement (Ex. 42).[24] None the less, the autograph sources of the last trio (K. 564 in G) suggest that the compositional process went from solo keyboard version towards the addition of string parts.[25] The autograph consists of two items: fragments of the keyboard part alone, and a manuscript score, the keyboard part of which is written by a copyist, and only the string parts are in Mozart's hand. After much debate in the Mozart literature, the opinion of the *NMA* editors, W. Rehm and W. Plath, is that the keyboard part of the piece must have been composed first, Mozart writing the string parts into the corrected copy later.[26]

Ex. 42 Score arrangement of the autographs of Mozart's keyboard trios

While Mozart wrote more duo-sonatas and trios than solo sonatas, Haydn's solo keyboard sonatas outnumber the accompanied ones (trios). The most prolific Viennese trio composer of the period was Leopold Koželuch. Sixty per cent of his total sonata output represents the accompanied type (sixty-three trios), and less than half is solo composition.

[23] See both versions in *JHW* XVII/3.

[24] C. P. E. Bach, a musician quite remote from the artistic world of Mozart, used the same layout in the composition of keyboard trios. See the autograph facsimile of the first page of H. 532 in Ernst Fritz Schmid, *Carl Philipp Emanuel Bach und seine Kammermusik* (Kassel, 1931), facing p. 144.

[25] A similar assumption arose about the genesis of K. 496, but according to present scholarly opinion, the piece was conceived as a keyboard trio. See Karl Marguerre, 'Zwei Abschriften Mozartscher Werke', *Die Musikforschung*, 13 (1960), 57–60.

[26] See Otto Jahn, *W. A. Mozart*, iv (Leipzig, 1859), 2; Einstein, *Mozart*, 263; Wilhelm Weismann, 'Zur Urfassung von Mozarts Klaviertrio KV. 564', *Deutsches Jahrbuch der Musikwissenschaft für 1958* (Leipzig, 1959), 35–40; Karl Marguerre, 'Mozarts Klaviertrios', *MJb* 1960–1, 192; Preface to *NMA* VIII/22, Abt. 2, p. xiii.

Publishers printed any sort of arrangements of original compositions, for the addition of accompanying part(s) was an unfailing attraction for consumers. Theobald Monzani, a London music dealer, published the following collection *c.*1803–5:

Mozart's Selection of Piano-Forte Music, Consisting of Single Sonatas, Duets, Trios, Quartetts, Airs with Variations, etc., with and without Accompaniments

The large album contains fifty-three compositions, among them the favourite A major sonata K. 331, 'with Violin and Vcello accompaniments, ad libitum'. But serious publishers took liberties with masterpieces, too: the posthumous first edition of K. 570 (Artaria, 1796) includes a violin part, which has nothing to do with Mozart.

Accompanied keyboard music seemed sadly inferior to the lofty ideals of clavichord-centred north German musicians. When the 25-year-old Christian Gottlob Neefe published his *12 Klaviersonaten* (Leipzig: Schwickert, 1773), he introduced it with a dedication 'An den Herr Kapellmeister Bach in Hamburg':

Seit der Zeit, da SIE, THEUERSTER HERR KAPELLMEISTER, dem Publikum IHRE meisterhaften und mit wahrem Geschmacke gearbeiteten Klaviersonaten geschenket haben, ist fast nichts Eigenthümliches für dieses Instrument wieder zum Vorschein gekommen. Die meisten Komponisten haben sich bisher mit Sinfonien, Trii, Quartetten, u. s. w. beschäftiget. Und ist ja dann und wann an das Klavier gedacht worden: so sind die Stücke meistentheils mit der, obschon öfters sehr willkührlichen Begleitung einer Violine versehen, und auf vielen andern Instrumenten eben so praktikabel gewesen, als auf dem Klaviere. Gleichwohl machen die Liebhaber des Klavichords, welche zu ihrem eigenen Vergnügen nichts mehr, als ein Solo interessiren kann, den grössten Theil aus. Diesen zu Gefallen habe ich bey leeren Stunden gegenwärtige Sonaten aufgeschrieben. Und wenn ich IHNEN dieselben zueigne, so geschicht es, um SIE von meiner Dankbarkeit öffentlich zu überzeugen, deren ich mich, wegen der Belehrung und des Vergnügens, welches Beydes ich aus IHREN theoretischen und praktischen Werken geschöpfet, schuldig erachte. Sollte mir dieser Versuch nicht ganz mislungen seyn, so haben SIE unstreitig den grössten Antheil daran.

Since the time that YOU, DEAREST HERR KAPELLMEISTER, gave to the public YOUR masterly keyboard sonatas, worked out with true taste, almost nothing has appeared especially for this instrument [clavichord]. Most of the composers have occupied themselves up to now with symphonies, trios, quartets, etc. And if the keyboard does get attention now and then, the pieces are usually provided with the accompaniment, often arbitrary, of a violin, and they become just as playable on many other instruments as on the keyboard. Yet, the majority of clavichord amateurs find interest and satisfaction in nothing but solos. To please them I have written the present sonatas during my spare time. And by dedicating them to YOU, I wish to express my gratitude publicly for the instruction and pleasure I gained from YOUR theoretical and practical works. If this effort of mine is not wholly unsuccessful, YOU have the greatest share in that.[27]

The revered *Kapellmeister*, C. P. E. Bach himself, had to yield to general demand later in the 1770s. He wrote in a letter to Forkel in September 1775:

Ich habe doch endlich müssen jung thun und Sonaten fürs Clavier machen, die man allein, ohne etwas zu vermissen, und auch mit einer Violin und einem Violoncello begleitet blos spielen kann und leicht sind.

Finally I had to keep up with fashion and compose easy sonatas for *Clavier*, which can be played alone without missing anything, and also with the accompaniment of a violin and a violoncello.[28]

His reluctance is more evident in a previous letter, where he reports that certain musicians ask for more fantasias from him:

allein noch habe ich wenig Lust dazu [Fantasien], eben so wenig, als zu Claviersonaten mit einem begleitenden Instrument nach dem jetzigen Schlendrian.

I have little inclination to it [composing fantasias], just as little as to keyboard sonatas with an accompanying instrument, according to the present slipshod practice.[29]

The last phrase sums up Bach's contempt for cheap fashion; but perhaps it voices the opinion of any ageing artist towards 'modern' taste.

After earlier violin and flute sonatas with harpsichord, C. P. E. Bach composed keyboard sonatas with optional accompaniment for the first time in the mid-1770s.[30] He published three sets in 1776–7:

Carl Philipp Emanuel Bachs Claviersonaten mit einer Violine und einem Violoncell zur Begleitung. Erste Sammlung (Leipzig, im Verlage des Autors, 1776) [H. 522–4; W. 90].

Carl Philipp Emanuel Bachs Claviersonaten mit einer Violine und einem Violoncell zur Begleitung. Zweyte Sammlung (Leipzig, im Verlage des Autors, 1777) [H. 531–4; W. 91].

Six Sonates for the Harpsichord or Piano Forte [accompanied by violin and cello] composed by C. P. E. Bach, Director of the Music at Hamburgh (London, printed and sold by R. Bremner, 1776) [H. 525–30; W. 89].

Subscribers for the first two sets included Charles Burney, Baron van Swieten, C. F. Cramer, and others; reviews appeared immediately. The *Staats- und gelehrte Zeitung des Hamburgischen unpartheyischen Correspondenten* wrote on the first set:

[27] Eng. trans. is partially taken from Newman, *The Sonata in the Classic Era*, 102, 377–8. Another paragraph of the dedication is cited in Ch. 4 above.

[28] Quoted in Bitter, *C. P. E. und W. F. Bach*, i. 343.

[29] Ibid. 341; letter of 10 Feb. 1775.

[30] For a recent survey of the keyboard chamber music of C. P. E. Bach, see Michelle Fillion, 'C. P. E. Bach and the Trio Old and New', in Stephen L. Clark (ed.), *C. P. E. Bach Studies* (Oxford, 1988), 83–104.

Original und Geistvoll, wie alle übrigen Werke unsres grossen C. Ph. Emanuel! Die Begleitung der Violine und des Violoncell kann zwar wegbleiben, besser aber ist es, wenn die Sonaten mit selbiger gespielt werden.

Original and ingenious, like all the other works of our great C. P. Emanuel! Although the accompaniment of the violin and the violoncello can be omitted, it is better when the sonatas are played with those.[31]

Report on the second set is equally laudatory:

Diese Bach'schen Sonaten mit Begleitung etc. sind, wie man leicht denken kann, voller Geist und Feuer, und obgleich in der Schreibart von den bekannten trefflichen Sonaten ohne Begleitung etwas verschieden, dennoch ganz original und des grossen Meisters völlig würdig. . . . Man kann diese Sonaten zwar ohne Begleitung der Violine und des Violoncells spielen, allein man wird wohl thun, wenn man beide Instrumente dabei nimmt. . . . Recensent hat das Vergnügen gehabt, diese Sonaten von dem Herrn Kapellmeister selbst auf einem Clavier von Friederici spielen zu hören, wo eine gedämpfte Violin und ein mit Discretion gespieltes Violoncell die Begleitung hatten.

These Bach sonatas with accompaniment are, as one can easily imagine, full of spirit and fire, and although in style somewhat different from the well-known excellent unaccompanied sonatas, they are wholly original, and completely worthy of the great master. . . . One can indeed play these sonatas without the accompaniment of the violin and the violoncello, but one would do better to use both instruments. . . . The present reviewer had the pleasure to hear these sonatas played by the Herr Kapellmeister himself on a *Clavier* by Friederici, at which a muted violin and a discreetly played violoncello gave the accompaniments.[32]

The latter report gives valuable evidence about performance. It seems that the delicate clavichord, considered mainly a solo instrument, was not excluded from *Kammermusik*—at least not in the personal practice of C. P. E. Bach.

The critic of the *Allgemeine deutsche Bibliothek*, reviewing the same two sets, sounds somewhat apologetic:

Man findet in diesen Sonaten . . . nicht das grosse, edle, planvolle, vollendete, durchaus Claviermässige, so den Charakter älterer Sonaten . . . dieses berühmten Komponisten bezeichnet, . . . sie sind in der neuern Manier gearbeitet, und reich an Annehmlichkeit, Abwechslung und brillanten Klavierfiguren. Folglich den Clavierspielern und Spielerinnen, die sich gerne produziren, ein sehr werthes Geschenk. Aber auch dem Kenner und Künstler ist es eine angenehme Erscheinung zu sehen, wie ein verständiger und geschmackvoller Komponist, das Leichte und Belustigende einer neuern Manier anwenden kann, ohne deshalb ihren Abgeschmacktheiten und nonsensikalischen Possenreissereyen zu huldigen.

In these sonatas one does not find . . . the great, the noble, the well-designed, the perfect, the properly *Clavier*-like, that is, the character . . . that distinguished the earlier sonatas of this famous composer, . . . they are written in the modern mode, and are rich in agreeableness, variation, and brilliant keyboard passages. Consequently, a valuable gift for the *Clavier*-players of both sexes, who like to perform. But the

[31] Quoted in Bitter, *C. P. E. und W. F. Bach*, i. 210. [32] Ibid. 210–11.

professionals and the artists can also be pleased to see how a composer of intelligence and good taste can apply the ease and amusement of a newer fashion, without bowing to its absurdities and nonsensical buffooneries.[33]

Johann Friedrich Reichardt, one of the greatest admirers of Philipp Emanuel, however, felt deeply disappointed about the 'English' keyboard trios. Concerning the *Six Sonates* [H. 525–30], he wrote in the *Musikalischer Beytrag zur Hamburger Neuen Zeitung*:

Wir verehren an H. C. Bach den grossen Original-Componisten, der an Adel und Hoheit und Würde und Erfindung über alle seine Zeitgenossen in der Kunst hoch hervor ragt. Muss es uns daher nicht kränken, wenn wir sehen, dass diese grosse Mann sich zu der Bequemlichkeit und dem Unvermögen des Volcks herablassen will? . . . Am mehresten fallen hier die kurzen, der Mode zu gefallen hineingeworfenen Andante-Sätze auf: wenn man diese mit den herrlichen Adagios in älteren Sonaten dieses grossen Meisters vergleicht! Von einem Meister fordert man Meisterstücke.

We revere Herr Kapellmeister Bach, the great original composer, who in nobility, dignity, and invention stands high above all his contemporaries in the arts. Should it then not offend us to see that this great man condescends to common convenience and weakness? . . . Most conspicuous are the short Andante movements, thrown in for fashion's sake, if one compares these with the splendid Adagios of the earlier sonatas of this great master! From a master one requires masterpieces.[34]

Actually, these sonatas make no more allowances for the market-place than some solo pieces of the composer. (See, for instance, short and easy pieces in the collections *Musikalisches Allerley*, *Musikalisches Mancherley*, etc.) After all, C. P. E. Bach always respected the claims of *Kenner & Liebhaber*, and although his artistic personality predestined him more towards the former, he contributed to the repertory of the latter as well.

A very unusual composition of C. P. E. Bach, the 'Clavier-Fantasie mit Begleitung einer Violine' (Hamburg, 1787; H. 536 = W. 80), should finally be mentioned. The last fantasia of the old master, in the rare key of F sharp minor, was written originally as a solo 'Freie Fantasie fürs Clavier' (H. 300 = W. 67), in 1787. Quite movingly, it bore the inscription 'Sehr traurig und ganz langsam'. Within the same year, Bach added a violin part to this composition. The fact is curious for two reasons: (1) free fantasia had always been a most personal, solo medium for Philipp Emanuel; (2) the genre itself was far from the light sonata/sonatina style that invited accompaniment. Why then the arrangement?[35]

[33] App. to vol. 25–6 (1779), 3030. Quoted in Schmid, *C. P. E. Bach und seine Kammermusik*, 80.

[34] No. 1 (1777), 3. Quoted in Schmid, *C. P. E. Bach und seine Kammermusik*, 79, 81–2.

[35] We face the same mystery in the Mozart fragment K. 396, subsequently called 'Fantasia'. The surviving autograph (1782?), with no title, shows a sonata exposition for keyboard, with violin accompaniment; the latter, however, is composed only for the last few bars (23–7). See *NMA* VIII/23/2, 181–3. The unfinished composition, completed by Maximilian Stadler, was published as a solo 'Fantaisie' by Cappi in Vienna, 1802.

The only hypothesis one can venture is a desire on the side of the composer for the most profound expression. Perhaps Philipp Emanuel, whose artistic aim throughout his career was a maximum *Empfindsamkeit* in composition and performance, at the end of his life found even the sensitive resources of his clavichord insufficient for the communication of his innermost feelings. 'C. P. E. Bachs Empfindungen', he wrote above the first system of his clavier–violin fantasia.

In the true manner of accompanied keyboard music, the violin adds little to the musical action.[36] But it sustains, it plays 'sigh' motives, it emphasizes expressive turns, and, at dramatic sections, it heightens the effect of passionate outbursts (see Ex. 43*a* and *b*).

Ex. 43 C. P. E. Bach, H. 536

(*a*)

(*b*)

[36] The duo version, however, is extended with a concluding Allegro in A major.

Then, if our reasoning is correct, we might find the *raison d'être* of this unusual fantasia-accompaniment in the 'Advertisement' of Charles Avison's Op. 7, quoted at the beginning of this chapter. Here, too, the solitary sound of the keyboard instrument will gain expression from the violin, 'for thus an effect results from the whole, as from the sound of one multiplied instrument'.

8

Questions of Interaction and Dissemination

MUSICAL culture and tradition evolved in widely different ways in the Habsburg Empire, in Germany, and in France and England during the eighteenth century. In the second half of that century, Italian influence was strongest in Vienna and London; Paris fought its battles for and against this influence; north Germany remained largely autonomous and isolated. Indeed it is ironic that Vienna, which seemed somewhat provincial and conservative at the time, produced the fundamental values of the 'classical style',[1] and, from a historical perspective, all other European trends and schools proved to be peripheral.

Local music printing and publishing started around 1780 in Vienna. Compared to other European centres (London, Paris, Amsterdam) this was late; music circulated mainly in manuscript form until the 1780s. As for keyboard instruments, when the new fortepiano began to replace the fashionable harpsichord, it was an instrument of light touch and tone, perfectly suited to the pleasant, graceful style that was favoured by the Viennese. In general, Viennese musicians disliked foreign tastes and manners. When the German writer and publisher, Friedrich Nicolai, travelled there in 1781, he remarked:

Zu den grössten Kennern der Musik unter den Liebhabern gehört der Herr Reichshofrath von Braun. Er schätzt besonders die Kompositionen des grossen Philipp Emanuel Bach. Er hat freylich darinn den zahlreichsten Theil des Publikums zu Wien wider sich. Ich selbst mache manche sonst eifrige und geschickte Liebhaber der Musick in Wien von Bach nicht allein mit Gleichgültigkeit, sondern auch mit innerm Widerwillen sprechen hören. Koželuch und Steffan waren ihnen für das Klavier alles.

One of the most knowledgeable of musical amateurs is the Imperial Counsellor Herr von Braun. He admires the music of the great Philipp Emanuel Bach especially. Needless to say he has the greater part of the Viennese public against him in this matter. I myself have heard many otherwise eager and skilful music-lovers in Vienna speak of Bach not only with indifference, but with outright hostility. Koželuch and Steffan are their idols among keyboard composers.[2]

[1] For a recent evaluation of the terms 'classical style', and 'Viennese classical style', see the Historiographical conclusion in James Webster, *Haydn's 'Farewell' Symphony and the Idea of Classical Style* (Cambridge, 1991), esp. 347–57.

[2] Friedrich Nicolai, *Beschreibung einer Reise durch Deutschland und die Schweiz im Jahre 1781* (Berlin, 1784), iv. 556. Quoted in Hans-Günter Ottenberg, *Carl Philipp Emanuel Bach* (Leipzig, 1982), 254; Eng. trans., Philip Whitmore (Oxford, 1987), 186.

…tly the Herr von Braun mentioned by Nicolai, and Baron van Swieten …e among the very few enthusiasts interested in something as anti-Viennese as the music of C. P. E. Bach.

Likewise, the strange virtuosity of Clementi, musical ambassador of London, made no lasting impression in Vienna. (During his Continental tour in the early 1780s, Clementi stayed six months in the imperial city.) If not everyone shared Mozart's negative reaction to the art of the famous visitor (see more on this in the final chapter), contemporary documents give almost no evidence of his presence there.[3] There is even less evidence that he had any compositional influence in Vienna. Other distinguished musicians resident in Paris or London rarely if ever travelled towards the Austrian parts of Europe.

However, there were some exceptional cases. Thomas Attwood, an English musician of moderate gift, did travel to Vienna in the 1780s to study composition with Mozart. As is usual with mediocre disciples, Attwood could only learn and imitate the very surface, and the outer manner of the art of his master. No one could seriously expect a pupil to emulate the wonderful depth of Mozart's inspiration.[4] But Attwood did carry a little bit of Mozartian ease and fluency back to London, and he subsequently published pretty sonatas (see Ex. 44, the main theme of Sonata No. 1 from the *Three Sonatas for the Piano Forte or Harpsichord, with accompanyments for a Violin and Violoncello, ad libitum*, Op. II*a*, Longman & Broderip, *c.*1791).

Ex. 44 Attwood, Sonata Op. 2/1, i

Not that Italianate rococo grace, one source of the Mozart style, was unknown in London. Established mainly by J. C. Bach, and continued by J. S.

[3] Notwithstanding the personal interest of the Emperor Joseph II; see Komlós, 'Mozart and Clementi', 7.

[4] See *Thomas Attwoods Theorie- und Kompositionsstudien bei Mozart*, ed. E. Hertzmann, C. B. Oldman, D. Heartz, and A. Mann, *NMA* X/30, 1 (Kassel, 1965).

Schroeter, this style lived on in the keyboard music of other *émigré* composers. The German-born Johann Baptist Cramer, who studied with Schroeter and Clementi, and toured the Continent from 1788 to 1791, was deeply affected by the art of Mozart. Although his composition seems to have gained stronger impulses from Haydn during the latter's London years, Cramer's playing, according to contemporaries, always retained a Mozartian quality.[5]

Perhaps the most cosmopolitan composer of the period was the widely travelled Ignaz Pleyel. Born with a clever business mind as well as compositional talents, later in his career Pleyel, like Clementi, carried on successful piano-making and music-publishing businesses. Pleyel published his music more extensively than any other composer of the time. His name was known equally in Italy, in Paris, in Vienna, and in London. The price of this success was of course a somewhat impersonal style, devoid of a strong character; a style that sought to please and to entertain. Charles Burney wrote about Pleyel as follows:

> There has lately been a rage for the music of Pleyel, which has diminished the attention of amateurs and the public to all other violin music. But whether this ingenious and engaging composer does not draw faster from the fountain of his invention than it will long bear, and whether his imitations of Haydn, and too constant use of semitones, and coquetry in *ralentandos* and *pauses* will not be soon construed into affectation, I know not; but it has already been remarked by critical observers, that his fancy, though at first so fertile, is not so inexhaustible, but that he frequently repeats himself, and does not sufficiently disdain the mixture of common passages with his own elegant ideas.[6]

Pleyel's music, then, represents to some degree the international, 'anonymous' language of the classical style.

For the European dissemination of keyboard music we must reconstruct the repertory of printed works, based on contemporary publishers' catalogues. A complete survey is, of course, not possible here, but a comparison of the major Viennese and London publishers gives an idea of the offerings of these two musical centres. I have selected the non-resident composers, in order to see the possible circulation of 'foreign' music at both places.

Of the London-oriented composers, Clementi was the most prominently represented in Vienna, especially by the largest publisher, Artaria; quite a few of the works were first editions (see Table 6).[7] Fifteen further Clementi compositions were published by Mollo, Hoffmeister, and Koželuch, but most of these were duplicates of Artaria editions. The pianoforte music of other London and/or Paris composers was printed only sporadically. Of the thirteen

[5] See Ch. 5 n. 19. [6] *General History*, ii. 951–2.

[7] The information in Table 6 is taken from reprints of contemporary publishers' lists; see Alexander Weinmann, *Beiträge zur Geschichte des Alt-Wiener Musikverlages*, 2nd series (Vienna, 1950–72), vols. 8 (1964), 12 (1968), 9a (1972); id., *Verzeichnis der Verlagswerke des Musikalisches Magazins in Wien* (Vienna, 1950), and *Vollständiges Verlagsverzeichnis Artaria & Comp.* (Vienna, 1952).

TABLE 6. Keyboard Works of London Composers Published in Vienna, 1780–1800

Publisher	*Composer*	*Number of Works*					*Total*
		Sonata				*Piano Piece*	
		Solo	*4-hand*	*Acc. (Duo)*	*Acc. (Trio)*		
Artaria	Clementi	42	3	—	22	5	72
	Cramer	6	—	—	3	4	13
	Steibelt	—	—	4	5	3	12
	Dussek	—	—	6	—	—	6
Mollo	Clementi	—	3*	—	—	—	3
	Cramer	4*	—	1	—	4*	9
Hoffmeister	Clementi	—	—	—	3*	3	6
Koželuch	Clementi	—	—	—	6*	—	6
Eder	Dussek	1	—	—	—	—	1

* Pub. by Artaria as well.

TABLE 7. Viennese/Bohemian Keyboard Composers in London Publishers' Catalogues, *c.*1785–1795

Publisher	*Composers*	
Birchall	*Works with accomp.* Koželuch	*Works without accomp.* Haydn, Vanhal, Mozart
Bland	Haydn, Koželuch, Mozart, Vanhal, Hoffmeister	
Dale	Haydn, Koželuch	
Longman & Broderip	*Concertos* Wagenseil	*Sonatas and Lessons* Haydn, Wagenseil, Mozart

Cramer compositions published by Artaria, a set of three sonatas and three sets of variations were published by Mollo as well. Daniel Steibelt, extremely fashionable elsewhere, is represented by a mere dozen pieces; and all that was available by Dussek were two sets of accompanied 'sonatinas', and the programme sonata entitled 'Die Seeschlacht' (C. 152), published by Joseph Eder.

The music of Pleyel was published in vast quantities in Vienna, as elsewhere; he had more original compositions and arrangements printed there than Haydn or Mozart.

London music publishing was a bigger enterprise and had a longer tradition. Regarding Viennese/Bohemian keyboard composers, a survey of the 'Piano Forte or Harpsichord Music' advertised by four major publishers, *c.*1785–95, shows that more or less the same names occur at the various dealers (see Table 7). Haydn and Koželuch appear frequently; these composers e vidently had stable relationships with English publishers. (Pirate editions, based on Viennese originals, were issued in great quantity, too.) Mozart was represented by considerably fewer works than his colleagues. The two sets of sonatas offered by Bland, and Longman & Broderip, respectively, were of the accompanied type;[8] the Variations on 'Lison dormait', K. 264, were published by Birchall and Bland as well. Two individual keyboard works appeared in 1788: the Variations for four hands in G, K. 501 (Bland), and the Quartet for fortepiano and strings in E flat, K. 493 (Longman & Broderip).[9]

The early appearance of a Mozart concerto is registered in the *Morning Post and Daily Advertiser* in 1786: K. 414, published the previous year in Vienna as Op. 4 (Artaria), was issued by W. Napier in London (not included in Table 7), together with another concerto composed by one Kloffler. The *Morning Post* noted: 'These are the two concertos which have been repeatedly performed by

[8] The 1786 Longman & Broderip version of the 1784 Torricella edn. of Op. 7 (= K. 333, 284, 454) adds violin accompaniment to the solo sonatas as well.

[9] For some of the above data I owe thanks to Professor Neal Zaslaw; the other source is Cliff Eisen, *New Mozart Documents* (London, 1991), 142–7.

Mr. Cramer, junr. at the Anacreontic Society.'[10] Apart from this, Mozart's music was a rare guest in London concert-halls; thus when the young Hummel made his London début as a pianist (5 May 1792) with a Mozart concerto, it must have seemed an unusual choice.

Besides serious publications, all sorts of amateur arrangements of masterpieces appeared in London. One example was *A Third Set of 6 Progressive Sonatas, for the Harpsichord or Piano Forte. Composed and compiled by John Relfe* (London: Goulding, *c.*1790). Lesson No. 1, in three movements, contains the following music, with no identification of the originals:

i = Finale of Mozart's *Klavierquartett* in G minor, K. 478, in an abridged form;
ii = Andante (by Relfe?);
iii = The first major section of the opening double variations of Haydn's Hob. XVI:40, with 'Allegro' inscription, arranged in a simple manner.

Mozart and Haydn were probably 'represented' by dozens of similar concoctions.

North German aesthetics of music in the latter half of the eighteenth century (cultivated mainly in Berlin) would be too vast a topic to cover here. As far as keyboard style is concerned, it represented a highly specialized manner, quite isolated from the surrounding European conventions. Heavily influenced by C. P. E. Bach, this style was in its own way just as idiomatic for the keyboard as the more familiar Viennese or London repertory—perhaps more. Anyone who has played C. P. E. Bach knows how excellently his instrumental writing lies under the hands, and how completely it shows up the sound and the profile of the instrument. One important reason behind this is the fantasia-like character of all genres of his keyboard music. Extemporization (*praeludiren*) is not only the expression of the process of invention, but it also aims at demonstrating the resources of the instrument; thus the improvisatory, rhapsodic writing stems directly from the nature of the keyboard, be it clavichord or fortepiano.

Another distinct quality of north German *Claviermusik* is the eschewing of operatic or orchestral effects. Instead of the use of conventional murky basses and tremolos, each little element of this music is part of a specific instrumental language that speaks in a personal and rhetorical manner to the listener. C. P. E. Bach, Hässler, Müthel, and others tried to express the very soul of the *Clavier*.

Highly praised by enthusiastic compatriots, north German style remained foreign and esoteric for the musicians of other nations. C. P. E. Bach himself had little experience of the culture of the surrounding countries. Like other

[10] See Eisen, *New Mozart Documents*, 140. Cramer played K. 414 at the Hanover Square Rooms, too, in Feb. 1786; ibid. 140–1.

composers who spent their lives in a confined geographical area, he gradually refined his own individual art. The development of his career was the result of circumstances rather than intentions, as we learn from his Autobiography:

> I have always remained in Germany and have taken only a few trips even in this, my fatherland. . . . I do not deny that it would have been of exceptional pleasure as well as advantage to me if I could have had the opportunity to visit foreign lands.[11]

As an earlier quotation in this chapter showed, C. P. E. Bach was little known or liked in Vienna. German *Empfindsamkeit*, and clavichord music in general, was even less familiar in England. Nevertheless, a certain respect, mainly from professionals, was forthcoming for the *Originalgenie* of the period. Charles Burney thought and spoke highly of him. A. F. Kollmann, a German-born London *émigré*, in his 1796 treatise *An Essay on Musical Harmony* referred to C. P. E. Bach as the single authority on the fantasia genre. Kollmann, who dedicated his work to Burney, states in his chapter xvii ('Of Fancy'):

> In any free fancy a certain *key* and *mode* must be fixed, in which the fancy ought to begin and to end. This is a rule which *Emanuel Bach* (one of the greatest fancy players and writers) gives in his treatise: *Versuch über die wahre Art das Clavier zu spielen*, Part ii.[12]

Bach's *Versuch* may have been known outside Germany; but it is not known whether London musicians played his fantasias and other compositions.

We noted in Chapter 5 that Haydn and Beethoven respected both C. P. E. Bach and Clementi. In Haydn's case, we may extend the compliments to J. L. Dussek, whose acquaintance he made in London.[13] We do not know whether Beethoven knew any music by Dussek, but we do know that he esteemed the instrumental expertise of J. B. Cramer. On his second Continental tour, 1799–1800, Cramer met Beethoven in Vienna, and the two musicians developed a friendly relationship with each other. The first two books of Cramer's *Studio per il Piano Forte* (forty-two *études*) were published by Haslinger in Vienna, 1804; twenty-one of these *études* became quite famous, through the later annotations of Beethoven.[14]

The notorious Anton Schindler reports that Beethoven, who was passionately interested in piano playing, intended to write a textbook on the subject himself.[15] He started to teach the young Czerny in 1801 on the basis of C. P. E.

[11] William Newman, 'Emanuel Bach's Autobiography', *MQ* 51 (1965), 367–8.

[12] *An Essay on Musical Harmony* (London, 1796), 121.

[13] See Haydn's letter of Feb. 1792 to Dussek's father, *CCLN* 130–1.

[14] See Johann Baptist Cramer, *21 Etüden für Klavier: Nach dem Handexemplar Beethovens aus dem Besitz Anton Schindlers*, ed. Hans Kann (Vienna, 1974). For a discussion of Beethoven's comments, see Harry Goldschmidt, 'Beethovens Anweisungen zum Spiel der Cramer-Etüden', in *Die Erscheinung Beethoven* (Leipzig, 1974), 115–29.

[15] Anton Schindler, *Beethoven As I Knew Him*, trans. Constance Jolly, ed. Donald W. MacArdle (Chapel Hill, NC, 1966), 379.

Bach's *Versuch*;[16] later, for the instrumental instruction of his nephew Karl, he used Cramer's *Studio*. It seems that he studied Cramer's etudes with particular care, and—so says Schindler—he considered them the best preparation for the playing of his own works.[17] The inscribed annotations that survive, in Schindler's hand, refer to accentuation and prosody, to legato playing, and to pseudo-polyphony in passage-work. Schindler's communication should not be taken at face value, of course, but it is unlikely to be pure fabrication. As William Newman has recently noted: 'The annotations in Schindler's document could very well be forgeries, yet still be largely true to and derived from Beethoven's own performance practices and intentions.'[18]

One may draw two conclusions from Beethoven's Cramer annotations. One is that his preoccupation with musical prosody, and with the *Klangrede* aspect of instrumental writing, indicates a true German trait in musical thinking, shared by his predecessors (C. P. E. Bach) and successors (R. Wagner) as well. The other inference is that Beethoven, who never left his chosen Vienna, received important impulses from the London Pianoforte School, through the personal acquaintance and the compositional influence of Clementi and Cramer.

A palpable manifestation of the British–Continental relationship in keyboard matters is the vast number of Scottish folksong arrangements made by Pleyel, Koželuch, Haydn, and Beethoven. Although such arrangements by local composers had looked back to a long tradition, when the Edinburgh publisher George Thomson started his project in 1792, he asked only Continental composers. The arrangements include Welsh and Irish songs as well, all of them for voice, and keyboard trio accompaniment. This popular kind of *Hausmusik* attracted masses of consumers, and Thomson evidently wanted to advertise the volumes with composers whose names were well established in the British Isles. Haydn wrote the most arrangements (*c*.400); towards his last years, however, some of the work was taken over by his pupil Sigismund Neukomm. Following English musical fashion, Thomson asked Beethoven to compose six sonatas on Scottish folksongs, but the idea must have seemed too frivolous for Beethoven: he never fulfilled the request.

[16] See Carl Czerny, 'Recollections from My Life', trans. Ernest Sanders, *MQ* 42 (1956), 307.

[17] Schindler–MacArdle, *Beethoven*, 379.

[18] William Newman, 'Yet Another Major Beethoven Forgery by Schindler?', *JM* 3 (1984), 414. For a new appraisal of the annotations, and the role of Schindler, see Barth, *The Pianist as Orator*, 124–6, 154–5.

Part Three
The Players

9

Kenner und Liebhaber

THE double term *connaisseur–amateur* (*Kenner–Liebhaber*) appeared, in connection with the appreciation of the arts, in the first half of the eighteenth century. However, as a result of historical and sociological developments, it became widely used from the mid-century on. Originally, the differentiation referred to listeners, and to critics of music: applied to listeners, *Kenner* implied the educated and rational, *Liebhaber* the uneducated and emotional; applied to critics, the same terms distinguished between professionals and laymen.[1] As the century proceeded, players themselves were more and more addressed or classified as *Kenner* or *Liebhaber*, and this new application of the terms fundamentally affected the composition and reception of music.

Compared to earlier periods, the second half of the eighteenth century saw a more widespread cultivation of music in Europe. Due to the ideals of the Enlightenment, political reforms brought more democratic conditions; at the same time, increasing industrial enterprise propelled economic development. With this arose a strong new middle class, which became an active participant in the social as well as cultural life of civilized Europe. In many ways, music became the symbol of a cultured existence, and listening no longer sufficed: one had to participate in making it.

The drastic decline in compositional complexity after J. S. Bach, along with the gradually rising status of instrumental music, happily coincided with the aspirations of this new class of music-lovers. Playing a keyboard instrument became a fashion in aristocratic and bourgeois homes, especially on the part of the ladies. The young daughter of any family of a respectable social status had to play the *Clavier* from an early age. *Hausmusik* for the amateur was composed and consumed perhaps in greater quantity during this half-century than at any other time in the history of music.

It cannot be sufficiently emphasized that classical keyboard music meant Mozart concertos or Beethoven sonatas for very few people at the time. Instead, it meant the sonatas and various pieces of a legion of *Kleinmeister*, some of whose names are hardly remembered today. The insatiable appetite of *Clavier-Liebhaber* demanded easy and simple music from composers and pub-

[1] See the excellent entry 'Kenner–Liebhaber–Dilettant' by Erich Reimer, in Hans Heinrich Eggebrecht (ed.), *Handwörterbuch der musikalischen Terminologie* (Wiesbaden, 1972–).

lishers alike. A brief collection of extracts, selected from contemporary sources, will demonstrate the general expectations of this musical society.[2]

The function of keyboard music as *Gebrauchsmusik* is clearly described in a 1786 review of the newly published keyboard sonatas by Vanhal (Op. 30; Vienna: Artaria):

Man muss billig in Verurtheilung musikalischer Werke auch darauf sein Augenmerk richten für was für eine Classe von Liebhabern er eigentlich das Stück componirt habe und ob er sich nicht nach ihren Fähigkeiten, und Geschmack richten müssen? . . . Der Verfasser gegenwärtiger Sonaten, hat diese gewiss für solche Liebhaber componirt, deren Hände noch nicht geübt genug waren, grosse Schwierigkeiten herauszubringen, und die doch gute empfindungsvolle Melodien liebten. Und in dieser Absicht sind sie vortreflich gesezt.

In fair judgement of musical compositions one must also keep in mind what kind of amateurs the piece is written for, and whether the composer should not have to adjust to their abilities and taste. . . . The composer of the present sonatas surely wrote them for amateurs whose hands are not yet practised enough to master great difficulties but who nevertheless enjoy good, expressive melodies. And in this respect they are excellently composed.[3]

In an earlier issue of the *Magazin der Musik* we find a review of the Op. 1 set by Koželuch:

Herr Koželuch ist ein treflicher Componist. In seinen Sonaten herrscht viel Erfindung, gute Melodie, und eine ihm eigne Modulation. Die geschwinden Sätze sind sehr brilliant und naiv, und die langsamen sehr sangbar. Wir können sie daher den Liebhabern des Claviers sicher empfehlen.

Herr Koželuch is an excellent composer. In his sonatas there is much invention, good melody, and a style of progression all his own. The fast movements are very brilliant and naïve, the slow ones very tuneful. Therefore we can certainly recommend them to amateurs of the *Clavier*.[4]

'For the lady dilettantes it is Koželuch who counts the most on the pianoforte,' stated a Viennese journal in 1788.[5] But, for some, even the pleasing style of Koželuch represented too high technical requirements, as a comment in the Salzburg–Viennese magazine *Pfeffer und Salz* shows (1786): 'His [Koželuch's] compositions bespeak an excellent mind, and no other fault is to be found with them than that they are too difficult.' [6]

A correspondent of Cramer's *Magazin der Musik*, writing about the Italian tour of the immensely popular Ignaz Pleyel, thought it necessary to empha-

[2] Some of the documents have been published in Katalin Komlós, 'The Viennese Keyboard Trio in the 1780s: Sociological Background and Contemporary Reception', *ML* 68 (1987), 222–34.

[3] *Magazin der Musik*, ii (Hamburg, 1786), 924. [4] Ibid. i (1783), 71.

[5] 'In der Liebhaberei der Damen gilt auf dem Pianoforte vor allen Koželuch.' *Journal des Luxus und der Moden* (1788), 230.

[6] 'Seine Compositionen verrathen indessen einen vortreflichen Kopf, und man kann ihnen keine andre Fehler ausstellen, als dass sie zu schwer sind.' Eng. trans. in Otto Erich Deutsch, *Mozart: A Documentary Biography*, trans. Eric Blom *et al.* (London, 1965), 270.

size that light style could very well be coupled with the serious craft of composition:

Er hat verschiedene schöne Clavier-Sonaten gesetzt, darnach man hier mit Ungeduld verlangt. Sein gefälliger Gesang darauf ist nicht so schwer wie Clementis und Mozarts Herereyen [*sic*]; er bleibt dabey mehr der Natur getreu, ohne desfals die Regeln des reinen Satzes hintenanzusetzen.

He [Pleyel] composed various beautiful keyboard sonatas which are in great demand here. The pleasant melody of these is not as heavy as in those of Clementi and Mozart; besides, he remains true to nature without neglecting the rules of strict composition.[7]

Pleyel was compared favourably not only with Clementi and Mozart, but with Haydn as well, on the pages of the *Morning Herald*. His approaching London visit prompted the following announcement in 1791:

Pleyel, the celebrated composer, certainly visits this country in the course of the approaching musical season. This composer, who is a pupil of the great Haydn, is becoming even more popular than his master; as his works are characterized less by the intricacies of science than the charm of simplicity and feeling.[8]

This comment, however, seems not to reflect the general opinion of the time, since Haydn's music held a universal attraction everywhere.

Haydn was the only great composer of the Classical period who could at once fulfil the expectations of both professionals and amateurs. It was a conscious ambition of his, and one of the secrets of his unparalleled success. The components of his personality, together with his high artistic integrity, made this exceptional achievement possible.

Prior to his London trips, Haydn wrote keyboard music for non-professional players. The wonderful variety of form and character in his solo and accompanied sonatas of this time is created through an instrumental idiom which is technically not too demanding on the performer.[9] Partly because of a kindly disposition, and partly because of his realistic sense for business, Haydn always showed special consideration for the amateur consumers of his music. He knew exactly for whom he composed, when he wrote to Artaria on 10 December 1785, concerning the poor engraving of his trios, Hob. XV:6–8: 'Even a professional would have to study before disentangling this passage, and then where would the dilettante be?'[10]

Contemporaries were aware of this rare quality in Haydn's music, as a relevant passage in the *Jahrbuch der Tonkunst von Wien und Prag* (1796) shows:

[7] *Magazin der Musik*, ii. 1378.

[8] Quoted in H. C. Robbins Landon, *Haydn: Chronicle and Works*, iii (Bloomington, Ind., 1976), 108.

[9] The relative technical 'easiness' of Haydn's pre-London keyboard music is deceiving for modern performers. Used to the heavy and virtuosic style of later periods, many of them find a Haydn sonata a mere trifle that can be tossed off with a minimal amount of preparation. Yet, to reproduce the refined rhetoric and articulation of this language requires painstaking work; without it, the music is meaningless.

[10] *CCLN* 51.

Wer ist so glücklich, wie er, lustige, schäckernde und reizende Thema zu erfinden, und wem ist es gegeben, selbige so natürlich, und doch so unerwartet, so einfach, und doch so künstlich aufzuführen? . . . Seine Klavierstücke sind meistens angenehm, einfach und leicht zu spielen, und eben aus diesem Grunde um so viel brauchbarer, da sich die heutigen Kompositeurs meistens auf Schwierigkeiten verlegen, und von dem Schüler die Kraft verlangen, welche dem Meister nicht selten schwer wird.

Who is so fortunate as he [Haydn], to invent such jolly, playful, and charming melodies, and to whom is granted the gift, to treat those so naturally, yet so unexpectedly, so simply, yet so artistically? . . . His keyboard compositions are mostly pleasant, simple, and easy to play, and, just for that reason, they are so much more useful; whereas today's composers strive mostly for difficulties, and they require such force from the student that would often be hard for the master.[11]

How admirably Haydn, later in his career in London, rose to the task of writing for professionals for the concert stage, has already been discussed in Chapter 6.

Mozart's music, as is well known, was criticized in its own time for being too complex. The always shrewd father, thoroughly versed in the ways of the world, tried to convey his thoughts on this fundamental question to his son during Wolfgang's unsuccessful Paris sojourn in 1778:

If you have not got any pupils, well then compose something more. . . . But let it be something short, easy and popular. Discuss the matter with some engraver and find out what he would best like to have . . . Do you imagine that you would be doing work unworthy of you? If so, you are very much mistaken. Did [Johann Christian] Bach, when he was in London, ever publish anything but similar trifles? *What is slight can still be great*, if it is written in a natural, flowing and easy style—and at the same time bears the marks of sound composition. Such works are more difficult to compose than all those harmonic progressions, *which the majority of people cannot fathom*, or pieces which have pleasing melodies, but which are *difficult to perform*. Did Bach lower himself by such work? Not at all. Good composition, sound construction, il filo—these distinguish the master from the bungler—even in trifles.[12]

Leopold Mozart was not at all averse to compromises in artistic questions; yet, it is hard to disagree with some of his statements. Two years later, in the midst of Wolfgang's preoccupations with the rehearsals of *Idomeneo* in Munich, he repeated his admonitions:

I advise you when composing to consider not only the musical, but also *the unmusical public*. You must remember that to every *ten real connoisseurs* there are a *hundred ignoramuses*. So do not neglect the so-called popular style, which tickles *long ears*.[13]

In fact, when writing for the keyboard, Mozart did distinguish between *Kenner und Liebhaber*.[14] His most brilliant and sophisticated compositions he

[11] pp. 21–2. [12] Letter of 13 Aug. 1778; see *Letters*, 599.
[13] Letter of 11 Dec. 1780, *Letters*, 685. [14] See also Ch. 5.

intended for himself. The concertos, and some of the variation sets especially, reflect the technical mastery and improvisatory character of his playing.[15] But many of the dedicatees of great concertos or sonatas of his were first-rate fortepianists. Barbara Ployer (recipient of K. 449 and 453) and Josepha Auernhammer (K. 448 was composed for her) were Mozart's students; K. 456 was dedicated to the celebrated Maria Theresia Paradis, a student of Richter and Koželuch.

At the same time, Mozart composed a great deal for amateur players. As a fortepiano teacher, he was obliged to supply his students with suitable material. He wrote the majority of his sonatas (occasionally marked 'für Anfänger') and various independent pieces for non-professionals. Still, his music had the general reputation of being above the capacity of the average *Liebhaber*. Chamber music with keyboard, a favourite field of amateurs, seemed to exceed their powers when composed by Mozart. Although speaking from the angle of the amateur, a review of one of the newly published keyboard quartets (K. 478 or 493) in the *Journal des Luxus und der Moden* (1788), shows remarkable insight towards the intrinsic value of the work. The article is characteristically called 'Über die neueste Favorit-Musik in grossen Concerten, sonderlich in Rücksicht auf Damen-Gunst, in Clavier-Liebhaberey'.

Es kam von einiger Zeit von ihm ein einzelnes Quadro (für Clavier, 1. Violin, 1. Viola (Bratsche) und Violoncell) gestochen heraus, welches sehr künstlich gesetzt ist, im Vortrage die äusserste Präcision aller vier Stimmen erfordert, aber bei glücklicher Ausführung doch nur, wie es scheint, Kenner der Tonkunst in einer Musica di Camera vergnügen kann und soll. . . . Manches andre Stück souteniert sich noch auch bey einem mittelmässigen Vortrage; dieses Mozartische Produkt aber ist wirklich kaum anzuhören, wenn es unter mittelmässige Dilettanten-Hände fällt, und vernachlässigt vorgetragen wird.

Some time ago a single *Quadro* by him [Mozart](for pianoforte, 1 violin, 1 viola and violoncello) was engraved and published, which is very cunningly set and in performance needs the utmost precision in all the four parts, but even when well played, or so it seems, is able and intended to delight only connoisseurs of music in a *musica di camera*. . . . Many another piece keeps some countenance even when indifferently performed; but this product of Mozart's can in truth hardly bear listening to when it falls into mediocre amateurish hands and is negligently played.[16]

The saleability of such works was dubious, therefore the publisher, Hoffmeister, withdrew his contract for additional compositions in the genre.[17]

The technical difficulty of Mozart's variation sets induced publishers and copyists to produce simplified or abridged versions for the *Liebhaber* clien-

[15] The question is discussed in detail in Komlós, '"Ich praeludirte und spielte Variazionen"'.
[16] Quoted in Deutsch, *Mozart: A Documentary Biography*, 318.
[17] See Georg Nikolaus von Nissen, *Biographie W. A. Mozarts nach Originalbriefen* (Leipzig, 1828), 633.

tele.[18] The C major variations on J. C. Fischer's Menuett (K. 179), for instance, are known in several simplified versions. Further examples include the 'Lison dormait' variations (K. 264), and the set composed on Duport's Menuett (K. 573). An early nineteenth-century Amsterdam print of the latter includes three variations only, 'approprié pour l'usage des élèves'. Mozart himself was aware that some compromise might further the immediate attraction of his music. When trying to offer his services at the electoral court in Mannheim, he sent a sample of his composition: 'I decided to take my six easiest variations on Fischer's minuet, which I had copied out here expressly for this purpose,' he wrote to Salzburg in November 1777.[19] Notwithstanding his efforts, his services were not wanted in Mannheim.

In Vienna, the double term *Virtuosen–Dilettanten* was used rather than *Kenner und Liebhaber*, with a more specific reference to players and composers.[20] The *Jahrbuch der Tonkunst von Wien und Prag* (1796) lists the names and activities of no fewer than 210 Viennese musicians under this title, in alphabetical order. There, among the entries under the letter B, we find 'Bethofen [*sic*], ein musikalisches Genie, welches seit zween [?] Jahren seinen Aufenthalt in Wien gewählet hat.'[21]

With Beethoven, the era of *Clavier-Liebhaberey* is more or less ended. His first *opera* must have shocked Viennese amateurs. If Joseph Haydn, always open to new impulses, rejected Beethoven's Op. 1 C minor trio, written approximately at the same time as his own wonderfully novel London trios, he must have felt strongly about it. And to recall Marianne von Genzinger again: if she, fine player as she was, found the crossing of the hands in the Adagio e cantabile of Hob. XVI:49 too difficult,[22] then what did her class of players make of Beethoven's Op. 2?

This is not to say that the amateur Fräulein of Biedermeier Vienna had no more music to play. On the contrary: *Hausmusik* on the fortepiano became more and more widespread. A multitude of ländler, German dances, waltzes, écossaises, and other pieces were composed for this purpose, not least by Franz Schubert. The Beethoven ideal, largely independent of the artistic tendencies of its time, remained an individual phenomenon.

In Germany, simple Lieder with keyboard accompaniment were a special part of the *Liebhaber* repertory. Numerous albums were printed, containing either songs alone, or songs mixed with solo instrumental compositions. Following

[18] See Komlós, '"Ich praeludirte und spielte Variazionen"', 42–3. The original data are taken from Kurt von Fischer, 'Mozarts Klaviervariationen', in *Hans Albrecht in Memoriam*, ed. Wilfried Brennecke and Hans Haase (Kassel, 1962), 168–73.

[19] *Letters*, 397.

[20] The term is already used by Georg Muffat, in the Preface to his *Auserlesene Instrumental-Music* (Passau, 1701), where Muffat recommends his series for 'Music-Liebhaber und Virtuosen'.

[21] p. 7. [22] See her letter of 11 July 1790 to Haydn, *CCLN* 108.

the success of the collections of the 1750s,[23] the various series published for amateurs usually offered Lieder, little dances or other pieces for *Clavier*, as well as easy duets for string or wind instruments. Such was the content of the *Musikalisches Allerley von verschiedenen Tonkünstlern* (printed in nine volumes), and the *Musikalisches Mancherley*, both published in Berlin, 1761–3. The composers included C. P. E. Bach, Graun, Marpurg, Quantz, Agricola, and others. Collections of this sort remained in fashion for the rest of the century, as is demonstrated by these characteristic titles from the 1780s:

Georg Benda, *Sammlung vermischter Clavier- und Gesangstücke für geübte und ungeübte Spieler* (Gotha and Leipzig 1780–7).
Johann Wilhelm Hässler, *Clavier- und Singstücke verschiedener Art* (Erfurt, 1782).

The importance of music, as part of the everyday life in a cultivated *bürgerlich* milieu, is depicted in Goethe's *Werther* (1774). 'If I am worried about something, I hammer out a *Contretanz* on my out-of-tune *Klavier*, and everything is all right again,' confesses Lotte to Werther, on the first night of their acquaintance.[24] Werther, who even performs the tuning of Lotte's clavichord,[25] feels a similar response to her playing and singing: 'There is a melody, a simple but moving air, which she plays on the *Klavier*, with angelic skill. It is her very favourite tune, and the moment she plays the first note I feel delivered of all my pain, confusion and brooding fancies.'[26]

Music can communicate sentiments that are inexpressible in words: such was the *ars poetica* of *Empfindsamkeit*. Nowhere is this more effectively suggested than in one of the excessively emotional scenes of Goethe's novel, formulated through Werther's words:

Sie [Lotte] fühlt, was ich dulde. Heut ist mir ihr Blick tief durchs Herz gedrungen. Ich fand sie allein; ich sagte nichts, und sie sah mich an. Und ich sah nicht mehr in ihr die liebliche Schönheit, nicht mehr das Leuchten des trefflichen Geistes; das war alles vor meinen Augen verschwunden. Ein weit herrlicher Blick wirkte auf mich, voll Ausdruck des innigsten Anteils, des süssten Mitleidens. . . . Sie nahm ihre Zuflucht zum Klavier und hauchte mit süsser leiser Stimme harmonische Laute aus ihrem Spiele.

[23] Marpurg, *Neue Lieder zum Singen beym Claviere* (1756), and *Berlinische Oden und Lieder* (1756–63); C. P. E. Bach, *Herrn Professor Gellerts geistliche Oden und Lieder mit Melodien* (1758); etc.

[24] 'Und wenn ich was im Kopfe habe und mir auf meinem verstimmten Klavier einen Contretanz vortrommle, so ist alles wieder gut.' Johann Wolfgang von Goethe, *Die Leiden des jungen Werther* (Leipzig, 1918), 35. Eng. trans. as *The Sorrows of Young Werther* by Michael Hulse (London, 1989), 39.

[25] *Die Leiden des jungen Werther*, 81; Eng. trans., 64.

[26] 'Sie hat eine Melodie, die sie auf dem Klavier spielt mit der Kraft eines Engels, so simpel und so geistvoll! Es ist ihr Leiblied, und mich stellt es von aller Pein, Verwirrung und Grillen her, wenn sie nur die erste Note davon greift.' Ibid. 62; Eng. trans., 53.

She senses what I am enduring. Today her gaze pierced my very heart. I found her alone; I said nothing, and she looked at me. And I no longer saw in her that gentle beauty, or the light of a great spirit; in my eyes, it had all vanished, and the vision that moved me, that gaze she turned upon me, was a more glorious one, full of the deepest compassion and the sweetest sympathy. . . . She retreated to the *Klavier* and accompanied her playing with harmonious sounds breathed forth in a sweet and tender voice.[27]

The paragraph is a perfect manifestation of eigthteenth-century German romanticism, literary and musical.

The leading German keyboard composer of the period, C. P. E. Bach, took *Liebhaber* quite seriously. His wonderful *Sechs Sonaten mit veränderten Reprisen* (1760) make no allowances in compositional standard; rather, they represent the model of the classical keyboard sonata. Yet, according to the author's Preface, they were intended for amateurs:

Bey Verfertigung dieser Sonaten habe ich vornehmlich an Anfänger und solche Liebhaber gedacht, die wegen gewisser Jahre oder anderer Verrichtungen nicht mehr Gedult und Zeit genug haben, sich besonders stark zu üben. Ich habe ihnen bey der Leichtigkeit zugleich auf eine bequeme Art das Vergnügen verschaffen wollen, sich mit Veränderungen hören zu lassen, ohne dass sie nöthig haben, solche entweder selbst zu erfinden, oder sich von andern vorschreiben zu lassen, und sie mit vieler Mühe auswendig zu lernen.

While composing these Sonatas I thought especially of beginners and of those amateurs who, on account of their years or of other business, have neither patience nor time enough to practice much. Apart from giving them something easy I wanted to provide them with the pleasure of performing alterations without having to resort to either inventing them themselves or getting someone else to write them and then memorizing them with much difficulty.[28]

Another title from ten years later announces the purpose of the volume more clearly: *Six Sonates pour le clavecin, à l'usage des Dames* (Amsterdam: Hummel, 1770).

The fundamental character of C. P. E. Bach's music, however, had more interest for connoisseurs, just as it has today. 'The wealth of ideas' of his sonatas and fantasias 'sooner frightens than attracts most *Musikliebhaber*,' wrote J. K. F. Triest, in the pages of the *Allgemeine musikalische Zeitung*.[29] Not unlike Mozart, C. P. E. Bach composed his real *Kenner* works for himself. He confesses in his Autobiography:

Because I have had to compose most of my works for specific individuals and for the public, I have always been more restrained in them than in the few pieces that I have written merely for myself.[30]

[27] *Die Leiden des jungen Werther*, 146–7; Eng. trans., 101.

[28] Quoted and trans. in *C. P. E. Bach: Sechs Sonaten mit veränderten Reprisen*, ed. Etienne Darbellay (Winterthur, 1976), p. xiii. See a detailed discussion of the Preface in Katalin Komlós, '"Veränderte Reprise": Aspects of An Idea', *MR* 51 (1990), 262–7.

[29] 3 (1800–1), 301.

[30] See Newman, 'Emanuel Bach's Autobiography', 371.

His most personal utterances, of course, are the fantasias. Those unique pieces reflect Bach's own improvisations, as we learn from several contemporary documents.

Real *Kenner*, however, must have been as scarce then as they are today. When pondering on this, Philipp Emanuel sounds quite sober, if not disillusioned:

Man will jetzt von mir 6 oder 7 Fantasien haben, wie das achtzehnte Probestück aus dem c-moll ist; ich läugne nicht, dass ich in diesem Fache gern etwas thun möchte, vielleicht wäre ich auch nicht ganz und gar ungeschickt dazu, . . . allein, wie viele sind deren, die dergleichen lieben, verstehen und gut spielen?

People now ask me for six or seven more fantasias like the final piece in C minor from the *Probestücke*; I do not deny that I should very much like to write something of this kind, and perhaps I am not altogether unqualified to do so; . . . the only difficulty is that one wonders how many people there are who like such music, understand it, and can perform it properly.[31]

What, then, does the famous C. P. E. Bachian designation 'für Kenner und Liebhaber', in the last six volumes of his solo keyboard music, really imply? Are certain pieces in the series intended for *Kenner*, others for *Liebhaber*? Is the entire series intended for *Kenner* as well as *Liebhaber*? Is it a mere cliché, with no particular message? Is it a catch-phrase, to attract more customers? (For that matter, the denotation 'fürs Fortepiano' in the titles of vols. ii–vi calls for similar investigation. Is it a genuine recommendation, or is it a mere response to new times, while the old master still thought in terms of his favourite clavichord?)

The sonatas, rondos, and fantasias in the 'Kenner und Liebhaber' series speak strictly to connoisseurs. In the case of C. P. E. Bach, this means the complexity of the musical syntax in the first place; the question of technical 'difficulty' is of secondary importance. Thus, one might wonder whether Philipp Emanuel uses the term in the spirit of his father, who, nearly half a century earlier, composed his *Clavierübung III* 'For Music Lovers and especially for Connoisseurs of such Work [*denen Liebhabern, und besonders denen Kennern von dergleichen Arbeit*], to refresh their Spirits'.[32] The comparison is still no great help for the better understanding of the apparent intention: more unsuitable music for amateurs than *Clavierübung III* would be hard to imagine.

Perhaps the intelligent J. F. Rochlitz perceived some truth when he tried to explain the same question, in his discussion of C. P. E. Bach's 'Kenner und Liebhaber' series:

Mit den Kennern meint er offenbar so wenig die . . . bei denen des Mäkelns kein Ende wäre u. s. w., als mit den Liebhabern die, welche in der Musik nichts, als einen artigen Zeitvertrieb, eine nicht unangenehme Unterhaltung suchen. Er meint Kenner, die

[31] Letter of 10 Feb. 1775 to Forkel; quoted in Ottenberg, *C. P. E. Bach*, 229–30; Eng. trans., 166–7.

[32] See facs. and trans. in Hans T. David and Arthur Mendel (eds.), *The Bach Reader*, rev. edn. (New York, 1966), 164–5.

zugleich wahre Liebhaber, oder, wie man in solchem Zusammenhange jetzt lieber spricht, wahre Kunstfreunde; und Liebhaber, die zugleich Kenner sind, oder das Wesen der Sache verstehen.

By 'professionals' he evidently means no more than those . . . who find fault with everything, as by 'amateurs' those who seek nothing but a good pastime, a not unpleasant amusement in music. He means professionals who are at the same time true amateurs, or rather, as one says today in this connection, true friends of the art; and amateurs who are at the same time professionals, that is, who understand the essence of things.[33]

Rochlitz already belonged to posterity when he wrote these thoughts, but he was still much closer in time to the mentality of the relevant period than we are today. To claim a perfect understanding of the artistic decisions of an enigmatic composer like C. P. E. Bach, however, would be presumptuous at any time.

In England, we find a less complicated situation. Here, the lively concert activities could boast dozens of professional pianists (many of whom were virtuosos in a more modern sense than their Continental colleagues), and the number of amateurs was legion. 'The daughters of the house are mostly musical, and highly skilled either in fortepiano playing, or in singing, and in this way they can pass the evenings very agreeably,' reported Adalbert Gyrowetz during his London sojourn of 1789–92.[34]

How exactly these evenings were passed, one can read in contemporary English novels. The loveliest scenes are recounted by Jane Austen.

There is no voluminous sociological dissertation that would introduce the late eighteenth- /early nineteenth-century social life of provincial England better than Austen's *Emma*. Here, among the several aspects of human existence, the pleasure of music is an important factor in people's lives, whether in a genuine or in an ironic sense. The social implications of pianoforte playing affect the position of Miss Woodhouse and Miss Fairfax, first and second young lady of the plot, respectively. The minute description of a large dinner-party, where the two ladies entertain the company by singing and playing at a grand pianoforte, abounds in subtle observations:

She [Emma Woodhouse] gave a proper compliance [to play]. She knew the limitation of her own powers too well to attempt more than she could perform with credit; she wanted neither taste nor spirit in the little things which are generally acceptable, and could accompany her own voice well. One accompaniment to her song took her agreeably by surprise; a second, slightly, but correctly taken by Frank Churchill. Her pardon was duly begged at the close of the song, and everything usual

[33] Johann Friedrich Rochlitz, 'Karl Philipp Emanuel Bach', *Für Freunde der Tonkunst*, 4 (Leipzig, 1832), 295.

[34] 'Adalbert Gyrowetz (1763–1850)', in Alfred Einstein (ed.), *Lebensläufe deutscher Musiker von ihnen selbst erzählt* (Leipzig, 1915), 74.

followed. He was accused of having a delightful voice, and a perfect knowledge of music, which was properly denied; and that he knew nothing of the matter, and had no voice at all, roundly asserted. They sang together once more: and Emma would then resign her place to Miss Fairfax, whose performance, both vocal and instrumental, she never could attempt to conceal from herself, was infinitely superior to her own.[35]

The emotional effect of music is expressed in the little scene of the following day, when the eligible young visitor, Frank Churchill, asks Miss Fairfax to play for him. '"If you are very kind," said he, "it will be one of the waltzes we danced last night; let me live them over again. . . . What felicity it is to hear a tune again which *has* made one happy!" Then, sorting through some music, he remarks to Emma: "Here is something quite new to me. Do you know it? Cramer. And here are a new set of Irish melodies. . . ." '[36]

Austen gives a wonderful portrayal of the *nouveau riche* couple, Mr and Mrs Cole. The subject of their musical snobbery is nothing other than a grand pianoforte, as we learn from Mrs Cole's narrative:

'It always has quite hurt me that Jane Fairfax, who plays so delightfully, should not have an instrument. It seemed quite a shame, especially considering how many houses there are where fine instruments are absolutely thrown away. This is like giving ourselves a slap, to be sure; and it was but yesterday I was telling Mr Cole I was really ashamed to look at our new grand pianoforte in the drawing-room, while I do not know one note from another, and our little girls, who are but just beginning, perhaps may never make anything of it; and there is poor Jane Fairfax, who is mistress of music, has not anything of the nature of an instrument, not even the pitifullest old spinnet in the world, to amuse herself with.'[37]

One of the most significant events of the novel, the unexpected arrival of a new Broadwood square pianoforte for Miss Fairfax, creates a sensation in the small community of Highbury:

Mrs Cole was telling that she had been calling on Miss Bates; and as soon as she entered the room, had been struck by the sight of a pianoforte, a very elegant looking instrument; not a grand but a large-sized square pianoforte: and the substance of the story, the end of all the dialogue which ensued of surprise, and inquiry, and congratulations on her side, and explanations on Miss Bates's, was that this pianoforte had arrived from Broadwood's the day before, to the great astonishment of both aunt and niece, entirely unexpected;

Mrs Weston, kind-hearted and musical, was particularly interested by the circumstance, and Emma could not help being amused at her perseverance in dwelling on the subject; and having so much to ask and to say as to tone, touch, and pedal.[38]

Miss Jane Fairfax, the lucky but confused recipient of the fine instrument, gives her first demonstration in the novel as follows:

[35] Jane Austen, *Emma* (London, 1816); modern edn. (London: Collins, 1953), 184.
[36] Ibid. 195–6. [37] Ibid. 175. [38] Ibid. 174, 178.

At last Jane began, and though the first bars were feebly given, the powers of the instrument were gradually done full justice to. Mrs Weston had been delighted before, and was delighted again; Emma joined her in all her praise; and the pianoforte, with every proper discrimination, was pronounced to be altogether of the highest promise.[39]

In Austen's wonderful novel, this instrument represents the role of music in contemporary society: it is made to appear as an *objet d'art*, and a parvenu at the same time.

In late eighteenth-century London pianoforte music, the difference in technical requirements between professional and amateur repertory was greater than elsewhere. There is no comparison between the representative concert sonatas, written for professionals by the most famous virtuosos (Clementi, Dussek, Cramer), and the vast amount of easy sonatinas and small pieces, intended for amateur players. While the latter were mostly produced by a host of second- and third-rate composers, the leading keyboard experts made their contributions, too.

As discussed in Chapter 7, the accompanied sonata was mainly the field of amateurs; to this we must add the various programme sonatas, pot-pourris, and shorter pieces. Programme sonatas were especially popular, and the range of subjects was wide. Franz Kotzwara, a Bohemian composer who lived in London and Dublin, started the vogue of 'battle pieces' with 'The Battle of Prague' for pianoforte, violin, violoncello, and drum *ad libitum* (*c.*1788). There is practically no London publisher's catalogue from the last dozen years of the eighteenth century that would not include Kotzwara's composition, arranged for solo pianoforte as well. Battle music became a fashion.[40]

Admiral Duncan's victory in 1797 occasioned two remarkable, large-scale works: a programme sonata by Dussek ('The Naval Battle and Total Defeat of the Grand Dutch Fleet by Admiral Duncan on the 11th of October 1797'), and a multipartite, descriptive composition by Steibelt, titled 'Overture in Commemoration of His Britannic Majesty's Solemn Procession to the Cathedral of St Paul's, to return thanks for Admiral Duncan's Victory'. The latter consists of seventeen separate sections, all in different tempos, with minute inscriptions that explain the programme, from 'The crowing of the cock' to the final 'Drums beat and Cannons'.[41]

James Hewitt, an English composer who emigrated to the United States in 1792, transplanted this fad there. He published 'The Battle of Trenton, a Favorite Historical Sonata' in 1797; another notable programme cycle of his is 'The 4th of July: A Grand Military Sonata For the Piano Forte, Composed in Commemoration of That Glorious Day' (1805).

[39] Jane Austen, *Emma*, 194.

[40] Descriptive and programme pieces were published in great quantities in Paris, too; see details, with musical examples, in Place, *Le Piano-Forte à Paris*, 105–13.

[41] See the complete reproduction of the programme in Harding, *The Piano-Forte*, 114–15.

Noisy military, and other percussive effects were achieved with the help of various stops and pedals on the pianoforte. Tambourine, drum and triangle, bassoon pedals, or janissary stops for 'Turkish' colour, became increasingly popular before and after the turn of the century, on the Continent as well as in England. Serious musicians considered such devices nonsensical, as Hummel and Czerny testify.[42] But, yielding to the demands of amateurs, instrument makers added more and more such mechanisms to their pianos.[43]

If not actually built into the pianoforte, tambourines as accompanying instruments were frequently prescribed for dance pieces. Steibelt, particularly fond of sensational effects, wrote waltzes for pianoforte with tambourine accompaniment. Fashion, however, tempted more serious composers too. Muzio Clementi, after the composition of his *Six Progressive Sonatinas for the Piano Forte* (Op. 36), published two sets of *Twelve Waltzes for Pianoforte, Tambourine and Triangle* (Op. 38, Longman & Broderip, 1798; Op. 39, Longman, Clementi & Co., 1800).

[42] Hummel, *A Complete Theoretical and Practical Course*, 62; Czerny, *Complete Theoretical and Practical Pianoforte School* (London, 1839), iii. 57, 65.

[43] See Harding, *The Piano-Forte*, 112–50.

10

Piano Tutors and Treatises[1]

THE nomenclature of the instruments in keyboard tutors published in the last two decades of the eighteenth century is more or less uniform. With few exceptions, English and French treatises offer instruction in 'harpsichord or pianoforte' playing, while German ones deal with the art of the *Clavier*. Generic as the latter term is, it still primarily indicates the clavichord. Thus the tutor of Johann Peter Milchmeyer, *Die wahre Art das Pianoforte zu spielen* (Dresden, 1797), which explicitly names the pianoforte, must be considered a milestone in the history of such treatises.[2] After 1800, nearly all such works indicated the pianoforte as their exclusive subject.[3]

To those who are familiar with the eighteenth-century German partiality for the clavichord (see Ch. 1), Milchmeyer's first statement must sound extraordinary:

halte ich den Flügel, so wie das Clavicord (das Clavier), gar nicht für die rechten Instrumente, auf denen sich ein gutes Spiel lernen lässt. Der Ausdruck, welchen man auf dem letztern hervorbringen will, verursacht unendliche Verdrehungen der Finger, und es ist gewiss selten, dass Personen, die sich lange auf dem Clavicord geübt haben, gute Pianoforte-Spieler werden. . . . Uebrigens wissen alle Liebhaber und Kenner der Musik, dass in Frankreich und England sehr grosse Tonkünstler sind, von denen ich nur die Herren Clementi und Steibelt erwähnen will. Ich fordere aber Jeden auf, zu sagen, ob er wohl in den neuern Zeiten in diesen Ländern ein Clavicord gesehen habe?

I regard neither the harpsichord, nor the clavichord as the right instrument for the learning of good keyboard playing. One can achieve expression on the latter, but it causes the endless twisting of the fingers, and it is surely rare that those who practise for a long time on the clavichord will become good pianoforte players. . . . Otherwise, all the amateurs and professionals of music know what outstanding musicians there are

[1] It is not the purpose of this chapter to give account of the vast material concerning performance practice. For a complete compendium of that area, including questions of dynamic and accentuation, articulation and touch, technique and fingering, pedals and ornaments, rhythms and tempo, readers must turn to Sandra Rosenblum, *Performance Practices in Classic Piano Music: Their Principles and Applications* (Bloomington, Ind., 1988).

[2] Two French treatises of about the same time also designate the pianoforte as their sole subject: B. Viguerie, *L'art de toucher le piano-forte*, Op. 5 (Paris, 1795), and L. Adam and L. W. Lachnith, *Méthode ou principe général du doigté pour le forté-piano* (Paris, 1798).

[3] Some German tutors, however, still did not dispense with the inclusion of the clavichord. See A. E. Müller, *Klavier und Fortepiano-Schule* (Jena, 1804); F. Guthmann, *Methodik des Klavier und Pianofortespiels* (Nuremberg and Leipzig, 1805).

in France and England, from whom I will name only Clementi and Steibelt. But I ask everyone, has anyone recently seen a single clavichord in these countries?[4]

One partial explanation for this is that the German author spent nearly two decades in France. The Preface reads thus:

Ich übergebe hier den Liebhabern und Anfängern des Pianoforte-Spieles ein Werk, in welchem ich die Grundsätze zergliedere, die ich durch einen 18 jährigen Aufenthalt in Paris und Lyon, und durch ein 24 jähriges unausgesetztes Studium dieses Instruments mir zu eigen gemacht habe.

Here I offer amateurs and beginning players of the pianoforte a work in which I discuss the principles thereof, acquired in the course of an eighteen-year sojourn in Paris and Lyon, and through twenty-four years of unceasing study of this instrument.[5]

Although Milchmeyer writes exclusively about the playing of the square piano,[6] just as, some years later, Andreas Streicher contributes his 'brief remarks' on fortepiano playing,[7] their instruction concerning the physical aspects of this art is hardly different from the early eighteenth-century descriptions of harpsichord playing. The position of the arm and hand, the primacy of finger technique, and the even touch achieved through the closeness of the fingertips to the keys are the same as prescribed by Rameau,[8] while the warnings about the negative result of too strong an attack echo François Couperin.[9] We find basically the same maxims in such late works as Louis Adam's *Méthode de piano-forte* (Paris, 1804), or even Hummel's *Ausführliche theoretisch–practische Anweisung zum Pianoforte-spiel* (Vienna, 1828), as in earlier treatises.

One crucial aspect of modern keyboard technique, the equal use of the thumb, is sanctioned in Chapter 1 of C. P. E. Bach's *Versuch über die wahre Art das Clavier zu spielen* (Berlin, 1753). Although applied earlier by J. S. Bach and Couperin, Philipp Emanuel's systematized fingering for all twenty-four keys, for right and left hands, became the point of departure for a new style of playing. Without the turning under of the thumb, pearly runs and passages in the *galanterie* style would hardly have been conceivable. One of Mozart's several malicious remarks about the playing of others concerns just this technical manœuvre. He ridicules the performance of the 8-year-old Nannette Stein thus:

When she comes to a passage which ought to flow like oil and which necessitates a change of finger, she does not bother her head about it, but when the moment arrives, she just leaves out the notes, raises her hand and starts off again quite comfortably.[10]

[4] Milchmeyer, *Die wahre Art*, 2. [5] Ibid., Preface. [6] See Ch. 1 above.

[7] *Kurze Bemerkungen über das Spielen, Stimmen und Erhalten der Fortepiano* (Vienna, 1801).

[8] *Pièces de clavecin, avec une méthode pour le mécanique des doigts* (Paris, 1724).

[9] *L'Art de toucher le clavecin* (Paris, 1716).

[10] Letter of 23 Oct. 1777, from Augsburg; *Letters*, 339–40.

Graceful, smooth flow of passage-work, however, is not the same as mechanical virtuosity. Classical musical language, still firmly rooted in the art of rhetoric and articulation, did not strive for the increased instrumental velocity of the next century, achieved through excessive technical training. Therefore, the opinion of Milchmeyer, according to which 'for beginners, one of the most important tasks is to be able to play scales in all twenty-four keys, as fast as possible, with the correct fingering, at once with both hands,'[11] seems a modern object. No less so than his categorical opposition to any sort of embellishment not prescribed by the composer. To be sure, several authors warned against extravagant ornamentation before Milchmeyer,[12] meaning, however, only a moderate application, instead of the total abstinence Milchmeyer requires:

möchte ich die Liebhaber des Pianoforte bitten, sich bey ihrem Spiele doch ja aller von den Componisten nicht angegebenen Auszierungen der musikalischen Gänge zu enthalten. . . . weder Meister, noch Liebhaber, noch Anfänger sollten je andere Musik, als die Musik grosser Meister spielen, und dann nicht das geringste von dem Ihrigen darzu thun.

I would like to ask the amateurs of the pianoforte to abstain from all ornamentation of musical passages not given by the composer. . . . Neither professionals, nor amateurs, nor beginners should play anything but the music of great masters, and then should not add the slightest of their own to it.[13]

Times were definitely changing. In 1796, a little-known London source voiced similar views concerning arbitrary embellishments:

Hamlet's request seems well adapted, as admonition, to such Gallopers over an Instrument. 'Speak the Speech, I pray you, as it is set down for you in the Book.'[14]

We know that Beethoven was against any alteration or addition to his music.[15] Customs die hard, nevertheless. Moscheles objected to the 'frequently trivial embellishments' in Cramer's otherwise beautiful Mozart performance,[16] and had we heard the famous Beethoven interpretations by Franz Liszt, we would likely have had a few surprises.

By the time the general notion of keyboard playing gave way to the specific technique of *pianoforte* playing, two important issues came to the front: legato touch, and the use of damper pedals. To some extent, both were dependent on

[11] 'Es ist für Anfänger eines der nöthigsten Stücke, verschiedene Läufe in den 24 Tonarten so geschwind als möglich mit den gehörigen Fingern und mit beyden Händen auf einmal machen zu können.' Milchmeyer, *Die wahre Art*, 11.

[12] C. P. E. Bach, Quantz, L. Mozart, Agricola, among others; see citations in Komlós, '"Veränderte Reprise"', 262–7.

[13] *Die wahre Art*, 8.

[14] 'Desultory Remarks on the Study and Practice of Music, Addressed to a Young Lady while under the Tuition of an Eminent Master', *European Magazine*, 30 (London, 1796), 180.

[15] See Carl Czerny, *Über den richtigen Vortrag der Sämtlichen Beethoven'schen Klavierwerke*, facs. edn. by Paul Badura-Skoda (Vienna, 1963), 26.

[16] *Recent Music and Musicians*, 34.

Ex. 45 Milchmeyer, *Die wahre Art das Pianoforte zu spielen*, Ch. 5

(*a*)

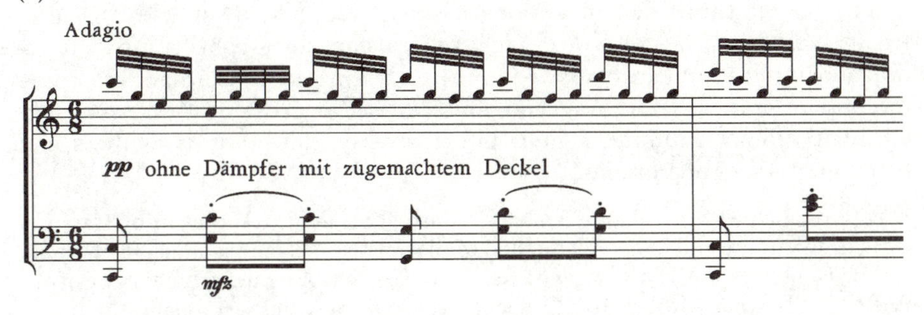

(*b*)

the mechanical development of the instrument, and once more, German/ Viennese and English pianos inspired different responses. A gradual tendency toward legato playing was discernible from the end of the century onwards (see more on this in the final chapter), and the more serious treatises registered the change. The practice of shortening the sound value of unmarked notes, explained so accurately by C. P. E. Bach and Türk, belonged to the past. The oft-quoted statement of Clementi, 'When the composer leaves the *legato*, and *staccato* to the performer's taste, the best rule is, to adhere chiefly to the *legato*,'[17] is only the verbal formulation of the new aesthetic of a new era.

The question of raised dampers seems more complex. Although described as early as 1762 by C. P. E. Bach,[18] it is not really treated in textbooks before the turn of the century. Operated by hand stop, knee-lever, or pedal, in the early period of the instrument, undamped register served only to give a special colour, rather than be used as a regular device.[19] The musical examples in Milchmeyer's work illustrate this very well (see Ex. 45*a*, *b*). Milchmeyer describes the different effect of the four pedals of his type of *Tafelklavier*,[20] but emphasizes that 'beginners should take all possible pains to achieve the entire

[17] *Introduction to the Art of Playing on the Piano Forte* (London, 1801), 8.

[18] *Versuch*, ii (Berlin, 1762), 327.

[19] See the discussion of the 'open Pedal' in Ch. 6. For a detailed account of the subject, see Rowland, 'Early Pianoforte Pedalling'.

[20] *Die wahre Art*, 58–65.

musical expression through the fingers, and only when that is wholly in their power, should they avail themselves of the . . . *Veränderungen*.'[21]

The use of the pedal, in a modern sense, was first dealt with in Louis Adam's *Méthode de piano-forte*.[22] Yet, a general consensus concerning its function and application hardly existed in the early nineteenth century. According to contemporaries, Beethoven and Dussek used a great deal of pedal, but Clementi did not. Hummel is more informative on this point than others, and he expresses a strong opinion:

> A performance with the dampers almost constantly raised, resorted to by way of a cloak to an impure and indistinct method of playing, has become so much the fashion, that many players would no longer be recognized, if they were debarred the use of the Pedals. . . . Neither Mozart, nor Clementi required these helps to obtain the highly deserved reputation of the greatest, and most expressive performers of their day.[23]

Before the time of Schumann and Chopin, it seems that pedalling was a matter of individual choice, not particularly linked to any 'school'. Czerny included the systematic treatment of the damper and the una corda pedal in his *Complete Theoretical and Practical Piano Forte School* (1839), based primarily on the works and performance practices of Beethoven.

The fundamental difference between eighteenth-century German and English keyboard tutors is that while the former concentrated on expression and execution, the latter focused on instrumental technique. 'It seems to me that music primarily must touch the heart, and the clavierist never can accomplish that through mere bluster, drumming and arpeggiating, at least not in my opinion,' said C. P. E. Bach.[24] His view accorded with the mentality of contemporary German musicians, and determined that of the next generation. In a work that was as influential in its own domain as C. P. E. Bach's in *Clavier* playing, Leopold Mozart summed up the essence of his violin instructions thus:

> The good performance of a composition according to modern taste is not as easy as many imagine, who believe themselves doing well if they embellish and befrill a piece right foolishly out of their own heads, and who have no sensitiveness whatever for the affect which is to be expressed in the piece.[25]

The most substantial final chapter of Türk's *Klavierschule* (1789) concerns execution ('Vortrag'), and the tenor of the Alsatian Hüllmandel's treatise, published in London in 1796, betrays the author's former studies with C. P. E.

[21] 'Indessen sollen . . . Anfänger sich alle nur mögliche Mühe geben, allen musikalischen Ausdruck durch die Finger hervorzubringen, und erst dann, wenn sie den Ausdruck mit dem Finger ganz in ihrer Gewalt haben, mögen sie sich . . . der Veränderungen bedienen.' *Die wahre Art*, 65–6.

[22] *Mëthode de piano-forte du Conservatoire de Musique* (Paris, 1804).

[23] *A Complete Theoretical and Practical Course*, 62.

[24] Newman, 'Emanuel Bach's Autobiography', 372.

[25] *Versuch einer gründlichen Violinschule* (Augsburg, 1756); Eng. trans., Editha Knocker, *A Treatise on the Fundamental Principles of Violin Playing*, 2nd edn. (Oxford, 1951), 215.

Bach in Hamburg. Nicolas Joseph Hüllmandel stresses the importance of good taste, and defines proper performance thus:

A fine execution consists not only in the sounds, their length, and the exactness of the time, but also in the expression and character proper for a movement or its various passages.[26]

The analysis of the artistic and philosophical value of C. P. E. Bach's *Versuch über die wahre Art das Clavier zu spielen* (Berlin, 1753 and 1762) is beyond the limits of this chapter. It is not only its clarity, conciseness, and pragmatism, but also the timeless validity of many of this work's thoughts that places it into a different category from other eighteenth-century treatises. In this respect, it can only be compared to the prose of Robert Schumann. Let the first paragraph of Philipp Emanuel's chapter on Performance ('Vortrag') speak for itself:

Keyboardists whose chief asset is mere technique are clearly at a disadvantage. A performer may have the most agile fingers, be competent at single and double trills, master the art of fingering, read skillfully at sight regardless of the key, and transpose extemporaneously without the slightest difficulty; play tenths, even twelfths, or runs, cross the hands in every conceivable manner, and excel in other related matters; and yet he may be something less than a clear, pleasing, or stirring keyboardist. More often than not, one meets technicians, nimble keyboardists by profession, who possess all of these qualifications and indeed astound us with their prowess without ever touching our sensibilities. They overwhelm our hearing without satisfying it and stun the mind without moving it. . . . Finger velocity must never be misused. It should be reserved for those passages that call for it, without advancing the tempo of the piece as a whole.[27]

The same year that Quantz's treatise on flute playing appeared,[28] Charles Avison published *An Essay on Musical Expression* (London, 1752). However, subsequent English instrumental textbooks paid little attention to the nuances of performance. Rather, they wanted to give quick aid to achieve a certain facility on the keyboard, and develop sufficient dexterity to the fingers to be able to play the popular tunes and pieces of the day. A few titles, to illustrate:

Robert Broderip, *Plain and Easy Instructions for Young Performers on the Piano Forte or Harpsichord* (Longman & Broderip, 1788?).[29]

James Hook, *Guida di Musica; being a Complete Book of Instructions for Beginners on the Harpsichord or Piano Forte, Entirely on a new plan, calculated to save a great deal of time and trouble both to Master and Scholar, to which is*

[26] *Principles of Music, Chiefly Calculated for the Piano Forte or Harpsichord* (London, 1796), 13.

[27] Eng. trans., W. J. Mitchell, *Essay*, 147.

[28] *Versuch einer Anweisung die Flöte traversière zu spielen* (Berlin, 1752).

[29] The title, borrowed from Thomas Morley (*A Plaine and Eaise Introduction to Practicall Musicke*, 1597), suggests a parallel; Broderip's tutor is, however, sadly inferior to Morley's comprehensive work.

added 24 progressive lessons in various keys, with the Fingering marked throughout (Preston, 1785).[30]

John Danby, *La Guida Della Musica Instrumentale, or the Rudiments of the Forte Piano or Harpsichord, Exemplified In a Clear and Concise manner. With 8 Exercises for forming the Hands, and the Fingering marked: To which are subjoined, 8 Progressive Lessons Constructed on pleasing familiar Airs. To conclude with a Lesson for 2 Performers on one Forte Piano. The whole Plan'd and Written with great Care and Attention to the immediate Improvement of all desirous of Acquiring a Perfect Knowledge of the above Instruments* (Smart, 1798).

C. P. E. Bach's maxim, according to which 'nothing fundamental can be learned without time and patience,'[31] was surely lost on these ambitious authors who wished 'to save a great deal of time and trouble' to the student, and promised 'immediate improvement' and 'perfect knowledge' of the instrument. Dozens of pianoforte tutors of similar character were published in London at the time, by Griffith Jones (1786), George Malme (1790), Matthew Camidge (1794), John Parsons (1794), John Hammond (1802), to name but a few.

Aspects of expression are missing from the instruction-books of Dussek and Clementi as well, the development of technique being the sole object of both. Dussek's work is clearly intended for beginners, as the long title suggests:

Instructions on the Art of Playing the Piano Forte or Harpsichord, Being a Compleat Treatise on the first Rudiments of Music, and containing General and Exemplified Rules and Principles on the Art of Fingering: Making the Compleatest Work ever offered to the Public, to which are added Op. 32 expressly Composed by Ignace Pleyel, Six progressive Sonatinas w. Violin accomp.ts ad Libitum; which the Author has so constructed, that the Passages are first immediately under the Performers Hand, not exceed.g in Compass one fifth, and gradually extended and connected w. the Improvement of the Pupil (London and Edinburgh: Corri, Dussek & Co., 1796).

The chief virtue of Clementi's *Introduction to the Art of Playing on the Piano Forte* (1801) is that it includes 'lessons . . . by composers of the first rank, ancient and modern'. Clementi's fine judgement is evident in the list of selected composers: J. S. Bach, Beethoven, Corelli, Couperin, Cramer, Dussek, Handel, Dr Haydn, Mozart, Paradies, Pleyel, Rameau, and Scarlatti. (Apparently, some authors considered the 'borrowing' of pieces from other composers not quite laudable, and boasted of their own invention. John Hammond, who affixed '24 progressive lessons' to his tutor, proudly announced that 'the original lessons, composed by the Author of the present work, have at least the

[30] Preston must have used the same title-page for different authors; a tutor by Richard Sharp, with almost identical title, appeared there in 1797.

[31] Open letter, *Hamburger unpartheiischer Correspondent*, 11 Jan. 1773; quoted by Mitchell in the Introduction of his trans. of the *Versuch*; see *Essay*, 4.

merit of being new, in the strictest acceptation of the term; not the smallest portion of them has been borrowed from former compositions'.)[32]

Considering the direction of pianoforte playing at the threshold of the nineteenth century, concentration on the technical aspect was perhaps more in keeping with the times than the insistence on the communication of the emotional content. However, a somewhat later English essay did focus on expressive performance. *A Treatise on Piano-Forte Expression, Containing the Principles of Fine Playing on that Instrument*, by W. S. Stevens (London, 1811), is quite unusual. It was also written for professionals, which distinguishes it from the vast number of booklets for amateurs.

Generally speaking, textbooks in any period are not written for professionals, but for those who wish to study, and perhaps eventually become professionals. But there are also 'methodology' books, primarily for the use of teachers, to help structure their work; and finally, of course, there are the short and simple brochures offering rudimentary information for amateurs. We can find this range of address among eighteenth-century keyboard tutors as well.

C. P. E. Bach declared his treatise to be written for professionals. He made this clear in the open letter of 1773, cited earlier: 'I divide all keyboard performers into two groups. In the first are those for whom music is a goal, and in the second, all amateurs who seek thorough instruction. My Essay is intended for the first group: no paragraph is superfluous.'[33] The more serious musicians intended their treatises for 'teachers and students'; Leopold Mozart,[34] for instance, or Türk, who even announced this in the title of his work: *Klavierschule, oder Anweisung zum Klavierspielen für Lehrer und Lernende* (Leipzig and Halle, 1789). Türk also expressed his hope that professionals would find his book useful, and consider it worthy of approbation.[35]

Milchmeyer, on the other hand, dedicated his treatise 'den Liebhabern und Anfängern des Pianoforte-Spieles'.[36] Although the range of topics he covers is not so different from that of Türk's *Klavierschule*, several of his statements and remarks make us smile today. His musical judgement is questionable, and even controversial. A special merit of the book is that a number of its musical examples are taken from Beethoven's Op. 2, published barely a year before the tutor itself. This suggests a sense of quality as well as an up-to-date spirit. However, while the author never identifies these examples with Beethoven's name, he does identify other excerpts as compositions of Clementi or Steibelt. Steibelt is in fact the undisputed hero of the book, and Milchmeyer dedicates pages to praising the pot-pourri, a genre inaugurated by Steibelt. Among other embarrassing comments, the one on the advantages of the accompanied sonata has already been cited in Chapter 7.

Several pianoforte tutors suggest that short preludes were often played

[32] John Hammond, *A Proper Guide to Music, being a Complete Book of Instructions for Beginners on the Piano Forte* (London, 1802).

[33] See n. 31 above; *Essay*, 8. [34] *Violinschule*, Preface. [35] *Klavierschule*, Introduction.

[36] See the section of the Preface cited at the beginning of this chapter.

before sonatas or other substantial compositions. English sources are chief among those referring to such a practice. For instance, the title page of a set of sonatas by Matthew Camidge reads: *Ten Easy Sonatas for the Piano Forte or Harpsichord, With an Accompaniment for a Violin (NB. Useful preludes are prefix'd to the Sonatas)* (Longman & Broderip, 1796). The publisher Joseph Dale issued a large collection in four volumes, between 1796 and 1801, called *Introduction to the Piano Forte, Harpsichord or Organ in 4 Books . . . to which is added Preludes in every key*. Among the composers represented we find Wagenseil, Schroeter, Storace, etc. Clementi's quizzical *Musical Characteristics* Op. 19, containing 'preludes and cadences' in the style of various composers, whether meant seriously or ironically,[37] reinforces the existence of quasi-improvisatory introductions.

In German tutors, the inclusion of preludes was less frequent. An early example, by Marianus Königsberger, was published a year before Leopold Mozart's *Violinschule*, in Augsburg:

Der wohl unterwiesene Clavierschüler, welchem nicht nur die wahre und sichere Fundamenta zum Claviere auf eine leichte Art beygebracht, sondern auch 8 Praeambula, 24 Versette und 8 Arien oder Galanteriestücke aus allen Tönen zur weitern Uebung vorgeleget werden (1755).

The description of the content also shows that 'quick and easy' methods were not exclusive to English publishers.

W. A. Mozart helped out his sister on many occasions by writing preludes for her. 'Bimperl, please be so good as to send me soon a short preambulum. But write one this time from C into B♭, so that I may gradually learn it by heart,'[38] wrote Nannerl in September 1777 to her brother, then staying in Munich. A year later, in connection with another 'preambulum', Wolfgang wrote from Paris:

I wanted to present my sister with a little Preambulum. The manner of playing it I leave to her own feeling. This is not the kind of Prelude which passes from one key into another, but only a sort of Capriccio, with which to test a clavier.[39]

Three autograph items are printed in the *NMA*: a completed piece in C (K. 284*a*), and two fragments ('Modulierendes Präludium', K. *deest*; 'Fragment eines Präludiums', K. 624 (626*a*) Anh I), all presumably from 1776–7.[40] Although we can not identify or date them precisely, their purpose is clear enough. Nannerl Mozart, not a bad player herself, wanted to show off with

[37] See Eva Badura-Skoda, 'Clementi's "Musical Characteristics" Op. 19', in H. C. Robbins Landon and Roger E. Chapman (eds.), *Studies in Eighteenth-Century Music: A Tribute to Karl Geiringer on his 70th Birthday* (London and New York, 1970), 62–6.

[38] *Letters*, 283. [39] Letter of 20 July 1778, *Letters*, 573.

[40] *NMA* IX/27/2, pp. 4–5, 5–9, 148–51. The other half of the 'Modulierendes Präludium' K. *deest* was recently identified in Krakow; see Christoph Wolff, 'Mozarts Präludien für Nannerl: Zwei Rätsel und ihre Lösung', in *Festschrift für Wolfgang Rehm zum 60. Geburtstag* (Kassel, 1989), 106–18.

some fashionable *praeludia* in Salzburg, where, it seems, the playing of preludes was as customary as elsewhere in Europe.[41]

When approaching the highest level of artistic questions and decisions, the limitations as well as the virtues of eighteeth-century treatises must be emphasized. While it is surely important to know the few central issues in these works, one must beware of relying on the musical/artistic judgement of some of the less brilliant authors.

Of the major topics, perhaps articulation comes first. Musical syntax, as Türk emphatically if prosaically explains it, leads to the intelligibility and expressivity of the performance. Ornamentation, somewhat overrated in importance in recent times, has its own function in the musical language of the eighteenth century, but only in context, and only when adjusted to the nature of the particular keyboard instrument. Its isolated treatment in instruction-books makes little sense, and one only rarely finds a comment like the following, of Hüllmandel: 'Taste is a better guide than Rules for determining the length of an Appoggiatura.'[42]

Beyond the obligatory knowledge of the conventions of rhythmic notation and other details, the tutors contain much practical information for the curious reader. It is, nevertheless, difficult to determine whether some 'rule' or other is merely a local custom or the personal opinion of a theorist of limited experience. When, for example, Milchmeyer declares that eight hours' practice per day for eight years is necessary for a student, does he voice a general expectation, or merely his own demands on students?

The perusal of the more important treatises, indispensable as it is, can never replace the thorough knowledge of the music itself. Only in the context of a rich and varied repertory will the character and the elements of any given piece of music reveal themselves. The best composers and thinkers of the time should guide one towards the maximum understanding of the style. What this understanding implies is set forth perhaps most authoritatively today by Nikolaus Harnoncourt:

Wenn der Musiker wirklich die Aufgabe hat, das gesamte musikalische Erbe—soweit es für uns interessant ist—darzustellen, und zwar nicht nur in seinen aesthetischen und technischen Aspekten, dann muss er das dafür notwendige Wissen erwerben. Daran führt kein Weg vorbei. Die Musik der Vergangenheit ist durch den Lauf der Geschichte, durch die Entfernung von der Gegenwart, durch das Losgerissensein von der eigenen Zeit in ihrer Gesamtheit zu einer Fremdsprache geworden. Einzelne Aspekte mögen allgemeingültig und zeitlos sein, die Aussage als solche aber ist zeitgebunden und kann nur wiedergefunden werden, wenn man sie in einer Art von Übersetzung in die heutige Zeit hineinbringt. Das heisst: Wenn die Musik

[41] For more details on Mozart's preludes see Komlós, '"Ich praeludirte und spielte Variazionen"', 27–9.

[42] *Principles of Music*, 16.

vergangener Epochen überhaupt noch in einem tieferen und weitergehenden Sinn für die Gegenwart aktuell ist, wenn sie in ihrer ganzen Aussage—oder doch zu einem grösseren Teil, als das normalerweise heute der Fall ist—dargestellt werden soll, muss das Verständnis dieser Musik von ihrer eigenen Gesetzmässigkeit her wieder erlernt werden. Wir müssen wissen, was die Musik sagen will, um zu erkennen, was wir *mit ihr* sagen wollen. Also muss jetzt zum rein Gefühlsmässigen, zur Intuition, das Wissen kommen. Ohne dieses historische Wissen kann historische Musik, kann unsere sogenannte 'Ernste Musik' nicht adaequat dargestellt werden.

If the musician really has the task of rendering our entire musical heritage—insofar as it is of any concern to us at all—and not just its aesthetic and technical aspects, then he must acquire the knowledge necessary to do so correctly. There is no other way. The music of the past has become a foreign language because of the progression of history, because of its remoteness from the present, and because it has been taken out of the context of its own period. Individual aspects of a piece of music may well be universally valid and timeless, but the message as such is linked to a particular time and can only be rediscovered when it is translated, as it were, into our contemporary idiom. This means that if the music of past epochs is in any way relevant to the present in a deeper and wider sense, if it is to be presented with its total message intact, or at least to a greater extent than is the case today, the understanding of this music has to be relearned from the principles that underlie its very essence. We have to know what music intends to express in order to understand what we want to say with it. Knowledge must therefore be added to the purely emotive and intuitive dimensions. Without such historical knowledge, neither historical music nor our own so-called 'serious' music can be performed properly.[43]

The infinite complexity of this knowledge can surely not arise from a fetishistic reliance on instrumental treatises.

[43] Nikolaus Harnoncourt, *Musik als Klangrede: Wege zu einem neuen Musikverständnis* (Salzburg and Vienna, 1982), 25–6; Eng. trans., Mary O'Neill, *Baroque Music Today: Music As Speech*, gen. ed. Reinhard G. Pauly (London, 1988; trans. © Amadeus Press, Portland, Ore., 1988), 23.

11

Aesthetics of Performance

THE first generation of pianoforte players started its keyboard activity on the older types of instruments. The harpsichord and the clavichord were the most likely choices, although the organ should by no means be excluded. To name only the greatest: W. A. Mozart professed the organ to be his favourite instrument,[1] and the young Ludwig van Beethoven had an organist's position in Bonn.

For keyboard technique and performance, the harpsichord and the clavichord required and taught entirely different approaches. The harpsichord developed strength and dexterity of the fingers, while the clavichord responded to a sensitive touch and produced fine shading of tone and dynamics. Ideally, a versatile keyboardist was supposed to be trained on both instruments. C. P. E. Bach gives a clear and rational explanation of this in his *Versuch*:

Every keyboardist should own a good harpsichord and a good clavichord to enable him to play all things interchangeably. A good clavichordist makes an accomplished harpsichordist, but not the reverse. The clavichord is needed for the study of good performance, and the harpsichord to develop proper finger strength. Those who play the clavichord exclusively encounter many difficulties when they turn to the harpsichord. In an ensemble where a harpsichord must be used rather than the soft-toned clavichord, they will play laboriously; and great exertion never produces the proper keyboard effect. The clavichordist grows too much accustomed to caressing the keys; consequently, his wonted touch being insufficient to operate the jacks, he fails to bring out details on the harpsichord. In fact, finger strength may be lost eventually, by playing only the clavichord. On the other hand, those who concentrate on the harpsichord grow accustomed to playing in only one colour, and the varied touch which the competent clavichordist brings to the harpsichord remains hidden from them. This may sound strange, since one would think that all performers can express only one kind of tone on each harpsichord. To test its truth ask two people, one a good clavichordist, the other a harpsichordist, to play on the latter's instrument the same piece containing varied embellishments, and then decide whether both have produced the same effect.[2]

Johann Friedrich Reichardt, one of C. P. E. Bach's most ardent admirers, often echoed the opinion of the Hamburg master. He compared Italian and German keyboard playing in a letter of 1776:

[1] Letter of 17 Oct. 1777, from Augsburg; *Letters*, 329. [2] *Essay*, 37–8.

Die Italiäner haben nie das Klavier bei sich im Gebrauch gehabt, sondern bedienen sich allein des Flügels; ihre Spielart muss also nur in Beziehung auf den Flügel betrachtet werden. . . . Bachs Spielart konnte ohne Klavier gar nicht erfunden werden, und er hat sie auch nur fürs Klavier erfunden; derjenige aber, der diese einmal innehat, der spielt auch ganz anders den Flügel als jener, der nie ein Klavier berühret, und für den können hernach auch Flügelsachen geschrieben werden, die unter den Händen des blossen Flügelspielers matt, oft unverständlich und unzusammenhängend werden. Für diese also, die nicht auf dem Klaviere gelernt haben, Töne zu verbinden, er sei durch Fingersetzung oder Verzierungen, für die müssen nur geschwinde Noten, gebrochene Akkorde—mit einem Worte, die Stücke, die sich für diese schicken sollen, können nur den Endzweck haben, durch Fertigkeit Bewunderung zu erregen.

Among the Italians the clavichord was never in use, they play only the harpsichord; their playing, therefore, can only be considered in relation to the harpsichord. . . . [C. P. E.] Bach's manner of playing could not have been evolved at all without the clavichord, and he created it only for the clavichord; he who once possesses this, however, will play on the harpsichord quite differently from those who never touch a clavichord, and then for these even harpsichord pieces can be written, which under the hands of mere harpsichord players, sound dull, often unintelligible and incoherent. Thus those who did not learn on the clavichord how to connect notes, through fingering or ornaments, will only aim at exciting admiration through their skills, apparent in pieces with rapid passages, broken chords, and the like.[3]

According to Reichardt, music played on the harpsichord sounds 'unintelligible and incoherent'. It seemed so to other contemporaries as well; the absence of dynamic and expressive nuances must have caused this reaction. The same negative qualities of the harpsichord, this time in relation to the fortepiano, are stated in the *Jahrbuch der Tonkunst von Wien und Prag* (1796), in the paragraph about the activity of Leopold Koželuch, who promoted the use of the fortepiano rather than the 'monotony and the muddled sound' of the harpsichord (see citation in Ch. 5).

It is well known that German musical thinking was strongly influenced by a partiality for the clavichord. Thus it is interesting that the Englishman Charles Burney, who heard a gifted young girl play on a *Tafelklavier* at a Viennese *Hauskonzert* in 1772, drew similar conclusions about the advantages of that instrument:

I went to Mr. L'Augier's concert, which was begun by the child of eight or nine years old, whom he had mentioned to me before, and who played two difficult lessons of Scarlatti, with three or four by M. Becke [Beecke], upon a small, and not good Piano forte. The neatness of this child's execution did not so much surprise me, though uncommon, as her expression. All the *pianos* and *fortes* were so judiciously attended to; and there was such shading off some passages, and force given to others, as nothing but the best teaching, or greatest natural feeling and sensibility could produce. I enquired of Signor Giorgio, an Italian, who attended her, upon what instrument she usually

[3] *Briefe eines aufmerksamen Reisenden die Musik betreffend*, ii (Frankfurt und Leipzig, 1776), 5.

practised at home, and was answered, 'on the Clavichord'. This accounts for her expression, and convinces me, that children should learn upon that, or a Piano Forte, very early, and be obliged to give an expression to lady Coventry's Minuet, or whatever is their first tune; otherwise, after long practice on a monotonous harpsichord, however useful for strengthening the hand, the case is hopeless.[4]

Times changed, however. Before the end of the century, the German Milchmeyer declared that clavichord training definitely harmed good pianoforte playing.[5] (He considered the harpsichord even worse.) This transitional period gradually gave way to the general use of the *Hammerklavier*, and keyboard practice, even for the youngest, started with the square or grand pianoforte.

The rich source material concerning the 1781 contest between Mozart and Clementi gives invaluable evidence about the relatively early period of piano playing, through the introduction of two outstanding, but opposed, artistic personalities.[6] As emphasized in Chapter 4, the harpsichord determined Clementi's early compositional and performing style; thus Mozart's condemnation of his playing ('ein blosser Mechanicus')[7] clearly referred to a certain lack of sensitivity which can be at least partially traced to Clementi's exclusive training on the harpsichord. A quarter of a century later Clementi related to his student, Ludwig Berger, that

in that earlier period he had taken particular delight in brilliant feats of technical proficiency, especially in those passages in double notes that were not common before his time, and in improvised cadenzas. It was only later that he adopted a more melodic and noble style of performance.[8]

As we read further in Berger's recollections, this later style resulted 'from the gradual perfection of the grand pianoforte—particularly the English one—whose faulty construction had previously almost totally precluded a more cantabile, legato style of playing.'[9] In 1781 Mozart was already well versed in fortepiano playing: his expectations presumably corresponded to the nature of that instrument.

Mozart's violent disapproval of Clementi's keyboard playing tells us a great deal about his (Mozart's) performance ideals, and these thoughts are formulated even more strongly one and a half years after the competition, in a letter to his father:

Well, I have a few words to say to my sister about Clementi's sonatas. Everyone who either hears them or plays them must feel that as compositions they are worthless. They contain no remarkable or striking passages except those in sixths and octaves.

[4] *The Present State of Music*, i. 282–3.
[5] *Die wahre Art*, 2. See the relevant passage cited in the previous chapter.
[6] See Komlós, 'Mozart and Clementi'. [7] *Letters*, 793.
[8] Berger, 'Erläuterung eines Mozartschen Urtheils'; quoted and trans. in Plantinga, *Clementi*, 65.
[9] Quoted in Plantinga, *Clementi*, 290–1.

And I implore my sister not to practise those passages too much, so that she may not spoil her quiet, even touch and that her hand may not lose its natural lightness, flexibility and smooth rapidity. For after all what is to be gained by it? Supposing that you do play sixths and octaves with the utmost velocity (which no one can accomplish, not even Clementi) you only produce an atrocious chopping effect and nothing else whatever. Clementi is a *ciarlatano*, like all Italians. . . . What he really does well are his passages in thirds; but he sweated over them day and night in London. Apart from this, he can do nothing, absolutely nothing, for he has not the slightest expression or taste, still less, feeling.[10]

A touch of jealousy may have coloured Mozart's opinion; nevertheless, his criteria for good fortepiano performance shine clearly through in these sentences. These criteria are a quiet, even touch; natural lightness, flexibility, and smooth rapidity of the hands; and expression, taste, and feeling.

Geschmack und Empfindung were indispensable for Mozart in the art of keyboard performance. From his usually sharp criticism of the playing of others we can learn further principles: precision; a thoroughly trained left hand; keeping strict time; and general abstention from rushed tempos.[11] 'She will never acquire the most essential, the most difficult, and the chief requisite in music, which is, time, because from the earliest years she has done her utmost not to play in time,' Mozart wrote about the 8-year-old Nannette Stein.[12] He added later in the same letter: 'Everyone is amazed that I can always keep strict time.' One gathers from the last remark that playing 'in strict time' must have been a rare virtue at the time. C. P. E. Bach makes the same prescription a quarter of a century earlier, in the performance chapter of his *Versuch*:

Every effort must be made despite the beauty of detail to keep the tempo at the end of a piece exactly the same as at the beginning, an extremely difficult assignment. There are many excellent musicians, but only a few of whom it can be said truthfully that in the narrowest sense they end a piece as they began it.[13]

This important discipline did not exclude the possibility of rubato playing, as both Mozart and C. P. E. Bach emphasized.

Mozart repeatedly warns against too fast tempos. It is, of course, impossible today to tell exactly what speed seemed 'too fast' to him; his letters, nevertheless, make it clear that the tempo must never be increased at the expense of intelligibility, clarity, and expression.[14]

A certain ease and lightness, essential qualities of Mozart's performance, characterized the playing of many German/Austrian clavierists of the time, even if not all of them reached the height of 'spirit and grace' which Clementi

[10] Letter of 7 June 1783, *Letters*, 850.
[11] See details in Komlós, '"Ich praeludirte und spielte Variazionen"', 52–4.
[12] Letter of 23–5 Oct. 1777, *Letters*, 340.
[13] *Essay*, 161.
[14] See letters of 26 Nov. 1777 and 17 Jan. 1778, *Letters*, 391, 448–9.

so sincerely admired in Mozart's playing.[15] The German-born Johann Samuel Schroeter retained this quality in his playing, although he spent the mature period of his life in London. W. T. Parke, writing in his memoirs about the 1787 concerts held by the Prince of Wales at Carlton House, describes Schroeter's playing as follows:

> Schroeter, who had retired from public practice, performed on the piano-forte on these occasions. His style, like his music, was expressive and elegant, and his execution was neat and rapid. He played in so graceful and quiet a manner, that his fingers were scarcely seen to move.[16]

According to contemporary evidence, the Germans Franz Xaver Sterkel and Friedrich Heinrich Himmel, and the Salzburg-born Joseph Wölfl, also played in a light and pleasant manner. By coincidence, all three came into contact, or even competed at the keyboard, with Beethoven. The well-known story of the 1791 encounter between Sterkel and the young Beethoven introduces the former as a fine keyboardist. 'His playing was light and very pleasant, and, as Father Ries expressed it, somewhat lady-like,' remembers Wegeler.[17] This opinion, however, was not at all unanimous. Mozart found not much to praise in Sterkel's performance; in fact, he considered it inferior to the playing of his young student, Rosa Cannabich.[18] The correspondent of Cramer's *Magazin der Musik* also wrote an uncomplimentary report on the 1782 Neapolitan sojourn of the composer, and declared that '[Sterkel] is in no position to play the easiest [C. P. E.] Bach sonata properly.'[19]

Beethoven made the acquaintance of Himmel in 1796 in Berlin, where Himmel was court Kapellmeister. In Beethoven's opinion, '[Himmel] possessed a quite well-educated gift, but nothing more; his clavier playing, elegant and pleasing as it was, could not at all be compared with that of Prince *Louis Ferdinand*.'[20] (For more about the music- and pianoforte-enthusiast Prince see Ch. 1.) The *Allgemeine musikalische Zeitung*, on the other hand, saw in Himmel's playing the epitome of delicate keyboard performance ('galantes, zierlich weichliches Spiel').[21]

Joseph Wölfl, who studied with Leopold Mozart and Michael Haydn in Salzburg, became Beethoven's rival as a pianist during the 1790s in Vienna.

[15] Quoted in Plantinga, *Clementi*, 65. [16] *Musical Memoirs*, 88.

[17] 'Sterkel spielte sehr leicht, höchst gefällig, und, wie Vater Ries sich ausgedrückt, etwas damenartig.' See Franz Gerhard Wegeler and Ferdinand Ries, *Biographische Notizen über Ludwig van Beethoven* (Koblenz, 1838; rev. edn., 1906), 22–3.

[18] *Letters*, 391.

[19] 'Er nicht im Stande ist, die leichteste Bachische Sonate gehörig zu spielen.' *Magazin der Musik*, i (Hamburg, 1783), 574–5.

[20] 'Er besitze ein ganz artiges Talent, weiter aber nichts; sein Clavierspielen sei elegant und angenehm, allein mit dem Prinzen *Louis Ferdinand* sei er gar nicht zu vergleichen.' See Wegeler and Ries, *Biographische Notizen*, 131.

[21] 9 (1807), 744.

Since his playing conformed more closely to Viennese taste and tradition than Beethoven's subversive style, general opinion favoured him. Ignaz von Seyfried, in his account of the 1799 contest between Beethoven and Wölfl, compares the two artists as follows:

Im Phantasieren verleugnete Beethoven schon damals nicht seinen mehr zum unheimlich Düstern sich hinneigenden Charakter; schwelgte er einmal im unermesslichen Tonreich, dann war er auch entrissen dem Irdischen . . . Wölfl hingegen, in Mozarts Schule gebildet, blieb immerdar sich gleich, nie flach, aber stets klar, und eben desswegen der Mehrzahl zugänglicher.

In improvisation Beethoven already showed his character, inclined towards the gloomy and the sinister; once he revelled in the immeasurable world of sound, then he was detached from earthly matters . . . Wölfl, on the other hand, trained in Mozart's school, always remained the same, never flat, but constantly clear, and because of that, more accessible to most.[22]

Towards the end of the century, a desire for fuller tone and more legato playing is discernible in keyboard performance (see also Ch. 3). As cited in the previous chapter, Clementi sanctioned the general rule of legato touch in his 1801 treatise, and emphasized the 'higher beauties of the legato'.[23] According to Moscheles, 'Clementi's pianoforte playing, when he was young, was famed for the exquisite legato, pearliness in touch in rapid passages, and unerring certainty of execution.'[24]

As the demand in the earlier years for an instrument that could produce dynamic differences by touch furthered the invention and development of the hammer mechanism, in later years the *sustaining* of the sound became the ideal in piano performance. And, as earlier, instrument makers were expected to be aware of this demand. Beethoven mentioned this explicitly in his 1796 letter to the eminent builder J. A. Streicher:

There is no doubt that so far as the manner of playing it is concerned, the *pianoforte* is still the least studied and developed of all instruments; often one thinks that one is merely listening to a harp. And I am delighted, my dear fellow, that you are one of the few who realize and perceive that, provided one can feel the music, one can also make the pianoforte sing. I hope that the time will come when the harp and the pianoforte will be treated as two entirely different instruments.[25]

In the Prefatory Observations to Cramer's 'new and enlarged edition' of his *Studio per il Piano Forte* (1835), the author stresses not so much the resources of the instrument, but rather the manner of playing it:

No one will excel as a Performer on the Piano Forte without a good touch, to acquire

22 *Ludwig van Beethovens Studien im Generalbass, Contrapunkt und in der Compositionslehre* (Vienna, 1832), Anh. 5.

23 *Introduction to the Art of Playing on the Piano Forte*, 8.

24 *Recent Music and Musicians*, 192.

25 *The Letters of Beethoven*, ed. and trans. Emily Anderson (London, 1961), i. 25–6.

which students must cultivate a *legato* style of performance, whereby the inability of sustaining sound on the Piano Forte is materially obviated.

Legato playing suited English pianofortes more than Viennese instruments; consequently, it was heard more in London than on the Continent. Beethoven, as in so many other aspects of keyboard art, was an exception; his legato manner of performance inspired admiration. Carl Czerny, recalling his pianoforte lessons with Beethoven during the early 1800s, remembers thus:

He . . . went through the various keyboard studies in [C. P. E.] Bach's book and especially insisted on legato technique, which was one of the unforgettable features of his playing; at that time all other pianists considered that kind of legato unattainable, since the *hammered*, detached staccato technique of Mozart's time was still *fashionable*.[26]

The peculiar feature of Beethoven's teaching seems to be that he combined the keyboard principles of C. P. E. Bach (then almost half a century old) with the most modern legato technique. Even if Czerny exaggerates in saying that 'all other pianists considered that kind of legato unattainable', it was probably a rarity in Vienna.[27]

Not so in London, where the famous pianoforte virtuosos set the concert halls and theatres on fire. There must have been something in the quality of his virtuosity that distinguished Dussek's playing from Mozart's. Mozart was by no means less of a virtuoso at the keyboard (there is plenty of evidence of that), but each component of a Dussek performance was different. He played different music from Mozart, on a different instrument, to a different audience. All this would determine the *style* of his performance, which approached nineteenth- rather than eighteenth-century ideals. The various recollections regarding Dussek's stage manner, and the feverish reactions (noted in Ch. 5), evoke the image of the romantic artist. An anonymous author in the *Allgemeine musikalische Zeitung* identified the new 'grand style' with Dussek's performance:

D[ussek]'s Spiel ist zum Erstaunen fertig, ist sicher, feurig, überhaupt affektvoll, es ist durchaus, was man jetzt das grosse Spiel nennet, um es durch diesen Namen zunächst von dem galanten, zierlich weichlichen (z. B. Himmels), zu unterscheiden.

D[ussek]'s playing is astonishingly accomplished; it is sure, fiery, always effective—it is what is now called the grand style, which name distinguishes it from the galant, elegant, and delicate manner of playing (Himmel's, for example).[28]

For specific information about the playing of the three celebrated London stars, Clementi, Cramer, and Dussek, we turn to contemporary sources. Some

[26] 'Recollections from My Life', 307.

[27] The various aspects of Beethoven performance are treated in detail in William Newman, *Beethoven on Beethoven: Playing His Piano Music His Way* (New York, 1988), esp. ch. 3, pp. 45–82. See also Peter Le Huray, *Authenticity in Performance: Eighteenth-Century Case Studies* (Cambridge, 1990), ch. 11, pp. 164–86.

[28] See n. 21 above; trans. in Craw, 'Biography and Thematic Catalogue', 141.

excerpts from the *Musical Memoirs* of Parke, principal oboist to the Theatre Royal, Covent Garden, follow:

Clementi [displayed] that rapid and surprising execution which proved that he was truly ambidexter, his left hand keeping pace with his right in the most difficult passages.[29] (Hanover Square Rooms, Feb. 1788.)

[At Salomon's subscription concerts] the solos were by Salomon, the leader on the violin, and J. B. Cramer on the piano-forte. The performance of the latter was much admired for the elegance of its style and brilliancy of its execution.[30] (Hanover Square Rooms, Mar. 1791.)

The opera concerts began this season under the direction of Viotti. . . . Dussek [played a concerto] on the pianoforte, which in brilliancy and taste was never surpassed.[31] (1797)

We can read German opinion in a December 1802 issue of the *Allgemeine musikalische Zeitung*, under the title 'Zustand der Musik in England, besonders in London'. (The article gives a somewhat belated description, as it includes passages about Dussek, who lived in London only until 1799.)

Das allgemein geliebte *Pianoforte* hat an der Spitze seiner Virtuosen das wackere Kleeblatt: Clementi, Dussek, Cramer. . . . Sollte ich das Spiel dieser drey wahren Meister zu charakterisiren versuchen, so muss ich es so: Alle drey leisten bewundernswürdig viel auf ihrem Instrumente. . . . Clementi's grösseste Stärke ist aber im charakteristischen, pathetischen Allegro, weniger im Adagio; Dussek spielt ganz vorzüglich brillante Allegrosätze mit ungeheuren Schwierigkeiten, trägt aber auch das Adagio sehr zart, gefällig und einschmeichelnd vor; Cramer beherrscht wohl nicht so viele Schwierigkeiten, hat aber ein äusserst nettes und sauberes Spiel in allem, was er vorträgt, und noch besonders etwas Seltsames, Eigenes, Pikantes in seinem Spiel, das sich augenblicklich empfinden, aber nicht durch Worte schildern lässt.

The universally favoured *pianoforte* can boast the brave triumvirate of its top virtuosos: Clementi, Dussek, Cramer. . . . If I had to attempt to characterize the playing of these three true masters, I would say the following: all three accomplish an admirable amount on their instrument. . . . Clementi's greatest strength lies with the characteristic, pathetic Allegro, less with the Adagio; Dussek plays brilliant Allegro movements of enormous difficulty quite excellently, but performs Adagios as well in a delicate, agreeable, and engaging manner; Cramer may not master so much difficulty, but he plays everything extremely neatly and clearly; there is also something peculiar, rare, and piquant in his performance that can be felt instantaneously, but cannot be described in words.[32]

The last passage (perhaps not a very lucid description of Cramer's playing) suggests that the musical personality of the German-born pianist-composer was unlike that of his colleagues. A keyboard student of Schroeter and Clementi, Cramer apparently retained a 'classical' quality in his playing.

[29] *Musical Memoirs*, 102. [30] Ibid. 143. [31] Ibid. 251. [32] 5 (1802), 196–7.

Moscheles praised his Mozart interpretation (quoted in Ch. 5); the fact that Cramer kept Mozart's works in his repertory is significant in itself. The minute description of Cramer's playing included in Moscheles' diaries continues thus:

> Those thin, well shaped fingers are best suited to legato playing; they glide along imperceptibly from one key to the other, and whenever possible, avoid octave as well as staccato passages. Cramer sings on the piano in such a manner that he almost transforms a Mozart Andante into a vocal piece.[33]

Two statements in this paragraph deserve attention. One is the quiet position of the hands, which Mozart also stressed; Schroeter, Cramer's earlier teacher, seems also to have played in this manner. Indeed, Cramer's fingers 'gliding along imperceptibly from one key to the other' recall Parke's observation on Schroeter's playing, quoted above: 'His fingers were scarcely seen to move.'[34] The other interesting point, Cramer's 'singing on the piano', coincides with Beethoven's desire for 'the pianoforte to sing'. (See his letter to Streicher, quoted above.) Cramer was one of the few musicians whom Beethoven regarded with approval. The reliable Ferdinand Ries notes that 'among clavier players he praised *one* as an excellent player: *John Cramer*. All others counted but little for him.'[35]

Johann Nepomuk Hummel may have played the pianoforte in a similar manner to Cramer, his senior by seven years. Somewhat provincial in character, he studied the instrument with Mozart and Clementi, and concertized extensively in Europe. Like Cramer, Hummel remained faithful to classical ideals, and his 1828 treatise is written in the spirit of eighteenth-century traditions. Czerny gives such a vivid report of Hummel's performance, it is worth citing in its entirety:

> For several years (*c.*1801–1804) my father and I visited Mozart's widow; every Saturday there were musical soirées at her house, where Mozart's younger son (a pupil of Streicher's) gave very skillful performances. On one occasion the party was a good bit larger than usual, and among the many elegant persons I was especially fascinated by a very striking young man. His unpleasant, common-looking face, which twitched constantly, and his utterly tasteless clothing (a light-gray coat, a long scarlet vest, and blue trousers) seemed to indicate that he was some village schoolmaster. But the many valuable diamond rings he wore on almost all fingers provided a most peculiar contrast. As usual there was music, and finally this young man (he might have been somewhat older than twenty) was asked to play. And what an accomplished pianist he turned out to be! Even though I had already had so many opportunities to hear Gelinek, Lipavsky, Wölfl, and even Beethoven, the playing of this homely fellow

[33] *Recent Music and Musicians*, 34.

[34] Of course, the instruction concerning a quiet hand originates in early 18th-cent. harpsichord tutors, as noted in the previous chapter.

[35] 'Unter den Klavierspielern lobte er mir *Einen* als ausgezeichneten Spieler: *John Cramer*. Alle andern galten ihm wenig.' See Wegeler and Ries, *Biographische Notizen*, 119.

seemed like a revelation. Never before had I heard such novel and dazzling difficulties, such cleanness and elegance in performance, nor such intimate and tender expression, nor even so much good taste in improvisation; when later he performed a few of Mozart's sonatas with violin (he was accompanied by Krommer), these compositions, which I had known for a long time, seemed like a completely new world. The information soon got round that this was the young *Hummel*, once Mozart's pupil and now returned from London, where for a long time he had been Clementi's student. . . . While Beethoven's playing was remarkable for his enormous power, characteristic expression, and his unheard-of virtuosity and passage-work, Hummel's performance was a model of cleanness, clarity, and of the most graceful elegance and tenderness; all difficulties were calculated for the greatest and most stunning effect, which he achieved by combining Clementi's manner of playing, so wisely gauged for the instrument, with that of Mozart. It was quite natural, therefore, that the general public preferred him as pianist, and soon the two masters formed parties, which opposed one another with bitter enmity. Hummel's partisans accused Beethoven of mistreating the piano, of lacking all cleanness and clarity, of creating nothing but confused noise the way he used the pedal, and finally of writing wilful, unnatural, unmelodic compositions, which were irregular besides. On the other hand, the Beethovenites maintained that Hummel lacked all genuine imagination, that his playing was as monotonous as a hurdy-gurdy, that the position of his fingers reminded them of spiders, and that his compositions were nothing more than arrangements of motifs by Mozart and Haydn. I myself was influenced by Hummel's manner of playing to the extent that it kindled in me a desire for greater cleanness and clarity.[36]

Czerny clearly appreciated neatness and clarity rather than flamboyance in keyboard performance. Later on in his reminiscences, a slightly disparaging remark shows his disapproval of mere 'virtuosos':

although I was, considering my age, quite proficient as a pianist, as a sight-reader, and in the art of improvisation, my playing lacked that type of brilliant, calculated charlatanry that is usually part of a travelling virtuoso's essential equipment.[37]

Czerny's long account of the soirée of Mme Mozart tells us as much about Beethoven's playing as about Hummel's. Beethoven, of course, was one of the outstanding pianists of the time. The various documents concerning his playing are more or less consistant in their content: they characterize his performance as unrefined but deeply moving, and passionate in an individual way. Interestingly, opinions changed little from Beethoven's early years in Bonn until his later thirties. The strength of his personality conformed as poorly in artistic as in social ways to the norms of the Viennese salons.

The earlier quoted account of the 1791 journey of Bonn musicians to Mergentheim, during which the young Beethoven heard Sterkel play and played for Sterkel in return, is introduced as follows:

Beethoven, der bis dahin noch keinen grossen, ausgezeichneten Klavierspieler gehört hatte, kannte nicht die feinern Nuancirungen in Behandlung des Instruments; sein Spiel war rauh und hart.

[36] 'Recollections from My Life', 308–9. [37] Ibid. 311.

Beethoven at that time had never heard a great excellent piano player and did not know the fine shading in treating the instrument; his playing was rough and hard.[38]

Fifteen years later Luigi Cherubini heard Beethoven, and, according to Schindler, 'he characterized his playing simply as "rough"'.[39]

Another recurrent criticism is that Beethoven's performance was 'unclear', or 'indistinct'. Presumably this means both that Beethoven's execution was imperfect and that he used the pedal extensively. One may surmise that some of Beethoven's horrendously difficult keyboard textures were conceived as *effects*, rather than as nice clavier passages that 'ought to flow like oil', to quote Mozart.[40] 'Beethoven's playing is extremely brilliant but has less delicacy, and occasionally he is guilty of indistinctness,' reported the *Allgemeine musikalische Zeitung* in April 1799.[41] Camille Pleyel heard Beethoven play for the first time in 1805, and related his impressions in a letter:

Enfin j'ai entendu Beethoven, il a joué une sonate de sa composition et Lamare l'a accompagné. Il a infiniment d'exécution, mais il n'a pas d'école, et son exécution n'est pas fini, c'est à dire que son jeu n'est pas pur. Il a beaucoup de feu, mais il tape un peu trop; il fait des difficultés diaboliques, mais il ne les fait pas tout á fait nettes. Cependant il m'a fait grand plaisir en préludant. Il ne prélude pas froidement comme Woelfl. Il fait tout ce qui lui vient dans la tête et il ose tout. Il fait quelquefois des choses étonnantes.

At last I heard Beethoven, he played one of his sonatas, and Lamare accompanied. He has tremendous execution, but he has no schooling, and his performance is not finished; that is, not clear. He has lots of fire, but he pounds a bit too much; he performs diabolical difficulties, but does not execute them quite distinctly. However, his improvisation gave me great pleasure. It is not cold like Wölfl's. He does everything that comes into his head, and he dares all. Sometimes he produces astonishing things.[42]

Clementi had a similar opinion. In Schindler's version he found Beethoven's playing 'insufficiently trained, often unrestrained, like himself, but always full of spirit'.[43]

We can learn specific details of Beethoven's performances from Ferdinand Ries:

Im Allgemeinen spielte er selbst seine Compositionen sehr launig, blieb jedoch meistens fest im Tacte, und trieb nur zuweilen, jedoch selten, das Tempo etwas. Mitunter hielt er in seinem *crescendo* mit *ritardando* das Tempo zurück, welches einen sehr schönen und höchst auffallenden Effekt machte.

In general, he played his own compositions capriciously, but mostly in firm tempo; only rarely did he increase the tempo somewhat. Now and then, in his crescendo, he

[38] Wegeler and Ries, *Biographische Notizen*, 22; trans. in Badura-Skoda, 'Clementi's "Musical Characteristics"', 62.

[39] Schindler, *Biographie von Ludwig van Beethoven*, 255.

[40] *Letters*, 339.

[41] Quoted in Alexander Wheelock Thayer, *The Life of Ludwig van Beethoven*, ed. and rev. Henry E. Krehbiel (New York, 1921), i. 215.

[42] Quoted in Theodor von Frimmel, *Beethoven-Studien*, ii (Munich and Leipzig, 1906), 254.

[43] Schindler, *Biographie von Ludwig van Beethoven*, 255.

would keep back the tempo with ritardando, which made a very beautiful and striking effect.[44]

A further remark of Ries is equally significant: 'Quite seldom did he add notes or an ornament [to the main text].'[45]

Until the nineteenth century, the real test of an instrumentalist was improvisation, especially on the keyboard. The numerous contests on organ, harpsichord, clavichord, and fortepiano gave occasion to show musical imagination as well as technical proficiency. In the second half of the eighteenth century, C. P. E. Bach, Mozart, and Beethoven won the highest praise for their extemporization. C. P. E. Bach, peerless clavichordist of the century, continued to practice his famous art on the *Hammerklavier* in his late years. Cramer's *Magazin der Musik* reported in 1786:

Wer den Herrn Capellmeister auf dem Fortepiano fantasiren gehört hat, und nur etwas Kenner ist, wird gerne gestehen, dass man sich kaum etwas Vollkommeners in dieser Art denken könne. Die grössten Virtuosen, welche hier in Hamburg gewesen, und neben ihm standen, wenn er grade in seiner Laune war, und ihnen so vorfantasirte, erstaunten über die Einfälle, Übergänge, kühne, nie gehörte und doch satzrichtige Ausweichungen, mit einem Worte, über die grossen Reichthümer und Schätze der Harmonien die ihnen Bach darlegte, und davon ihnen selbst viele noch unbekannt gewesen, rieben sich die Stirne und bedauerten—dass sie nicht auch solche Kenntnisse besässen.

Anyone who has heard the Herr Kapellmeister improvising on the fortepiano, if he is a connoisseur of such matters, will gladly admit that greater perfection in this art could scarcely be imagined. The greatest virtuosos who have lived here in Hamburg, and have witnessed his improvisations when he was in just the right frame of mind for them, have been astounded at his bold ideas and transitions, his daring, unprecedented, and yet technically correct modulations, in a word at the great wealth and rich variety of harmony with which Bach presented them, much of which was previously unknown to them; they have mopped their brows and expressed regret that they did not also possess such knowledge themselves.[46]

Musicians of more modest gifts did not possess such harmonic knowledge and imagination. Marvellous pianist though he was, as an improviser Dussek did not exactly excite his audiences. 'His fantasia, which consisted mainly of mere broken chords, was utterly worthless,' wrote Tomášek of a concert held in October 1802 in Prague, in which the 'Extemporaneous Fantasia by Dussek' was supposed to be the highlight of the programme.[47] Later in the same year, Dussek played in Leipzig and Brunswick, and his concerts always included

[44] Wegeler and Ries, *Biographische Notizen*, 127.

[45] 'Allein äusserst selten setzte er Noten oder eine Verzierung zu.' Ibid. 127.

[46] Quoted in Ottenberg, *C. P. E. Bach*, 230; Eng. trans., 167–8.

[47] 'Seine Phantasie, die meistentheils in gebrochenen Akkorden bestand, war ohne allen Werth.' Quoted and trans. in Craw, 'Biography and Thematic Catalogue', 128.

improvisations. The *Zeitung für die Elegante Welt* reported in November 1802: 'In free improvisation there are other artists who accomplish more.'[48] Of the 'mehrere Konzerte und Fantasien' performed in Brunswick, the *Allgemeine musikalische Zeitung* wrote: 'Our young organists will not praise the latter [die Fantasien].'[49] Presumably in Germany, where organ and clavichord improvisation had a long artistic tradition, expectations were not easily satisfied by pretty arpeggio passages.

Nor did the improvisations of Daniel Steibelt, judged by contemporary documents, reach remarkable heights. 'He . . . improvised, and made very much effect with his *Tremulando's*, which were a novelty at the time,' wrote Ferdinand Ries, when Steibelt challenged Beethoven to a contest on the pianoforte during his visit to Vienna in 1800.[50] It seems that Steibelt achieved his short-lived fame as a pianist mainly through 'calculated charlatanry', to quote Czerny's apt observation.

A humorous occurrence in Berlin during Beethoven's visit there in 1796 informs us about the extempore style of Kapellmeister Himmel. Ferdinand Ries relates the story as follows:

Als sie eines Tages zusammen waren, begehrte Himmel, Beethoven möge etwas phantasiren, welches Beethoven auch that. Nachher bestand Beethoven darauf, auch Himmel solle ein Gleiches thun. Dieser war schwach genug, sich hierauf einzulassen. Aber nachdem er schon eine ziemliche Zeit gespielt hatte, sagte Beethoven: 'Nun, wann fangen Sie denn einmal ordentlich an?'

Himmel hatte Wunders geglaubt, wie viel er schon geleistet, er sprang also auf und beide wurden gegenseitig unartig.

Beethoven sagte mir: 'Ich glaubte Himmel habe nur so ein bischen präludirt.' Sie haben sich zwar nachher ausgesöhnt, allein Himmel konnte verzeihen, doch nie vergessen.

When one day they were together, Himmel asked Beethoven to improvise a little, and Beethoven did. Afterwards he insisted that Himmel should do the same. The latter was weak enough to be persuaded. But after he had played for some time, Beethoven said, 'Now, when will you finally begin for real?'

Himmel believed that he had already accomplished a great deal, so he jumped up, and both became impolite to each other.

Beethoven said to me, 'I thought that Himmel had just preluded a little.' Later they became reconciled, but Himmel, although he forgave, never forgot.[51]

Beethoven's reaction (surely not amusing for Himmel) suggests a definite distinction between *phantasiren* und *präludiren*. By the latter, he meant simply a kind of introduction—perhaps a few passages with which to test the instru-

[48] 'In der Phantasie gibt es Künstler, die . . . mehr leisten.' Ibid. 130.

[49] 'Unsre jungen Organisten wollen die Letztern nicht loben!' Ibid. 133.

[50] 'Er . . . Phantasirte und machte mit seinen *Tremulando's*, welches damals etwas ganz Neues war, sehr viel Effect.' See Wegeler and Ries, *Biographische Notizen*, 96. On the infamous tremolando technique of Steibelt, see Rowland, 'Early Pianoforte Pedalling', 5–17.

[51] Wegeler and Ries, *Biographische Notizen*, 131.

ment.[52] A real extemporization, as Beethoven's comment implies, is something more substantial. Whether in the *gebundenen* or the *freien* manner, it is supposed to demonstrate the fertile musical and creative invention of the player.

Vogler's definition of *Fantasieren* as 'Ausführung eines gegebenes Themas'[53] is surely just one version of this freest of arts. W. A. Mozart, at any rate, usually referred to his own improvisations as 'variations'.[54] If not actually playing in an 'orglmässig' (Mozart's term for 'strict') style, his extemporizations, especially on the fortepiano, took the form of a series of free variations on popular songs or operatic tunes of the day. Such productions were the most eagerly anticipated numbers of his concerts, public or private. In fact, several of Mozart's surviving variation sets (certainly K. 398 and 455, and hypothetically K. 354, 264, and 613) originate in keyboard improvisations.

Mozart's extempore performances, however, must have included a large variety of forms and styles. An account by Mozart's friend the Abbé Maximilian Stadler gives an idea of these splendid productions:

> In the art of free improvisation Mozart had no equal. His improvisations were as well-ordered as if he had had them lying written out before him. This led several to think that, when he performed an improvisation in public, he must have thought everything out, and practised it, beforehand. Albrechtsberger thought so too. But one evening they met at a musical soirée; Mozart was in a good mood and demanded a theme of Albrechtsberger. The latter played him an old German popular song. Mozart sat down and improvised on this theme for an hour in such a way as to excite general admiration and shew by means of variations and fugues (in which he never departed from the theme) that he was master of every aspect of the musician's art.[55]

Beethoven's improvisations, like his artistic character in general, must have been entirely different. Ignaz von Seyfried's comment, quoted above in connection with his contest with J. Wölfl, indicates that his improvisation 'inclined toward the gloomy and the sinister'; Pleyel described it as 'daring' and 'astonishing'. 'That young fellow must be in league with the devil. I've never heard anybody play like that!' declared the Abbé Joseph Gelinek, one of the fashionable fortepianists in late eighteenth-century Vienna, who likewise competed with Beethoven on the keyboard.[56] Gelinek's expression evokes a certain Dionysian quality which Beethoven's performance doubtless possessed.

It is very likely that Beethoven's extemporizations lacked the 'well-ordered' manner Stadler emphasized in Mozart's improvisations. His originality and his predelection for shocking effects must have dominated his extempore productions. Ferdinand Ries, who heard Beethoven repeatedly in this capacity, summed up his impressions thus:

[52] See Wolfgang Mozart's letter from Paris, 20 July 1778, quoted in the previous chapter.

[53] Georg Joseph Vogler, *Betrachtungen der Mannheimer Tonschule* (Mannheim, 1778), ii. 290.

[54] This paragraph is a short résumé of my essay, ' "Ich praeludirte und spielte Variazionen" '.

[55] Quoted in Deutsch, *Mozart: A Documentary Biography*, 543.

[56] See Czerny, 'Recollections from My Life', 304.

[Beethoven's Phantasiren] war freilich das Ausserordentlichste, was man hören konnte, besonders wenn er gut gelaunt oder gereizt war. Alle Künstler, die ich je phantasiren hörte, erreichten bei weitem nicht die Höhe, auf welcher Beethoven in diesem Zweige der Ausübung stand. Der Reichthum der Ideen, die sich ihm aufdrangen, die Launen, denen er sich hingab, die Verschiedenheit der Behandlung, die Schwierigkeiten, die sich darboten oder von ihm herbeigeführt wurden, waren unerschöpflich.

[Beethoven's improvisation] was of course the most extraordinary that one could hear, especially when he was well disposed or attuned. None of the artists that I heard could reach Beethoven's height in this sort of performance. The wealth of ideas that poured from him, the whims he indulged in, the variety of treatments, the difficulties that arose or were brought about by him, were inexhaustible.[57]

Perhaps the long and fantasia-like coda sections of the early variation sets, as noted in Chapter 5, reflect some of those ephemeral Beethovenian moments. WoO 68, 71, 72, 73, and 75 especially, abound in sudden shifts of texture, tonality, or dynamics. Such devices, however, are also present in the early sonatas. The magnificent cadenza of the opening movement of Op. 2 No. 3, starting fortissimo with the deceptive cadence on the lowered vi degree (A flat), and the similar moment of the Adagio of the same sonata (the fortissimo C major appearance of the E major main theme), are striking examples.

And, of course, there is the Fantasia Op. 77 in G minor, which opens in that key, stays there for a few bars, then never returns to it again. It would be surprising if the capricious mood and the rhapsodic style of this piece did not resemble Beethoven's improvisations. Reviewing the composition in the *Allgemeine musikalische Zeitung*, J. F. Rochlitz wrote:

Die Phantasie ist recht eigentlich eine freye, und hat—in Neuheit mehrerer Ideen, in Kühnheit und Ueberraschung der Modulationen, in gelehrter Führung der Stimmen, und auch im Abgebrochenen der Schreibart—am meisten Aehnlichkeit mit denen des herrlichen Ph. Eman. Bach.

The fantasy is truly a free one, and has—in the newness of its several ideas, in daring and surprise of modulation, in learnedness of part-writing, and even in abruptness of style—the most kinship with those of the magnificent Philipp Emanuel Bach.[58]

It may very well be that the rhetoric of Beethoven's improvisation was closer to the art of his German predecessors, to C. P. E. Bach in particular, than to the polished style of his Viennese contemporaries.

[57] Wegeler and Ries, *Biographische Notizen*, 119.

[58] 13 (1811), 548. Quoted and trans. in E. Eugene Helm, 'The "Hamlet" Fantasy and the Literary Element in C. P. E. Bach's Music', *MQ* 58 (1972), 277.

References

ADAM, LOUIS, *Méthode de piano-forte du Conservatoire de Musique* (Paris, 1804).

ADLUNG, JAKOB, *Anleitung zur musikalischen Gelahrtheit* (Erfurt, 1758).

Allgemeine musikalische Zeitung, 1st series (Leipzig, 1798–1848).

AVISON, CHARLES, *An Essay on Musical Expression* (London, 1752).

BACH, CARL PHILIPP EMANUEL, *Versuch über die wahre Art das Clavier zu spielen* (2 vols.; Berlin, 1753, 1762); Eng. trans., William J. Mitchell, *Essay on the True Art of Playing Keyboard Instruments* (New York, 1949).

BADURA-SKODA, EVA, 'Clementi's "Musical Characteristics" Op. 19', in H. C. Robbins Landon and Roger E. Chapman (eds.), *Studies in Eighteenth-Century Music: A Tribute to Karl Geiringer on his 70th Birthday* (London and New York, 1970), 53–67.

—— 'Prolegomena to a History of the Viennese Fortepiano', *Israel Studies in Musicology*, 2 (1980), 77–99.

—— and BADURA-SKODA, PAUL, *Mozart-Interpretation* (Vienna, 1957); Eng. trans., Leo Black, *Interpreting Mozart on the Keyboard* (London, 1962).

BARTH, GEORGE, *The Pianist as Orator: Beethoven and the Transformation of Keyboard Style* (Ithaca, NY, and London, 1992).

BEETHOVEN, LUDWIG VAN, *The Letters of Beethoven*, ed. and trans. Emily Anderson (3 vols.; London, 1961).

BERGER, LUDWIG, 'Erläuterung eines Mozartschen Urtheils über Muzio Clementi', *Caecilia*, 10 (1829), 238–9.

BILSON, MALCOLM, 'The Viennese Fortepiano of the Late Eighteenth Century', *EM* 8 (1980), 158–62.

—— 'Keyboards', in Howard Mayer Brown and Stanley Sadie (eds.), *Performance Practice: Music after 1600* (London, 1989), 223–38.

BITTER, CARL HERMANN, *Carl Philipp Emanuel und Wilhelm Friedemann Bach und deren Brüder* (2 vols.; Berlin, 1868).

BRODERIP, ROBERT, *Plain and Easy Instructions for Young Performers on the Piano Forte or Harpsichord* (London, 1788?).

BROWN, A. PETER, *Joseph Haydn's Keyboard Music: Sources and Style* (Bloomington, Ind., 1986).

BURNEY, CHARLES, *The Present State of Music in Germany, the Netherlands, and United Provinces* (2 vols.; London, 1773; facs. repr. of 1775 edn., New York, 1969).

—— *A General History of Music from the Earliest Ages to the Present Period* (4 vols.; London, 1776–89); modern edn. by Frank Mercer (2 vols., London and New York, 1935).

CLEMENTI, MUZIO, *Introduction to the Art of Playing on the Piano Forte* (London, 1801).

COLE, WARWICK HENRY, 'Americus Backers: Original Forte Piano Maker', *Harpsichord and Fortepiano Magazine*, 4 (1987), 79–85.

CRAMER, CARL FRIEDRICH (ed.), *Magazin der Musik* (Hamburg, 1783–7; facs. repr., 5 vols.; Hildesheim and New York, 1971–4).

CRAMER, JOHANN BAPTIST, *Instructions for the Piano Forte* (London, 1812).
CRAW, HOWARD ALLEN, 'A Biography and Thematic Catalog of the Works of J. L. Dussek (1760–1812)', Ph.D. diss. (Univ. of S. California, 1964).
CZERNY, CARL, *Complete Theoretical and Practical Piano Forte School* (3 vols.; London, 1839).
—— 'Recollections from My Life', trans. Ernest Sanders, *MQ* 42 (1956), 302–17.
—— *Über den richtigen Vortrag der sämtlichen Beethoven'schen Klavierwerke: Czerny's 'Erinnerungen an Beethoven' sowie das 2. und 3.Kapitel des IV. Bandes der 'Vollständigen theoretisch–practischen Pianoforte-Schule, Op. 500'*, facs. edn. by Paul Badura-Skoda (Vienna, 1963).
DANBY, JOHN, *La Guida Della Musica Instrumentale, or the Rudiments of the Forte Piano or Harpsichord* . . . (London, 1798).
DAVID, HANS T., and MENDEL, ARTHUR (eds.), *The Bach Reader* (New York, 1945; rev. edn., 1966).
DEUTSCH, OTTO ERICH, *Mozart: Die Dokumente seines Lebens, gesammelt und erläutert* (Kassel, 1961); Eng. trans., Eric Blom *et al.*, *Mozart: A Documentary Biography* (London, 1965).
DOLINSZKY, MIKLÓS, 'Transition from Solo to Ensemble Genres in Chamber Music with Obbligato Keyboard in the Middle of the Eighteenth Century', *Hungarian Music Quarterly*, 3 (1990), 2–11.
—— 'A műfaj problémája a 18. század közepének billentyűs kamarazenéjében', diss. (Budapest, 1992).
DUSSEK, JAN LADISLAV, *Instructions on the Art of Playing the Piano Forte or Harpsichord* . . . (London and Edinburgh, 1796).
EHRLICH, CYRIL, *The Piano: A History*, 2nd edn. (London, 1990).
EINSTEIN, ALFRED (ed.), *Lebensläufe deutscher Musiker von ihnen selbst erzählt* (Leipzig, 1915).
—— *Mozart: His Character, His Work* (New York, 1945),
EISEN, CLIFF, *New Mozart Documents* (London, 1991).
FILLION, MICHELLE, 'C. P. E. Bach and the Trio Old and New', in Stephen L. Clark (ed.), *C. P. E. Bach Studies* (Oxford, 1988), 83–104.
FISCHER, KURT VON, 'Mozarts Klaviervariationen', in *Hans Albrecht in Memoriam*, ed. Wilfried Brennecke and Hans Haase (Kassel, 1962), 168–73.
FORKEL, JOHANN NIKOLAUS (ed.), *Musikalischer Almanach für Deutschland auf das Jahr 1782* (Leipzig, 1782; facs. repr., Hildesheim and New York, 1974).
FRIMMEL, THEODOR VON, *Beethoven-Studien* (2 vols.; Munich and Leipzig, 1905–6).
FULLER, DAVID, 'Accompanied Keyboard Music', *MQ* 60 (1974), 222–45.
FULLER, RICHARD, 'Andreas Streicher's Notes On the Fortepiano, Chapter 2: "On Tone" ', *EM* 12 (1984), 461–70.
GEIRINGER, KARL, *Haydn: A Creative Life in Music* (New York, 1946).
GERLACH, SONJA, 'Haydns Orchestermusiker von 1761 bis 1774', *HSt* 4 (1976–80), 35–48.
GLEICH, CLEMENS VON, *Pianofortes uit de Lage Landen* (The Hague, 1980).
GOLDSCHMIDT, HARRY, *Die Erscheinung Beethoven* (Leipzig, 1974).
GRIESINGER, GEORG AUGUST, *Biographische Notizen über Joseph Haydn* (Leipzig, 1810); modern edn., Franz Grasberger (Vienna, 1954).

GROSSMAN, ORIN, 'The Piano Sonatas of Jan Ladislav Dussek (1760–1812)', Ph.D. diss. (Yale Univ., 1975).
HAMMOND, JOHN, *A Proper Guide to Music, being a Complete Book of Instructions for Beginners on the Piano Forte* (London, 1802).
HARDING, ROSAMOND, 'The Earliest Pianoforte Music', *ML* 13 (1932), 194–9.
—— *The Piano-Forte: Its History Traced to the Great Exhibition of 1851*, 2nd edn. (Cambridge, 1978).
HARNONCOURT, NIKOLAUS, *Musik als Klangrede: Wege zu einem neuen Musikverständnis* (Salzburg and Vienna, 1982); Eng. trans., Mary O'Neill, *Baroque Music Today: Music As Speech*, gen. ed. Reinhard G. Pauly (London, 1988).
HAYDN, JOSEPH, *Gesammelte Briefe und Aufzeichnungen*, ed. Dénes Bartha (Kassel, 1965).
HELM, E. EUGENE, 'The "Hamlet" Fantasy and the Literary Element in C. P. E. Bach's Music', *MQ* 58 (1972), 277–96.
—— *Thematic Catalogue of the Works of Carl Philipp Emanuel Bach* (New Haven, Conn., and London, 1989).
HILLER, JOHANN ADAM (ed.), *Wöchentliche Nachrichten und Anmerkungen die Musik betreffend* (Leipzig, 1766–70; facs. repr., Hildesheim and New York, 1970).
HOOK, JAMES, *Guida di Musica; being a Complete Book of Instructions for Beginners on the Harpsichord or Piano Forte . . .* (London, 1785).
HÜLLMANDEL, JOSEPH NICOLAS, *Principles of Music, Chiefly Calculated for the Piano Forte or Harpsichord* (London, 1796).
HUMMEL, JOHANN NEPOMUK, *Ausführliche theoretisch–practische Anweisung zum Piano-Forte Spiel* (Vienna, 1828); Eng. trans., anon., *A Complete Theoretical and Practical Course of Instruction on the Art of Playing the Pianoforte* (London, 1828).
JAHN, OTTO, *W. A. Mozart* (4 vols.; Leipzig, 1856–9).
JANDER, OWEN, 'Beethoven's "Orpheus in Hades": The *Andante con moto* of the Fourth Piano Concerto', *19th-Century Music*, 8 (1984–5), 195–212.
KALKBRENNER, FRIEDRICH, *Méthode pour apprendre le pianoforte à l'aide de guidemains* (Paris, 1830); Eng. trans., anon. (London, 1862).
KENYON DE PASCUAL, BERYL, 'Francisco Pérez Mirabel's Harpsichords and the Early Spanish Piano', *EM* 15 (1987), 503–13.
KIDD, RONALD, 'The Emergence of Chamber Music with Obbligato Keyboard in England', *AM* 44 (1972), 122–44.
KIRKPATRICK, RALPH, *Domenico Scarlatti* (Princeton, NJ, 1953, rev. edn., 1968).
KOCH, HEINRICH CHRISTOPH, *Musikalisches Lexikon* (Frankfurt am Main, 1802).
KOLLMANN, AUGUST FRIEDRICH, *An Essay on Musical Harmony* (London, 1796).
KOMLÓS, KATALIN, 'Haydn's Keyboard Trios Hob. XV:5–17: Interaction Between Texture and Form', *SM* 28 (1986), 351–400.
—— 'The Viennese Keyboard Trio in the 1780s: Studies in Texture and Instrumentation', 2 vols., Ph.D. diss. (Cornell Univ., 1986).
—— 'The Viennese Keyboard Trio in the 1780s: Sociological Background and Contemporary Reception', *ML* 68 (1987), 222–34.
—— 'On the New Fortepiano in Contemporary German Musical Writings', *Harpsichord and Fortepiano Magazine*, 4 (1988), 134–9.
—— 'Mozart and Clementi: A Piano Competition and its Interpretation', *Historical Performance*, 2 (1989), 3–9.

—— ' "Veränderte Reprise": Aspects of An Idea', *MR* 51 (1990), 262–7.

—— 'The Function of the Cello in the Pre-Beethovenian Keyboard Trio', *Studies in Music*, 24 (1990), 27–46.

—— ' "Ich praeludirte und spielte Variazionen": Mozart the Fortepianist', in R. Larry Todd and Peter Williams (eds.), *Perspectives on Mozart Performance* (Cambridge, 1991), 27–54.

LANDON, H. C. ROBBINS (ed.), *The Collected Correspondence and London Notebooks of Joseph Haydn* (London, 1959).

—— *Haydn: Chronicle and Works* (5 vols.; London and Bloomington, Ind., 1976–80).

LATCHAM, MICHAEL, 'The Check in Some Early Pianos and the Development of Piano Technique Around the Turn of the Eighteenth Century', *EM* 21 (1993), 29–42.

LE HURAY, PETER, *Authenticity in Performance: Eighteenth-Century Case Studies* (Cambridge, 1990).

LIBIN, LAURENCE, 'Keyboard Instruments', *Metropolitan Museum of Art Bulletin*, 47 (1989), 5–56.

LOWENS, IRVING, 'Haydn in America', in Jens Peter Larsen, Howard Serwer, and James Webster (eds.), *Haydn Studies* (New York, 1981), 35–48.

LÜTGE, WILHELM, 'Andreas und Nannette Streicher', *Der Bär* (Jahrbuch von Breitkopf & Härtel), 4 (1927), 53–69.

MARGUERRE, KARL, 'Zwei Abschriften Mozartscher Werke', *Die Musikforschung*, 13 (1960), 57–60.

—— 'Mozarts Klaviertrios', *MJb* 1960–1, 182–94.

MATTHESON, JOHANN, *Critica musica*, ii (Hamburg, 1725).

MAUNDER, RICHARD, 'The Earliest English Square Piano?', *Galpin Society Journal*, 42 (1989), 77–84.

—— 'J. C. Bach and the Early Piano in London', *JRMA* 116 (1991), 201–10.

MEER, JOHN HENRY VAN DER, *Germanisches Nationalmuseum Nürnberg: Wegweiser durch die Sammlung historischer Musikinstrumente*, 3rd edn. (Nuremberg, 1982).

—— *Musikinstrumente* (Munich, 1983).

MILCHMEYER, JOHANN PETER, *Die wahre Art das Pianoforte zu spielen* (Dresden, 1797).

MOBBS, KENNETH, 'Stops and Other Special Effects on the Early Piano', *EM* 12 (1984), 471–6.

MONTANARI, GIULIANA, 'Bartolomeo Cristofori: A List and Historical Survey of his Instruments', *EM* 19 (1991), 383–96.

MOSCHELES, IGNAZ, *Recent Music and Musicians As Described in the Diaries and Correspondence of Ignatz Moscheles*, ed. Charlotte Moscheles, trans. A. D. Coleridge (New York, 1873).

MOZART, LEOPOLD, *Versuch einer gründlichen Violinschule* (Augsburg, 1756); Eng. trans., Editha Knocker, *A Treatise on the Fundamental Principles of Violin Playing* (London, 1948; 2nd edn., Oxford, 1951).

MOZART, WOLFGANG AMADEUS, *The Letters of Mozart and his Family*, ed. and trans. Emily Anderson, 3rd edn. (London, 1985).

Musik in Geschichte und Gegenwart, Die ed. Friedrich Blume (14 vols.; Kassel, 1949–68).

New Grove Dictionary of Music and Musicians, The, ed. Stanley Sadie (20 vols.; London, 1980).

New Grove Dictionary of Musical Instruments, The, ed. Stanley Sadie (3 vols.; London, 1984).

NEWMAN, WILLIAM, 'Concerning the Accompanied Clavier Sonata', *MQ* 33 (1947), 327–49.

—— *The Sonata in the Classic Era* (Chapel Hill, NC, 1963).

—— 'Emanuel Bach's Autobiography', *MQ* 51 (1965), 363–72.

—— 'Beethoven's Pianos versus his Piano Ideals', *JAMS* 23 (1970), 484–504.

—— 'Yet Another Major Beethoven Forgery by Schindler?', *JM* 3 (1984), 397–422.

—— *Beethoven on Beethoven: Playing His Piano Music His Way* (New York, 1988).

NISSEN, GEORG NIKOLAUS VON, *Biographie W. A. Mozarts nach Originalbriefen* (Leipzig, 1828).

OTTENBERG, HANS-GÜNTER, *Carl Philipp Emanuel Bach* (Leipzig, 1982); Eng. trans., Philip Whitmore (Oxford, 1987).

PAPENDIECK, CHARLOTTE, *Court and Private Life in the Time of Queen Charlotte* (2 vols.; London, 1837).

PARKE, WILLIAM THOMAS, *Musical Memoirs* (London, 1830).

PARRISH, CARL, 'Criticisms of the Piano when it was New', *MQ* 30 (1944), 428–40.

PLACE, ADÉLAÏDE DE, *Le Piano-Forte à Paris entre 1760 et 1822* (Paris, 1986).

PLANTINGA, LEON, 'Clementi, Virtuosity, and the "German Manner"', *JAMS* 25 (1972), 303–30.

—— *Clementi: His Life and Music* (London, 1977).

POLLACK, HOWARD, 'Some Thoughts on the "Clavier" in Haydn's Solo *Claviersonaten*', *JM* 9 (1991), 74–91.

POLLENS, STEWART, 'The Pianos of Bartolomeo Cristofori', *Journal of the American Musical Instrument Society*, 10 (1984), 32–68.

—— 'The Early Portuguese Piano', *EM* 13 (1985), 18–27.

QUANTZ, JOHANN JOACHIM, *Versuch einer Anweisung die Flöte traversière zu spielen* (Berlin, 1752); Eng. trans., Edward R. Reilly, *On Playing the Flute* (London, 1966).

REESER, EDUARD, *De klaviersonate mit vioolbegeleiding in het Parijsche musiekleven ten tijde van Mozart* (Rotterdam, 1939).

REICHARDT, JOHANN FRIEDRICH, *Briefe eines aufmerksamen Reisenden die Musik betreffend* (2 parts; Frankfurt and Leipzig, 1774–6; facs. repr., Hildesheim and New York, 1978).

REIMER, ERICH, 'Kenner–Liebhaber–Dilettant', in Hans Heinrich Eggebrecht (ed.), *Handwörterbuch der musikalischen Terminologie* (Wiesbaden, 1972–).

RESTLE, KONSTANTIN, *Bartolomeo Cristofori und die Anfänge des Hammerclaviers: Quellen, Dokumente und Instrumente des 15. bis 18. Jahrhunderts* (Munich, 1991).

RICE, JOHN A., 'The Tuscan Piano in the 1780s: Some Builders, Composers and Performers', *EM*, 21 (1993), 4–26.

RIMBAULT, EDWARD FRANCIS, *The Pianoforte: Its Origin, Progress and Construction, with Some Account of the Clavichord, Virginal, Spinet, Harpsichord etc.* (London, 1860).

RINGER, ALEXANDER, 'Beethoven and the London Pianoforte School', *MQ* 56 (1970), 742–58.

ROCHLITZ, JOHANN FRIEDRICH, 'Karl Philipp Emanuel Bach', *Für Freunde der Tonkunst*, 4 (Leipzig, 1832), 271–316.

ROSEN, CHARLES, *The Classical Style* (New York, 1971).

ROSENBLUM, SANDRA, *Performance Practices in Classic Piano Music: Their Principles and Applications* (Bloomington, Ind., 1988).

ROWLAND, DAVID, 'Early Pianoforte Pedalling: The Evidence of the Earliest Printed Markings', *EM* 13 (1985), 5–17.

RUMMENHÖLLER, PETER, *Die musikalische Vorklassik: Kulturhistorische und musikgeschichtliche Grundrisse zur Musik im 18. Jahrhundert zwischen Barock und Klassik* (Kassel, 1983).

SADIE, STANLEY (ed.), *The Piano* (The New Grove Musical Instruments Series; London, 1988).

SCHILLING, FRIEDRICH GUSTAV, *Encyclopädie der gesammten musikalischen Wissenschaften oder Universal-Lexikon der Tonkunst* (6 vols.; Stuttgart, 1835–8).

SCHINDLER, ANTON, *Biographie von Ludwig van Beethoven* (Münster, 1840); Eng. trans., Constance S. Jolly, ed. Donald W. MacArdle, *Beethoven As I Knew Him* (Chapel Hill, NC, 1966).

SCHMID, ERNST FRITZ, *Carl Philipp Emanuel Bach und seine Kammermusik* (Kassel, 1931).

SCHOLZ-MICHELITSCH, HELGA, *Das Orchester- und Kammermusikwerk von G. C. Wagenseil: Thematischer Katalog* (Vienna, 1972).

SCHÖNFELD, JOHANN FERDINAND VON, *Jahrbuch der Tonkunst von Wien und Prag* (Vienna, 1796; facs. edn. by Otto Biba, Munich and Salzburg, 1976).

SEYFRIED, IGNAZ VON (ed.), *Ludwig van Beethovens Studien im Generalbass, Contrapunkt und in der Compositionslehre* (Vienna, 1832).

SOMFAI, LÁSZLÓ, *Joseph Haydn zongoraszonátái* (Budapest, 1979; Eng. trans., Univ. of Chicago Press, forthcoming).

SPOHR, LOUIS, *Autobiography* (London, 1878).

STEVENS, RICHARD JOHN SAMUEL, 'Recollections' (MS in Pendlebury Library, Cambridge); modern edn., *Recollections of R. J. S. Stevens: An Organist in Georgian London*, ed. Mark Argent (London, 1992).

STEVENS, WILLIAM SEAMAN, *A Treatise on Piano-Forte Expression, Containing the Principles of Fine Playing on that Instrument* (London, 1811).

STREICHER, ANDREAS, *Kurze Bemerkungen über das Spielen, Stimmen und Erhalten der Fortepiano, Welche von [Nannette Streicher] [geborne] Stein in Wien verfertiget werden* (Vienna, 1801).

TAGLIAVINI, LUIGI FERDINANDO, 'Giovanni Ferrini and his Harpsichord "a penne e a martelletti"', *EM* 19 (1991), 399–408.

THAYER, ALEXANDER WHEELOCK, *The Life of Ludwig van Beethoven*, ed. and rev. Henry E. Krehbiel (3 vols.; New York, 1921; rev. Elliot Forbes, Princeton, 1964).

TÜRK, DANIEL GOTTLOB, *Klavierschule, oder Anweisung zum Klavierspielen für Lehrer und Lernende* (Leipzig and Halle, 1789); Eng. trans., Raymond Haggh, *School of Clavier Playing* (Lincoln, Nebr., 1982).

TYSON, ALAN, *Thematic Catalogue of the Works of Muzio Clementi* (Tutzing, 1967).

Verzeichnis des musikalischen Nachlasses des Verstorbenen Capellmeisters Carl Philipp Emanuel Bach (Hamburg, 1790). See also Rachel W. Wade below.

VOGLER, ABBÉ GEORG JOSEPH, *Betrachtungen der Mannheimer Tonschule* (3 vols.; Mannheim, 1778–81; facs. repr., Hildesheim and New York, 1974).

WADE, RACHEL W. (ed.), *The Catalog of Carl Philipp Emanuel Bach's Estate* (New York, 1981).

WAINWRIGHT, DAVID, *Broadwood by Appointment: A History* (London, 1982).

WALTER, HORST, 'Haydns Klaviere', *HSt* 2 (1969–70), 256–88.

WEBSTER, JAMES, 'Schubert's Sonata Form and Brahms's First Maturity', *19th-Century Music*, 2 (1978–9), 18–35; 3 (1979–80), 52–71.

—— 'On the Absence of Keyboard Continuo in Haydn's Symphonies', EM 18 (1990), 599–608.

—— *Haydn's 'Farewell' Symphony and the Idea of Classical Style* (Cambridge, 1991).

WEGELER, FRANZ GERHARD, and RIES, FERDINAND, *Biographische Notizen über Ludwig van Beethoven* (Koblenz, 1838; rev. edn., 1906).

WEINMANN, ALEXANDER, *Beiträge zur Geschichte des Alt-Wiener Musikverlages*, 2nd series (Vienna, 1950–72), vols. 8 (1964), 12 (1968), 9a (1972).

—— *Verzeichnis der Verlagswerke des Musikalischen Magazins in Wien, 1784–1802, Leopold Koželuch* (Vienna, 1950).

—— *Vollständiges Verlagsverzeichnis Artaria & Comp.* (Vienna, 1952).

WEISMANN, WILHELM, 'Zur Urfassung von Mozarts Klaviertrio KV. 564', in *Deutsches Jahrbuch der Musikwissenschaft für 1958* (Leipzig, 1959), 35–40.

WENKE, WOLFGANG, 'Das "clavecin roial" des Dresdener Instrumentenmachers Johann Gottlob Wagner von 1774', in Günter Fleischhauer, Walther Siegmund-Schultze, and Eitelfriedrich Thom (eds.), *Studien zur Aufführungspraxis und Interpretation von Musik des 18. Jahrhunderts*, Beilage zum Heft 29: *Zur Entwicklung der Tasteninstrumente in der zweiten Hälfte des 18. Jhs.* (Blankenburg, 1986), 13–15.

WILLIAMS, PETER, 'The Earl of Wemyss' Claviorgan and its Context in Eighteenth-Century England', in Edwin M. Ripin (ed.), *Keyboard Instruments: Studies in Keyboard Organology, 1500–1800* (New York, 1971), 77–87.

—— 'Some Developments in Early Keyboard Studies', *ML* 52 (1971), 272–86.

WITTMAYER, KURT, 'Der Flügel Mozarts: Versuch einer instrumentenbaugeschichtlichen Einordnung', in Rudolph Angermüller, Dietrich Berke, Ulrike Hofmann, and Wolfgang Rehm (eds.), *MJb 1991: Bericht über den Internationalen Mozart-Kongress 1991* (2 vols.; Kassel, 1992), i. 301–12.

WOLFF, CHRISTOPH, 'New Research on Bach's *Musical Offering*', *MQ* 57 (1971), 379–408.

—— 'Mozarts Präludien für Nannerl: Zwei Rätsel und ihre Lösung', in *Festschrift für Wolfgang Rehm zum 60. Geburtstag* (Kassel, 1989), 106–18.

Index of Names